PERSPECTIVES ON THE INFORMAL ECONOMY

Monographs in Economic Anthropology, No. 8

Edited by

M. Estellie Smith

Contributing Editors

Leo A. Despres
William L. Leap
Larissa Lomnitz

Society for
Economic
Anthropology

UNIVERSITY
PRESS OF
AMERICA

Lanham • New York • London

University Press of America®, Inc.
4720 Boston Way
Lanham, Maryland 20706

3 Henrietta Street
London WC2E 8LU England

Co-published by arrangement with
the Society for Economic Anthropology

Library of Congress Cataloging-in-Publication Data

Perspectives on the informal economy / edited by M. Estellie Smith.
   p.   cm. — (Monographs in economic anthropology ; no. 8)
   Papers presented at the 6th annual meeting of the Society for
   Economic Anthropology, held in 1986.
   Includes bibliographical references.
  1. Informal sector (Economics)—Congresses. 2. Informal sector
(Economics)—Case studies. I. Smith, M. Estellie, 1935–   .
II. Society for Economic Anthropology (U.S.). Meeting (6th : 1986)
                   III. Series.
  HD2341.P44   1990   381—dc20   90–11933 CIP

ISBN 0–8191–7752–0 (alk. paper)
ISBN 0–8191–7753–9 (pbk. : alk. paper)

ACKNOWLEDGEMENTS

The papers appearing in this volume were presented on April 14-16 at the ninth annual meeting of the Society for Economic Anthropology. Walter Neale of the Department of Economics, University of Tennessee, Knoxville was the host of the program. The general organizer and coordinator of the program was M. Estellie Smith (Department of Anthropology and Sociology, SUNY-College at Oswego); Leo Despres (Kellogg Institute of International Studies, University of Notre Dame) organized and chaired the segment on "The informal sector in developing societies"; William Leap (Department of Anthropology, The American University) organized and chaired the segment on "Hidden economies in pluralistic social settings"; and Larissa Lomnitz (Centro para la Innovación Tecnológica, Universidad Nacional Autónoma de México) organized and chaired the segment on "The second economy in centrally planned societies."

Thirty-nine papers were presented in the four formal sessions, the poster session, and the Harold Schneider Commemorative session. Though, for varied reasons, not all the papers or the lively discussion and commentary contributed by the audience, could be included in this volume, the Society wishes to thank them for their participation.

SEA MONOGRAPHS

Monographs of the Society for Economic Anthropology are conference proceedings of the annual meetings of the Society.

No. 1. Ortiz, Sutti, ed.
Economic Anthropology: Topics and Theories. Monographs in Economic Anthropology. Lanham MD: University Press of America and Society for Economic Anthropology.

No.2. Greenfield, Sidney M. and Arnold Strickon , eds.
Entrepreneurship and Social Change. Monographs in Economic Anthropology. Lanham MD: University Press of America and Society for Economic Anthropology.

No. 3. Machlachlan, Morgan, ed.
Household Economies and Their Transformations. Monographs in Economic Anthropology. Lanham MD: University Press of America and Society for Economic Anthropology.

No. 4. Plattner, Stuart, ed.
Markets and Marketing. Monographs in Economic Anthropology. Monographs in Economic Anthropology. Lanham MD: University Press of America and Society for Economic Anthropology.

No. 5. Bennett, John W. and John R. Bowen, eds.
Production and Autonomy: Anthropological Studies and Critiques of Development. Monographs in Economic Anthropology. Lanham MD: University Press of America and Society for Economic Anthropology.

No. 6 Rutz, Henry J. and Benjamin S. Orlove, eds.
The Social Economy of Consumption. Monographs in Economic Anthropology. Lanham MD: University Press of America and Society for Economic Anthropology.

No. 7. Gladwin, Christina and Kathleen Truman, eds.
Food and Farm: Current Debates and Policies. Monographs in Economic Anthropology. Lanham MD: University Press of America and Society for Economic Anthropology.

CONTENTS

Introduction
"A MILLION HERE, A MILLION THERE, AND
PRETTY SOON YOU'RE TALKING REAL MONEY "
M.ESTELLIE SMITH.. 1

THE INFORMAL SECTOR IN COMPARATIVE PERSPECTIVE
BRYAN   ROBERTS... 23

THE INFORMAL ECONOMY AND THE STATE IN TANZANIA
AILI MARI TRIPP.. 49

INFORMAL SECTOR HOUSING: SOCIAL STRUCTURE AND THE
STATE IN BRAZIL
WILLIAM P. NORRIS...................................... 73

MACROTHEORIES, MICROCONTEXTS, AND THE INFORMAL
SECTOR; CASE STUDIES OF SELF-EMPLOYMENT IN THREE
BRAZILIAN CITIES
LEO A. DESPRES.. 97

POPULAR RELIGION, PATRONAGE, AND RESOURCE
DISTRIBUTION IN BRAZIL: A MODEL OF AN HYPOTHESIS
FOR THE SURVIVAL OF THE ECONOMICALLY MARGINAL
SIDNEY M. GREENFIELD and RUSSELL R. PRUST.......... 123

CRISIS AND SECTOR IN OAXACA, MEXICO: A COMPARISION
OF HOUSEHOLDS 1977-1987
ARTHUR D. MURPHY AND MARTHA W. REES with
Karen French, Earl W. Morris, Mary Winter, and Henry Selby... 147

THE NEED FOR A RE-EVALUATION OF THE CONCEPT
"INFORMAL SECTOR": THE DOMINICAN CASE
MARTIN F. MURPHY..................................... 161

COMMUNITY GROWTH VERSUS SIMPLY SURVIVING; THE
INFORMAL SECTORS OF CUBANS AND HAITIANS IN MIAMI
ALEX STEPICK...................................... 183

ECONOMIC CRISIS AND THE INFORMAL STREET MARKET
SYSTEM OF SPAIN
ANTHONY OLIVER-SMITH with Joaquin Beltrán Antolín,
María Angeles Lorenzo Quintela, María Victoria Martínez Saez,
María Teresa Pedruelo Pedruelo, and María Dolores Rosell
Vaquero.. 207

CONTENTS

BLACK MARKETS AND WELFARE IN SCANDINAVIA; SOME
METHODOLOGICAL AND EMPIRICAL ISSUES
    GUNNAR VIBY MOGENSEN...................................... 235

SELF-EMPLOYMENT VS. WAGE EMPLOYMENT IN HONG KONG:
A RECONSIDERATION OF THE URBAN INFORMAL ECONOMY
    JOSEPHINE SMART...................................... 251

HIDDEN DIMENSIONS OF THE BURMESE WAY TO SOCIALISM
    NICOLA TANNENBAUM and*E. PAUL DURRENBERGER.* 281

BUNDLES OF ASSETS IN EXCHANGES: INTEGRATING THE
FORMAL AND INFORMAL IN CANAL IRRIGATION
    ROBERT C. HUNT...................................... 301

A CROSS-CULTURAL TREATMENT OF THE INFORMAL
ECONOMY
    RHODA H. HALPERIN and *SARA STURDEVANT*............... 321

INDEX.. 343

"A MILLION HERE, A MILLION THERE, AND PRETTY SOON YOU'RE TALKING REAL MONEY"[1]

M. Estellie Smith
Department of Anthropology and Sociology
SUNY-College at Oswego

Introduction.

In this century, economists and economic data have played an ever more important role in national planning. Beginning in the 1960s, there began to be a broad awareness that the economic data and modeling of economists increasingly were providing the information basis for people engaged in making decisions in a wide range of contexts—from the individual and the household, through the associational level (e.g., firms; unions; religious, educational, health care, or reseach institutions), to the national and international level (e.g., local/regional/national agencies and legislatures; private and public international investment programs). Through reports of varying levels of sophistication, economic "facts" and "scenarios" were then used to plan national budgets, increase or decrease investment, expand/contract work forces or capital expenditures in both the private and public sectors—in short, to engage in the fine art of "futurology." Across the board, there was a sense of hubris as to the extent that we could manage economic management to improve the quality of whatever it was we wanted to improve (and, of course, in whatever direction it was determined was right and desirable). There was no particular ideological foundation for this growing commitment;[2] simply a general acceptance that the forces of production shaped sociocultural contexts and provided the bases for

---

[1]This well known quote is attributed to Senator Everett Dirksen.

[2]Indeed, the well-known managerial expert, Peter Drucker (1989), has agreed with others (e.g., Albert Camus, Raymond Aron, and Daniel Bell) that the second half of the 20th century has been marked by non- and even anti-ideological political and economic manifestos.

1

the cognitive evaluation of (1) past performances as successful, satisfactory, or dismal, (2) smart choices now; and (3) futures to seek or avoid.

The use of such data was particularly critical to those in or concerned with governmental and political decisions. To what kinds of decisions did the growing mountain of economic data relate? Government personnel at all levels talked of such matters as GNP or the balance of payments and how to "fine tune the economy"; the prime interest rate was raised or lowered to address inflation, to encourage consumer spending, investment or savings; legislators, their staffs, bureaucrats, and private consultants spent much government time in such matters as juggling the unemployment rate (and with it the entitlement budgets), allocating subsidies or tariffs to support flagging businesses, or designing foreign aid programs to encourage economic growth in other countries so they might better be able to afford our own exports. Corporations, labor organizations, trade associations used such figures as the basis for tough or moderate contract negotiations, capital investment, and their stance on immigration or tariff legislation. And, increasingly, the ordinary decisions of individual householders were influenced by news of whether the rates for employment, auto sales, the balance of trade, or bank loans were up or down. Such news not only affected decisions on saving versus going into debt and on how to spend discretionary income, it influenced people in their perceptions of their political leaders and how they would vote, along with whether the electorate felt buoyed, complacent, or pessimistic about their future and that of generations to come.

The challenge to economic models.

By the early 1970s, however, cautionary voices began to be heard—in other social sciences as well as within economics itself, in government, in business, wherever.[3] There emerged a small

---

[3]Some of the earliest material came out of eastern Europe where studies of centrally planned economies (e.g., Berliner 1957) revealed that, despite stringent control, and rigorous oversight, even the most formalized operations were ridden with informal structures and processes and the distinct odor of entrepreneurial capitalism. Thus, some of the earliest writings on this newly discovered economic

congeries of reports that questioned not only the models that provided the frameworks for gathering and analyzing the data but, indeed, the very data themselves. We were, for example,writing tax laws, planning agency budgets, and allocating resources up or down the line, often using some figures that, admittedly, were "guess-timates" expanded or diminished by some formula, and fed into models grounded in questionable assumptions and a sweeping inventory labeled *"ceteris paribus."*

These were serious enough concerns for so-called first world or industrialized countries but the issues were even more critical in other parts of the world.[4] Industrial world models, both inadequate and inappropriate, were used to evaluate the economies of Latin America, Africa, and Asia. Even with the dubious assumption that such models were adequate in first world contexts, it became increasingly clear that not a few of these other states had economies of sufficiently different structure that projections based on the analyses they produced—even if the data were accurately gathered by well-trained and conscientious technicians—were worse than none at all given the extent to which analysts were blindsided to major areas of economic activity. So, for example, these inquiries ignored the whole sector of petty commodity production (e.g., cottage industries), as well as street hawking, casual labor, and the activities of the elderly, children, and women in home, field or roadway, as their labor was bartered and sold in exchange for household goods and services.

---

sphere—this "underground [black, parallel, second, unregistered, private] economy"—dealt with the way it intermeshed or articulated with the "bureaucratic capitalism" of those national economies in which surplus value was received only by those in the governing sector (see Grossman 1988).

[4]Noting the array of activities ignored by planners and bureaucrats, various anthropologists—e.g., the Banfields 1958, Geertz 1963, and Swift 1965—had suggested that third world "take off," the leap from small to large scale production for economic development, could not take place unless and until those bottlenecks to large-scale structures were by-passed or eliminated.The "bottlenecks" were what were labeled "traditional" individualistic and familial organizations that predated the colonial period but persisted within westernized cities and nations.

Anthropologists and sociologists[5] were among the earliest and most sensitive voices to be heard, probably because our studies have tended to focus on the everyday lives of ordinary folk—and such research gives clear evidence of the extent to which, at the microlevel of sociocultural reality, such people "make do" and "make out" in ways that simply do not fit the macro-models of institutionally-oriented economists, statisticians, technical analysts, or political scientists. Anthropologists, especially, were involved: First, much of their work was in the third world areas where challenges to economic canons initially emerged; secondly, their research emphasized the gathering of data that to a greater or lesser extent included material on those structures and processes that are now considered to be an integral part of the informal sector,i.e., details of subsistence activities usually existing outside the institutionalized market system. Goods and services were exchanged as gifts or barter between kin and neighbors but individuals or families also bought and sold necessary services as well as cottage crafts or manufactured goods. Whether tribal peoples or peasants/farmers in the hinterlands of an encapsulating State, small villages and towns, or the neighborhoods and ethnic enclaves of urban settings, the ethnographic literature held a vast array of material describing the activities surrounding forms of production, distribution, and consumption. The majority of these data however, were trivialized, dismissed and overlooked by those concerned with the national statistics of those polities within which such activities took place.

To be sure, not all such transactions had been ignored: Some forms of vending were licensed and even minimally managed; some were criminalized, though authorities turned a blind eye or themselves earned income from bribes or other types of pay-offs. However, even when formalized, the admittedly sketchy, incomplete data on such inputs were deemed too small to matter at the macroeconomic level. It was viewed as unimportant that many of the people needed the resources of what came to be called "the informal sector" to stretch inadequate incomes; maintain ties with rural kin and neighbors as insurance; secure, from a myriad of

---

[5]See, for example, Ferman and Ferman 1973; Stack 1974; and, as noted later in the text, a seminal paper by Hart 1973.

4

invisible entrepreneurs, goods and services essential to urban (even rural) poor but too costly or unavailable in the formal sector; and that, in not a few cases, these activities served to shore up a polity structure in such disarray that, in any practical sense, the State had ceased to function. Did "non-working" household members or "unemployed"people receiving entitlements (if such existed) earn undeclared incomes by tending children, doing odd jobs, and selling at flea markets? It was too small an amount to matter. Did rural folk, newly arrived in the city, work and receive monies that never showed up in employment or earnings statistics? It was too small an amount to matter. Did children labor in backroom sweatshops, run errands, sell flowers or cigarettes to those stopped in traffic and did peasant women provide a significant though non-accountable portion of the labor necessary to the production of resources and household maintenance? It was too small an amount to matter. Did fishermen peddle a few pounds of fish a day at the docks, tribespeople sell a few handcrafted items to tourists, peasants take an unplanned, irregularly available "surplus" to markets to sell? All these represented activities too small to matter—or so said officialdom, economists, experts in national/international finance, and development planners.

Yet, as Hart (1973) showed in a paper that provided a major paradigmatic shift, these might be the very elements that were analytically critical to understanding why the post World War II growth industry of third world development was showing a disappointing (and, worse, unpredictable) success/failure ratio. His own fine-grained research in Ghana took account of what he labeled the dual economy, a formal and informal sector working in tandem. He identified the informal as characterized by self-employed individuals entering into enterprises that were small-scale, tending to focus on less profitable activities, with little access to credit for expansion (thus, marked by greater risk and uncertainty), and frequently substituting for what many see as more desirable wage work that provides more income on a predictable basis. Hart maintained that only irrational "rational" development would discount such activities. The inventory of "relevant data" as currently configured allowed, he claimed, for a rather tautological exercise in which economists equated "significant economic activity" with whatever it was that economists chose to measure (1973:84). In point of fact, however, in what might be more the rule than the exception, plans to expand or alter the formal national economy would succeed, stumble along, or fail, to the extent that an informal sector underwrote and provided an infrastructure to support the total economic endeavor—in short, to the extent such endeavors complemented or contradicted formal sector effort. Thus, for example, if the transition period of development required a pool of free, urban labor, how would those from that pool survive during periods of unemployment (cf. Uzzell 1980)? Further, who would provide basic services to those newly incorporated into the changing economic scene, i.e., if rural males moved to cities for industrial work, who would wash and mend their clothes, how would their meals be prepared, with what leisure activities could they relax—and to what extent would they abandon the work site or work at a low level of efficiency if such were not available?[6]

Hart (1973:84-85) raised some questions—most of which we are still addressing—that provoked attention in a number of quarters. What was the relationship between, on the one hand, the formal economy (that official inventory of economic "facts" that are identified, tracked, collated and managed, and—perhaps most important—from which the polity extracts resources and employs in planning for the future) and, on the other hand, the informal economy (which was everything else)? What are the determinants of growth in the informal sector, and is the demand curve perfectly elastic? If the curve is downwards sloping, to what extent does the increase of labor seeking informal work decrease average income— and is this a relatively stable or dynamic situation? What is the transactional structure between the two sectors and what normative (even institutionalized) processes prevail? In terms of its dependence

---

[6]In addition to that cited elsewhere in this paper, some of the material I found especially useful relative to data of this sort may be found in: Benedict 1972, especially pp. 83, 91; Brush 1977; Clark 1988; Hicks 1972, especially p.77; Hoyman 1987; Jones 1988; Lomnitz 1977; Long and Richardson 1978; Mayer 1961, 1980; McGee 1973a, b, 1976a, b; Meillassoux 1971, 1981; Mintz 1955, 1957, 1959; Pahl and Wallace 1985; Santos 1979; Saunders and Mehenna 1986; Sethuraman 1976, 1981a, b, c; Shankland 1977, 1980; Swetnam 1980; Trager 1985, 1987; Van Dikj 1980; Velez-Ibanez 1983, 1988; Vinay 1985; Wedel 1986.

on outside factors, is the scale of third world informal economies similar to that of first world countries? Is there a net transfer of resources between formal/informal sectors? What are the relationships with the rural sector? Finally, what are the income distribution effects of informal activities?

The ripple effect of these questions—these attempts to get control of the structural and processual characteristics of third world economies—soon began to be felt across a broad spectrum of individuals in the private and public sector alike. Concerns with "the informal economy," became increasingly common as a growing mountain of evidence revealed that there was an extraordinarily productive system of goods and services, and of social resources, whose dimensions included a wide range of production, circulation, and consumption activities that engaged people—wholly or in significant measure outside the ken of the government.[7]

The economists have second thoughts.

Two seminal papers by economists (Gutmann 1977; Feige 1979) targeted the same issues raised by Hart but from the perspective of lost or wasted State resources.[8] Gutmann noted that, in 1976, the average American family of four had $1522.72 of currency circulating outside of banks—an sum of cash so large one could only assume it was necessary for "lubricating a vast amount of nonreported income and unreported work and employment, a whole subterranean economy, untaxed and substantially ignored." In 1976, it amounted to a GNP of $176 billion while reported individual

---

[7]One debate generated was centered within anthropology and is summarized in Smith 1989 in the section on petty commodity production (cf. Long and Richardson 1978) . Another issue still to be resolved—whether the informal sector is the "traditional" system not yet incorporated into the formal economy or, contrariwise, is an innovative response to the formal sector—is reviewed by Trager 1987.

[8]However, as studies such as those of the Fermans (1973) showed, the State could actually benefit from such endeavors since, for every dollar lost in revenues or "excess" entitlement payments, there was at least an entitlement dollar saved by the self-help strategies developed by the poor, the elderly, children—when, indeed, there were entitlements at all (since, in many of the world's countries, these are available only at a minimal level and, too often, are inadequately delivered by an incompetent or corrupt bureaucracy).

income taxes totaled only $142 billion on $1073 billion of reported income tax (1977: 26-27) The paper caused an international furor.[9]

Feige (1979) tested Gutmann's thesis and, agreeing, was even more critical of his colleagues. He charged that economists and those who relied on them were faced with a growing lack of confidence in the ability of any to manage the economic system properly: "Either our theories are defunct...or our data base is so distorted that we are misperceiving the economic realities in our midst" (1979:5). He opted for the latter explanation and credited sociologist Louis Ferman's research on the irregular economy[10] with providing the clue to what were the "economic realities" (1979:6).[11] This was a phenomenon he said "affecting all the developed nations of the world" (1979:12) and was significantly linked to economic efficiency because information costs would rise relative to productivity.[12]

Tanzi (1980).expressed the major concern of economic managers (public or private) when he noted that informal economy activities "will succeed in attracting resources from the formal sector

---

[9]Entitlement programs, especially, came under attack since Gutmann's work not only challenged the reliability of unemployment statistics but noted that, despite that "most illegal income is probably produced by those also employed in recorded jobs," if "even a minimal 10% of the subterranean economy came from those not otherwise employed, total employment still exceeded official statistics by some 820,000 persons" (1977: 27, 34).

[10]He stated that he hoped the use of this term would avoid "the evocative connotations of terms like 'subterranean' or 'underground,' which lend themselves all too readily to journalistic sensationalism" (Feige 1979: 6).

[11]One economist, J.S.Cramer of the Faculty of Actuarial Science and Econometrics, University of Amsterdam, rejected Gutmann's thesis but noted (1980:4), " ...there is probably no alternative to the extensive probing of specific areas by means of sample surveys and other fieldwork, leading up to the direct measurement of missing entries"—which, of course, anthropologists and sociologists had been doing right along, only to have their data largely ignored by economists.

[12]He noted that barter was a major component of the informal sector, despite that it was "a highly inefficient means of conducting economic intercourse, entailing high costs of transaction and information gathering" (1979:12) and despite, I would add, the growing utilization of it in public and private international trade at times of monetary volatility and internal scarcity of foreign currency.

8

[and] these activities may be less productive in a social (rather than a private) sense" (1980:35). Revenues from formal sector assessments provide the wherewithal for all of society's services and entitlements, e.g., education, housing, caretaking of those unable to provide for themselves; highways; public parks and the infrastructure of the transportation system; defense (national and in terms of the police and juridical system); environmental protection; scientific research and support for the arts. Whatever diminishes the resource base from which funds for all these are drawn, diminishes a government's ability to provide them. Individual households may benefit but, said Tanzi, society—and thus all its individual members—must, in the long run, suffer for it. Further, the polity as a whole will suffer; ultimately, all will have to pay increased caretaking costs. Formal sector workers will find it more difficult if not impossible to receive fair wages and may lose employment due to job diversion to the informal sector, Those working in the latter sector are more likely to be forced to find work in unsafe/unhealthy conditions and receive few if any entitlements. There is an increased probability of consumers receiving flawed, toxic, or dangerous goods and services. There is a high potential for environmental degradation under non-monitored conditions. Finally, scarce resources will have to be diverted to inhibit if not eliminate the informal sector.[13]

The state of the art.

The disagreements and diversity among the papers presented here reflect the volatile—some might label it "pre-paradigmatic"—state of the field. However, there are many issues and difficulties involved in exploring the informal sector. (1) Even assuming the ability to track all the relevant research within (let alone across) disciplines, researchers in these different disciplines utilize non-comparable data and non-conformable assumptions and analytical

---

[13]However, this argument assumes, e.g., that (1) the State uses a major portion of the funds to provide well monitored, efficiently delivered public services and, (2) State monies are used for socially approved expenditures rather than diverted to feed corrupt practices or perquisites of position and power. It must also be noted that, within the governing sector of the polity, there are institutionalized informal practices (see Bennett and Di Lorenzo 1983 for a study of the underground economy of the U.S. government).

models. For example, there is no consensus on what is or is not part of the informal sector—which probably accounts for the multiplicity of titles for the sector. At the moment studies may focus on an extraordinary range of activities, running the gamut from bribery, blackmail, public corruption, through "creative bookkeeping" and *ad hoc* solutions to government red tape, to necessary survival tactics of minimal income households, or such activities as children selling fishing worms (and not collecting/forwarding a sales tax) or occasional income of the elderly from baby sitting or garage sales. (2) The very nature of the informal sector makes it difficult to research. Obviously, one is not surprised to encounter misdirection, subterfuge and secrecy when trying to gather data (and one must use such data with a greater degree of scepticism than one normally applies). (3) Ethical concerns are always omnipresent, particularly when it comes time for the public dissemination of the material: What should be revealed or concealed; how well have we protected those with whom we worked; how much can and must be concealed to protect informants without seriously damaging the scientific legitimacy of the data thereby causing others to question the soundness of our research; or what should be done about our personal ethical and legal dilemmas (e.g., what should one do with information on practices that not only violate one's personal code of ethics but which, if knowingly withheld from the authorites, make one subject to legal action)? (4) Finally, there are ideational or ideological biases—self-conscious and out-of-awareness—that skew research, lead to the selection of one context and not another, and influence our assessments of participants and their activities so as to present some hostilely and others sympathetically.

Despite these problems, work on the informal economy has mushroomed over the past decade and our understanding of it has grown as the data have multiplied, the analyses have increased in sophistication, the networks among those working on the subject have expanded, and the debates (usually heated) have flourished. The conference represented by these Proceedings was representative of all of these developments. This sampling of the papers gives a perspective on current research.

The contributions to this volume fell into a natural order. The first, by Roberts, uses a comparative perspective to look at, especially, the material from Latin America but with a tangential look at the influential African context. His essay is particularly apt as an introduction to the four papers that follow, beginning with the contribution by Tripp which, set in Africa, provides a contrast for the next three on Brazil. Her paper focuses on the interface between the informal economy and the State in Tanzania and emphasizes the extent to which informal activities not only function to sustain an inadequately functioning State sector but also force governing personnel to come to an accommodation with and change in response to informal sector activities.

The next three papers (Norris, Despres, and Greenfield) all focus on Brazil. Latin America has been the target for much of the research on the informal economy but Despres (as contributing editor) chose to concentrate on an articulated view of the informal economy in one country. In the first of the trio, Norris, like Tripp, is concerned with the role of the State but, while the Tanzania study centers on urban workers and subsistence needs, Norris looks at the issue of housing within the context of social structure. Interestingly, both Tripp and Norris reveal the vulnerability of governing personnel (too often reified as "the State") to the actions of an aroused citizenry. The next paper, Despres's comparision of self-employment patterns in three Brazilian cities, stresses the diversity among these patterns. It provides a useful antidote to the abused practice of focusing on one locale (usually a primate city) and taking it as representative of the whole—with the result that an entire polity formation is viewed as a homogeneous entity. The last paper in this group, Greenfield's study of popular religion, patronage, and resource distribution, demonstrates how the informal sector is a blend of the traditional and the innovative, of hierarchical patron/client relations and, I would suggest, the popular Portuguese strategy of making a *cuñha* (literally, a plug used to split a piece of wood or a wedge such as is used to hold open a door) i.e., having someone help you obtain some desired end by "putting in a plug for you"—and, at least ideally, doing it not to indebt you but because it's the friendly, generous, or honorable thing to do.

The next two papers still focus on Latin America. A. D. Murphy and Rees, et al., juxtapose two time frames, 1977 and 1987, a period of national economic crisis and, thus, intense economic change in the city of Oaxaca, Mexico. Various factors are reviewed in order to illustrate the extent to which the economic structure of the city, its employment market, and its constituent households do not simply reflect but move to respond actively to national economic change. Similarly, in the next paper, M. F. Murphy centers on the city of Santo Domingo, Dominican Republic, to compare changes in the sociocultural patterns of mobile retail produce vendors—using 1982 and 1987 as the two temporal contexts.. Where the authors of the Oaxaca paper concentrate on testing the extent to which particular sociocultural factors are dependent or independent variables in informal sector changes, the Dominican data are used to test the utility of the three principle schools of thought concerning the informal sector—and concludes that all can be found wanting.

Though Miami is a "first world" city, in Stepick's (as in Despres's) paper we see how inadequate can be our analysis if we gloss over the historical and sociocultural specificity of one city, region, or polity relative to another. Not only is Miami a "kind of" Latin American city (though Cubans are very different from, say, Puerto Ricans or Colombians), it is home to a diverse population that includes, among others, a Haitian enclave. Avoiding the lumping of Cubans and Haitians into a single category—say, "Informal sector immigrant workers"—Stepick demonstrates how each ethnic group has made a unique adaptation to contextual conditions at time of arrival. As with all the other papers, we see how fluid and situationally responsive are informal strategies—and, indeed, it is their externality to the rigid, cumbersome formal system that not only differentiates them from the latter but permits a fairly immediate adjustment to market (and other social) forces.

The same is true of Oliver-Smith's paper on the street market system of Spain. As in Oaxaca, a national economic crisis (beginning in 1974) brought significant structural change to the informal sector. Whether traditional street hawker or refugee from a shrunken formal employment sector, the flexible perimeters of the informal economy offered opportunities for "making do" in the face of the inadequacy of or outright opposition from those in the formal sector.

Viby Mogensen's paper concentrates on the Danish informal economy set within the comparative context of similar material from Norway and Sweden—three countries that have long had generous entitlement programs. In addition to raising issues of the effect of "cheating" on the caretaking system, this study reminds us that the informal sector may exist despite a viable economy coupled with high employment levels, and what most maintain is a generous entitlement program. The desire to escape taxation is one factor at work here—and this reminds us that similar sociocultural pheneomena may be driven by different processes.

The next paper, Smart's study of Hong Kong's street hawkers, is akin to Viby Mogensen's in questioning the effectiveness of the State's attempts at social engineering. Further, like Pahl (whose work in the U.K. revealed that the employed rather than unemployed were more likely to be found in the informal sector [1984]), she challenges the simplistic correlation between unemployment and informal sector. She argues that it is active resistance to proletarianization that draws recent Hong Kong immigrants to street hawking.

In complementary fashion, in the following paper—where Tannenbaum and Durrenberger discuss the Burmese government's "Way to Socialism"—we see that it is the existence of government planning that has created a shortage of consumer goods and encouraged the wide-spread informal sector entrepreneurialism that marks life in this southeast Asian country. And, carrying the irony one step further, it is U.S. sponsored drug suppression campaigns that provide the resources that encourage participation in the international drug trade! Their analysis conforms with that of Hunt who, in the next paper, presents the thesis that the formal and informal economies are inextricably linked in the day-to-day determinations that are actualized in the operation of India's canal irrigation system. Hunt shows that the informal sector can be deeply integrated into the center of a major institution. In large measure, the formally structured system (in this case, water management) creates the complex structure of interdependent—perhaps even symbiotic—formal/informal assets.[14]

The role of the State in defining (if not actually creating) the informal sector is a broad thread that runs through all the papers. The last essay, however, questions what the other contributors simply assume: Is the State the fulcrum for what is now being identified as the formal/informal economic dyad; i.e., without the State, would one or the other or both not exist? Halperin and Sturdevant provide an ethnographically grounded comparison that has as its core, the provocative proposition that,"if one defines the informal economy as the anti-economy, then all economies have informal components." I have taken the same position (Smith 1989), holding that all sociocultural systems have a formal and informal economy in that every society makes at least some rules concerning production, distribution or consumption of resources—material and non-material. These rules can be said to constitute the formal system. Individuals are monitored, sometimes by the community at large, sometimes by specially designated individuals to insure obedience. When people violate these public rules, they become actors in what can be cross-culturally and cross-temporally defined as the informal sector of any sociocultural formation. In short, the informal sector is characterized by activities that do not conform with the rules set down by those who serve as the social arbiters of/for the dictums for managing what are deemed public resources (cf. Mattera 1985: 1). Such arbiters may, for example, consist of all the society's members (as, say, in a foraging group), a single despot, or a vast cadre of governing personnel.

Conclusion.

The last two decades have witnessed increasing attention given to a wide range of activities that had been ignored or had escaped survey by economists and governing officials. We are now aware of

---

[14]He also raises the issue of how to differentiate the centralized polity writ large from sub-structures within it—states and provinces. I have anticipated the issue by adopting the editorial convention of using the term "State" when referring to the central governmental structure and "state" when referring to a regional component.

how extensive is the informal sector and how truly vast is the amount of resources flowing through it. We must ask why the crystalization of this awareness happened now and not sooner or later. The answer would seem to lie, on the one hand, in the intensifying demands on the State to expand its caretaking duties and, on the other hand, in the concomittant need of polity managers to optimize their efficient capture of available resources. The list of public services grows daily: the expanding world population,[15] environmental concerns, the swelling sector of aged and disabled (and relative decrease in the income-producing) citizens, crumbling urban infrastructures, and on and on. Aside from the current fad of *ad hoc* (and often ill-conceived) attempts at privatization, officialdom can do only two things: It can decrease waste costs (by, say, having better information—a process aided by the computer revolution), and it can widen its resource-foraging scope. In such a context, the State cannot afford to ignore or trivialize activities that may provide revenues, reduce unnecessary entitlements, and badly skew planning—as well, by their very presence, encourage others similarly to elude the State.

For the foreseeable future, there will be an inevitable increment in the range and depth of the State's monitoring, both for purposes of assessment and quality control. As the formal sector expands, it will become more costly and require greater resources to maintain—not the least because that very expansion will create greater waste through inefficiency and opportunities for corruption. In addition, however, greater enforcement costs are likely to be incurred as the citizenry responds to this growing intrusiveness of the State by inventing new ways to circumvent structures and processes they consider inimical to their own special and private interests. The tension and disjuncture as well as complementarity between the formal and informal sectors are, therefore, not likely to diminish and it is likely that we shall be hearing more about them both.

---

[15]And, given international concerns as well as world population movements, it is irrelevant that, in any given polity, population may be declining.

References.

Banfield, E.C. and L.F. Banfield
1958   The Moral Basis of a Backward Society. Glencoe, IL: Free Press.

Benedict, Peter
1972   Itinerant Marketing: An Alternative Strategy. In E. N. Wilmsen, ed., Social Exchange and Interaction. Anthropological Papers No. 46, Museum of Anthropology. Ann Arbor: University of Michigan, pp. 81-94.

Bennett, James T. and Thomas J. DiLorenzo
1983   Underground Government: The Off-budget Public Sector. Washington, D. C.: The Cato Institute.

Berliner, Joseph
1957   Factory and Manager in the USSR. Cambridge: Harvard University Press.

Brush, Stephen
1977   The Myth of the Idle Peasant: Employment in a Subsistence Economy. In R. Halperin and J. Row, eds., Peasant livelihood. New York: St. Martin's press, pp. 60-78.

Clark, Gracia, ed.
1988   Traders versus the State: Anthropological Approaches to Unofficial Economies. Westview Special Studies in Applied Anthropology. Boulder CO: Westview Press.

Cramer, J. S.
1980   The Regular and Irregular Circulation of Money. Paper presented at the 1980 meeting of the American Econometric Association, Denver.

Drucker, Peter F.
  1989   The New Realities: In Government and Politics/ In Economics and Business/ In Society and World View. New York: Harper and Row.

Feige, Edgar L.
  1979   The Irregular Economy: Its Size and Macro-economic Implications. Madison: University of Wisconsin.

Ferman, Patricia R. and Louis A.
  1973   The Structural Underpinning of the Irregular Economy. Poverty and Human Resources Abstracts 8: 3-17.

Geertz, Clifford
  1963   Peddlers and Princes. Chicago IL: U. of Chicago Press.

Grossman, Gregory, ed.
  1988   Studies in the Second Economy of Communist Countries. Berkeley: University of California Press.

Gutmann, Peter
  1977   The Subterranean Economy. Financial Analysts Journal, November/December, pp. 26-27, 34.

Hart, Keith
  1973   Informal Income Opportunities and Urban Employment in Ghana. Journal of modern African studies 11: 61-89.

Hoyman, Michele
  1987   Female Participation in the Informal Economy: A Neglected Issue. In L.A.Ferman, S. Henry, M. Hoyman, eds., The Informal Economy. The Annals of the American Academy of Political and Social Science. Newbury Park CA: Sage Publications, pp. 100-119.

Jones, Yvonne V.
1988   Street Peddlers as Entrepreneurs: Economic Adaptation to an Urban Area. Urban Anthropology 17: 143-170.

Lomnitz, Larissa Adler
1977   Neworks and Marginality: Life in a Mexican Shantytown. New York: Academic Press.

Long, Norman and Paul Richardson
1978   Informal Sector, Petty Commodity Production, and the Social Relations of Small-scale Enterprise. In John Clammer, ed., The New Economic Anthropology. New York: St. Martin's Press, pp. 176-209.

Mattera, Philip
1985   Off the Books: The Rise of the Underground Economy. New York: St. Martin's press.

Mayer, Philip, ed.
1961   Xhosa in Town: Studies of the Bantu-speaking Population of East London, Cape Province. Vol. 2. Institute of Social and Economic Research, Rhodes University. Cape Town: Oxford University Press (2d ed.).
1980   Black Villagers in an Industrial Society: Anthropological Perspectives on Labor Migration in South Africa. Cape Town: Oxford University. Press.

McGee, T.G.
1973   Peasants in the Cities: A Paradox, a Most Ingenious Paradox. Human Organization 32: 135-142.
1974   Hawkers in Hong Kong. Hong Kong: Center of Asia Studies.
1976a   The Persistence of the Proto-proletariat. Progress in Geography 9: 3-38.
1976b   Hawkers and Hookers: Making Out in the Third World City: Some Southeast Asian Examples. Manpower and Unemployment Research 9.

Meillassoux, Claude, ed.
  1971   The Development of Indigenous Trade and Makets in
          West Africa. London: Oxford University Press.

Mintz, Sidney
  1955   The Jamaican Internal Marketing Pattern. Social and
          Economic Studies 4: 95-103.
  1957   The Role of the Middleman in the Internal Distribution
          System of a Caribbean Peasant Economy. Human
          Organization 15: 18-23.
  1959   Internal Market Systems as Mechanisms of Social
          Articulation. In V. Ray, ed., Intermediate Societies,
          Social Mobility and Communication. Proceedings, The
          American Ethnological Society. Seattle: University of
          Washington, pp. 20-30.

Pahl, Raymond E.
  1984   Divisions of Labor. Oxford: Basil Blackwell.

Pahl, R.E. and C. Wallace
  1985   Household Work Strategies in Economic Recession. In
          N. Redclift and E. Mingione, eds., Beyond
          Employment: Household, gender and subsistence.
          Oxford: Basil Blackwell, pp. 189-227.

Sampson, Steven L.
  1987   The Second Economy of the Soviet Union and Eastern
          Europe. In L. A. Ferman, S. Henry and M. Hoyman,
          eds., The Informal Economy. The Annals of the
          American Academy of Political and Social Science.
          Vol. 493, pp. 120-136.

Santos, Milton
  1979   The Shared Space: The Two Circuits of the Urban
          Economy in Underdeveloped Countries. London:
          Methuen.

Saunders, Lucie and Sohair Mehenna
1986   Unseen Hands: Women's Farm Work in an Egyptian
        Village. Anthropological Quarterly 59: 105-114.

Sethuraman, S.V.
1976   The Urban Informal Sector: Concept, Measurement
        and Policy. International Labor Review 114: 69-81.
1981a   The Urban Informal Sector in Developing Countries:
        Employment, Poverty and Environment. Geneva:
        International Labor Office.
1981b   The Role of the Urban Informal Sector. In S. V.
        Sethuraman, ed., The Urban Informal Sector in De-
        veloping Countries: Employment, Poverty and
        Environment, Geneva: International Labor Office, pp.
        3-8.
1981c   Summary and Conclusions: Implications for Policy and
        Action. In S.V. Sethuraman, ed., The Urban Informal
        Sector in Developing Countries: Employment, Poverty
        and Environment.   Geneva: International Labor
        Office, pp. 188-208.

Shankland, Graeme
1980   Our Secret Economy.   London: Anglo German
        Foundation.

Smith, M. Estellie
1989   The Informal Economy. In S. Plattner, ed., Economic
        Anthropology.   Stanford CA: Stanford University
        Press (in press).

Stack, Carol B.
1974   All Our Kin: Strategies for Survival in a Black
        Community. New York: Harper and Row.

Swetnam, John J.
1980   Disguised Employment and Development Policy in
        Peasant Economies. In Human Organization 39: 32-
        39.

Swift, M. G.
1965 Malay Peasant Society in Jelebu. London School Economics Monographs on Social Anthropology. London: Athlone Press.

Tanzi, Vito
1982 The Underground Economy in the United States and Abroad. Lexington MA: D.C.Heath.

Trager, Lillian
1985 From Yams to Beer in a Nigerian City: Expansion and Change in Informal Sector Trade Activity. In Stuart Plattner, ed., Markets and Marketing. Monographs in Economic Anthropology, No.4. New York: University Press of America, pp. 259-286.
1987 The Urban Informal Sector in West Africa. Canadian Journal of African Studies 21: 238-255.

Udy, Stanley H., Jr.
1959 Organization of Work: A Comparative Analysis of Production Among Nonindustrial Peoples. New Haven CN: HRAF Press.

Uzzell, J. Douglas
1980 Mixed Strategies and the Informal Sector: Three Faces of Reserve Labor. Human organization 39: 40-49

Van Dikj, Pieter
1980 La Réussite des Petits Entrepreneurs dans le Secteur Informel de Ouagadougou (Haute-Volta). Tiers Monde 21: 373-386.

Vélez-Ibañez, Carlos
1983 Rituals of Marginality. Berkeley: U. of California Press.
1988 Networks of Exchange Among Mexicans in the U.S. and Mexico: Local Level Mediating Responses to National and International Transformations. In E. J. Arnould and T. R. McGuire, eds., Indigenous

Responses to Economic Development. Urban Anthropology 17: 27-52.

Vinay, Paola
1985   Family Life Cycle and the Informal Economy in Central Italy. International Journal of Urban and Regional Research 9:82-98.

Wedel, Janine
1986   The Private Poland. New York: Facts on File Publications.

THE INFORMAL SECTOR
IN COMPARATIVE PERSPECTIVE

Bryan Roberts
Department of Sociology
University of Texas at Austin

Introduction.

My aim in this paper is to provide an overview of the nature of the informal sector in urban Latin America. This task is made difficult by disagreements over definition and by the different issues which the concept is used to address. Researchers have often found the concept hopelessly imprecise and confused (Moser 1978; Breman 1985). It has been attacked by those on the left as exploitative of the poor, and praised as a possible source of economic self-empowerment. For the right, it is often seen as the economic activity *par excellence* of the dangerous classes and, at other times and places, as an exemplar of initiative in the face of excessive State control of the economy (De Soto 1986). However, the concept of the informal sector continues to be used by researchers and policy makers and the reality it describes—that of the large numbers of the Latin American urban population who remain outside the world of full-time, stable employment—shows little sign of diminishing with time.

I focus on three major approaches to the analysis of the informal sector in Latin America. They are not exclusive of each other, but each has concentrated on a somewhat different set of issues. The first of these approaches is concerned with the formal rationality of the informal sector, looking at product and labor markets, and emanating from the International Labor Office (ILO) and its Latin American agency, PREALC. I will use this approach to provide a general overview of the informal sector and to raise issues about its definition.

The second approach takes a political economy perspective and focuses on the external determinants of the informal sector, especially State regulation. The final approach is that concerned with the substantive rationality of the informal sector and is based, on the work of anthropologists and sociologists concerned with how the poor make out in the cities of developing countries.

Formal rationalities.

The ILO has approached the issue of the informal sector in terms of the problems of job creation in developing countries. The country missions of ILO in the late 1960s and early 1970s came to the conclusion that the central problem underlying poverty in the urban economies was not so much unemployment, as the type of employment available to much of the population (ILO 1972). Their own research and the case studies emanating from anthropologists and sociologists convinced the ILO that the economic activities of the informal sector made a contribution both to the growth of the urban economy and to sustaining the growing urban population. The problem, as the ILO saw it, was the very low income generated by such activities. From the beginning, the ILO adopted a policy stance of improving income *within* the informal sector as a solution to poverty, by cooperative credit or marketing schemes that would reduce overheads. The growth of employment opportunities in the formal sector was also advocated by the ILO, but such growth was thought likely to be too slow to be an adequate short or medium-term solution to poverty, given the capital investments required. From the ILO's perspective, informal sector activities made a useful contribution to the urban economy and, because of the low capital to labor ratios involved, could make a significant and cost effective contribution to absorb the rapidly growing urban labor forces.

In Latin America, PREALC carried out a number of general and country studies of the informal sector during the 1970s and 1980s. The early discussions viewed the informal sector as a relatively clearly defined economic sector constituted by enterprises with certain types of characteristics. These enterprises were characterized as small-scale, based on a rudimentary technology, with little capital investment. From PREALC's viewpoint (1976:

35), the informal sector contained workers and enterprises in "unorganized activities," meaning both that there was no clear-cut distinction between capital and labor, making use of family labor so that salary was often not the predominant retribution of work, and that employment was not regulated by legal obligations such as observance of social security laws, labor contracts, and so on. These characteristics, and the relatively low levels of qualification associated with them, made for ease of entry into the sector which, consequently, was highly competitive and poorly remunerated. The enterprises occupied sectors of the market which were too unstable and unprofitable for formal sector enterprises or were at the bottom of the supply pyramid of the oligopolistic markets in which formal sector enterprises act.

Though PREALC sponsored case studies of informal enterprises, their data are mainly drawn from sample surveys or tabulations of population and economic censuses. This has resulted in empirical data which, at best, only provided indirect measures of the informal sector as an enterprise sector. PREALC's standard definition has been to class as informal sector the self-employed, unpaid family workers, domestic servants and those working in enterprises of less than five persons.[1] The data gathered by PREALC demonstrated that the informal sector so defined was disproportionately made up by people with particular characteristics: women, rural migrants, the young and the old. These findings and others suggesting that a high proportion of the informal sector was made up of employees of small-scale enterprises, led, in later PREALC analyses, to a greater emphasis on the structure of urban labor markets in Latin America, and their segmentation (Tokman 1986). The low incomes associated with the informal sector result not only from the disadvantages faced by small-scale enterprises but

---

[1]For reasons of data comparability and availability, PREALC analyses rarely use all these categories; the most frequent indicators used are self-employment and unpaid family labor. Some PREALC studies have used income (usually defining the informal sector as that earning below the minimum income) as their indicator. The justification used by PREALC researchers for using employment characteristics as indicators of type of enterprise is that the individual self-employed or the domestic servant could be considered as offering goods and services on a market made up of purchasers such as middle class households (Tokman, 1986).

also from the individual characteristics (education, gender, age) of those within it. There is, to be sure, a sectoral effect in that for any given characteristic, those working in the informal sector had lower incomes than those working in the formal sector. PREALC (1976: 36) cited studies from Asunción and San Salvador which compared workers of identical age, gender and educational profiles, and showed that those in the informal sector earned between 30% and 60% less than those in the formal sector.

Using definitions based on employment status, PREALC monitored the informal sector throughout Latin America. Three major conclusions have emerged. First, and possibly most important, the informal sector shows no sign of disappearing with time. Thus, in most Latin American countries, the proportion of urban workers in the informal sector has remained relatively constant. From 1950 to 1980, the proportion of urban informal employment (defined in this case as self-employment and unpaid family labor in non-agricultural activities) declined only by two percentage points, from 30.7% to 28.7% (Tokman 1986). To emphasize that Latin America is unusual in this respect, Portes (1985) shows that the decline of the informal sector in Latin America, measured by various indices, is much slower than it was in the United States at the comparable period. Thus, in the 30 years beginning with 1900, when the level of informal sector employment was similar to that of Latin America in 1950, informal employment in the United States declined by almost 20 percentage points.

With the debt crises of the early 1980s, informal sector employment has increased at an annual rate of 6.8%, compared with 2% in the formal urban sector (PREALC 1987, Table 2). In only two of the countries surveyed, Argentina and Chile, has there been a decrease in the absolute levels of informal sector employment between 1980 and 1985, and, in these, for only some of these years. In all nine countries (which include Brazil and Mexico), the informal sector has increased its proportion of the employed non-agricultural population (PREALC 1987, Table 6).

Despite the persistence of the informal sector, the PREALC analyses emphasized that the informal sector did not act as an independent or counter-cyclical source of wealth and job creation. With the generalized recession of the 1980s, there is little evidence that the informal sector has acted to absorb the decline in employment in the formal sector, since there have been substantial increases in the rates of open unemployment in urban areas from 6.8% in 1970 to 11.1% in 1985 (PREALC 1987, Table 3; Marshall 1987). Further, in manufacturing, where the independent dynamic of the informal sector should be observed, informal sector employment is clearly pro-cyclical, indicating a dependence on sub-contracting and other exchanges with the formal economy (Marshall 1987). In the recession, the evidence suggests that informal sector employment has increased most in the low-income, easy-entry occupations of the service sector, especially commerce and personal services.

PREALC and other surveys have made clear that the informal sector is heterogeneous, with considerable variation in the income of its members and in the capital of its enterprises. Tokman (1986) reports findings from Costa Rica, Colombia, and Peru indicating substantial differences in income between owners of informal shops, the self-employed, workers in informal workshops and domestic servants. The variation in income is such that, for some categories of informal sector workers such as shop owners, earnings are higher than for workers in the formal sector. These findings are similar to those of Portes et al. (1986) for Montevideo, Uruguay. Escobar's (1986: 88) detailed case studies of formal and informal labor markets in Guadalajara, Mexico, also show the complex working careers produced by the heterogeneity of income opportunities in that city. Depending on stage in life cycle and changes in needs, people move from the informal sector to the formal and back again, even, at times, migrating internationally. Though these moves are not typical of the working population, they happen because people make choices between the flexible but volatile income opportunities and working conditions in the informal sector, and the secure (including welfare protection), steady, but inflexible, working conditions and incomes of the formal sector.

Despite the general uniformity of the trends and characteristics of the informal sector in Latin America, there are significant differences in the proportions of the urban labor force that are classed as informal. In the least developed and industrialized countries, such as Paraguay, these were estimated at 57% of the urban labor force, with the lowest estimate being 30.3% for Brazil (PREALC 1978: 298, Cuadro 3).

There are also differences among cities in the prevalence of the informal sector. In a study of Mexico, for example, PREALC (1978: 157-170) showed significant differences between Guadalajara, Monterrey, and Mexico City. Guadalajara had the largest informal sector and Monterrey the smallest. These differences relate to contrasts in the industrial structure of the three cities (Arias and Roberts 1985; Roberts 1989a). Guadalajara's manufacturing industry is heavily concentrated in basic goods industries and, compared to the other two cities, contains a disproportionate number of small-scale enterprises. Guadalajara, for instance, supplies a high proportion of the domestic demand for shoes in Mexico; such production is often carried out in workshops, especially in lines such as women's shoes where there are frequent changes in styling.

The major factors, then, accounting for the informal sector in the PREALC analysis are economic ones related to the level and type of economic development found in Latin America. The abundant supply of urban labor, combined with the limitations on employment growth in the formal sector, create an environment suited to low-wage employment in a host of services and workshops. These provide useful services both directly and indirectly to the formal sector, and are not competitive with that sector but, because of low productivity and high internal competition, generate low incomes. The predominantly low-income clientele of cities of developing countries inhibits the rationalization of markets.

In recent publications, PREALC has come to see this situation as reflecting a structural and more permanent characteristic of current patterns of economic development, both in Latin America and worldwide. The argument is that technological change—including the worldwide phenomenon of rapid industrial restructuring—is making manufacturing industry more capital and less labor intensive, and shifting employment growth to the service sector. Both trends lead to the worldwide growth of what the ILO calls non-standard forms of employment—self-employment, part-time employment, and casual labor—so that, even in developed countries, only about half of the labor force is now in full-time, protected employment (Marshall 1987; Roberts 1989b). Though the most dynamic growth occurs in the so-called modern services (producer and social), the small size and labor intensiveness that characterizes service firms add to rather than diminish the informal sector. For instance, such operations often have a polarized income structure in which the high income of the owners, professionals and technical staff contrast with the low incomes of the unskilled and, often, part-time staff. Both in the service and the manufacturing sector, fierce international competition leads firms to seek increasing control over labor and greater flexibility in its allocation. Certain parts of the productive process become more technologically sophisticated, requiring a highly skilled but relatively reduced number of operatives, other routine and labor intensive parts are "put out" to workshops or homeworkers and frequently located in countries with an available supply of cheap labor (Benaría and Roldan 1977)

The State and the informal sector.

One of the factors that those associated with PREALC and the ILO stressed in their definitions of the informal sector is the nature of the State regulation. Thus, in PREALC's 1976 publication, the informal sector is in part defined as unorganized in the legal sense, unregulated by the State. The formal sector is the protected sector, receiving preferential credits from banks and government, while the informal sector is unregistered, and avoids taxation as well as the obligations imposed by social security laws. It is a short analytic step from this position to see the existence of an informal sector, and differences between cities and countries in its extent, as resulting from the essentially political compromises attending industrialization in Latin America. Though this position is not explicitly developed in PREALC's analyses, it is the focus of those concerned with the political economy of urbanization in Latin America (Portes and Walton 1981: 84-87). Throughout the continent, governments in the import-substitution phase of industrialization made alliances with sectors of the urban work force, permitting trade unions, providing health and some social security coverage, plus establishing labor contracts. The labor and accompanying social security legislation have not, however, been based on universal principles of coverage, but have tied benefits to employment. Typically, key workers in key sectors of the economy received earliest coverage. Thus, as Latin America began to urbanize, a distinction emerged between protected and unprotected workers.

Marshall (1987) points to the inflexibility of this legislation, usually providing similar coverage and rights to temporary or part-time workers as to regular full-time workers. The consequence has been, on the one hand, a reluctance on the part of employers to use part-timers or temporary workers to gain flexibility in the face of fluctuations in demand, so that in Argentina overtime by regular workers has been the normal means of increasing production temporarily. On the other hand, there has been a widespread avoidance of legal requirements through informal agreements with workers. Unlike most European countries where, within the same firm, there are legal gradients of employer commitment to workers, the Latin American situation has tended to present a sharper contrast between the formal and protected workers and the informal, unprotected worker.

The informal sector is dynamic because there are few overhead costs, such as social security or the observance of health, safety or zoning ordinances. It is attractive both to those who seek to set up an enterprise but are without capital reserves, as well as to those formal sector firms that wish to cut costs and gain flexibility by putting-out work. Thus, the informal sector is functional for the formal sector both directly and indirectly: It serves the latter sector directly by providing a cheap and flexible source of goods and services for formal sector firms and, further, gives indirect support by lowering the subsistence costs, and thereby the wage demands, of all urban workers (Portes and Walton 1982). From this perspective, the vitality of the informal sector depends primarily on the shifting alliances among State personnel, formal sector employers, and formal sector workers. If formal sector employers are relatively free to set wages, to operate flexible labor contracts, and have low social security overheads, then the economic advantages of informality are less. Conversely, where trade unions or political parties seeking the support of the organized working class have established a substantial protective legislation for formal sector workers, as happened in Peru in the 1960s or in Argentina under Peron, then becoming informal brings substantial economic advantages—to the extent that formal firms in certain lines such as textiles or shoe production may not be able to compete. In Brazil, in the last years of the recent military government, the increasing costs of social security coverage were shifted to employers (Malloy 1985). As this occurred, so the incidence of subcontracting and other informal employment practices increased.

From the political economy perspective, the formal/informal distinction serves to illustrate the slow development of citizenship in Latin America. In the early stages of urbanization and industrialization, when few had effective citizen rights, the formal/informal distinction had little salience since most workers were subject to arbitrary dismissal and casual working careers. The formal/informal distinction becomes most prominent when rights become dependent on certain types of employment and, because of the weakness of democratic pressure groups, are not extended to the general urban population. Informal activities, in this context, substitute for formal State welfare provision in various spheres of urban life: providing access to a bare subsistence income, to housing, and social security. The implication of this argument is that the disappearance of the informal sector depends on the extension of the citizenship to Latin American urban dwellers to assure basic welfare rights, not tied to employment.[2]

---

[2]Such an extension would not necessarily lead to full employment in the formal sector, but could result, as in the British case, in high levels of unemployment but without an informal sector. See Roberts (1989b) for a comparison of Britain, Spain, and Mexico on these dimensions. Whether there is an informal sector in Britain remains a subject of controversy, but there is no evidence for an informal sector there of the Latin American type—one in which the main support of households is derived from unregulated economic activities.

3 1

Substantive rationalities.

Most of the analyses dealing with the general characteristics of the informal sector in Latin America, have focused on individual behavior when not dealing with enterprise characteristics. This is particularly true in the case of PREALC whose surveys have noted such individual characteristics as education, income, and employment status. The sources have skewed the data in that non-individual units of analysis such as the household, kinship or friendship networks and the community are rarely considered by PREALC in relation to the informal sector.

It is to these other units of analysis, and to the related concern with the substantive rationality of the informal sector, that I now turn. This concern is traceable at least as far back as the work of Boeke on dualism in Indonesia (1942, 1953) and, especially, to Geertz's (1963) contrast between the economies of the bazaar and the firm. The issue that Geertz takes up is that of the different rationalities of the two economies. The bazaar economy uses labor intensely and in apparently economically irrational ways, but its logic is to minimize risk rather than maximize profit. Consequently, the time spent in maintaining relationships and obtaining information, while often having little direct economic payoff, serves to guarantee some economic stability and predictability in a highly competitive economic environment. In contrast, the economy of the firm allocates resources in an economically rational way to maximize profits. It is capital rather than labor intensive. The firms have a dominant market position, and usually rely on government regulation to make the economic environment stable and calculable.

Analyzing the non-market rationalities that influence the economic behavior of city dwellers is essential to understanding why the informal sector persists during economic modernization. It provides a "bottom-up" view of the opportunities of the urban economy, suggesting why such an impoverished and exploitative sector of the economy engenders positive commitments on the part of its members. I suggest that we need to see the urban economy as presenting those seeking subsistence with a set of opportunity structures, and not, as is customary in much labor market analysis, with a set of positions to which people are fitted according to the match between position and their socioeconomic characteristics.[3] It is not jobs *per se* but how jobs combine with other key elements in urban subsistence—e.g., housing, the division of labor within a household and the household's consumption patterns of social networks—that provide different opportunity sets for people in broadly similar economic positions. Often, this has the effect of leading even the urban poor to see themselves as being confronted by choice as well as constraint in the labor market.

These issues were developed by Keith Hart (1973, 1975) in a series of articles based upon field work in Ghana in the 1960s in which he introduced the term "informal sector" to describe the insertion of the Frafra of Ghana in the urban labor market. In his 1973 article, Hart sought to demonstrate that apparently marginal and, at times, illegal economic activities were an integral and normal part of the Accra economy which contributed to the growth in incomes of the urban poor. To Hart, the key distinction was the degree of rationalization of work, the formal sector being that where labor is recruited on a permanent and regular basis for fixed rewards, while the informal consisted of more casual and irregular forms of employment and in self-employment. Illegitimate activities were classed as informal.

The existence of the informal sector in Accra was based on an uneven economic development in which migration outpaced the growth in formal employment opportunities. The vitality of the informal sector was due to the particular needs, qualifications and aspirations of urban migrants. Hart (1975) showed the importance of cooperation and exchange amongst the Frafra for their survival in both town and country. Migrants retained interests in land and

---

[3] I am following Przeworski's (1982) line of analysis in which he argues that the behavior of any group in an objectively similar economic position, such as the manual working class, always involves choices as well as constraints. In part, this is because of the different ways in which "needs" can be defined and met. In part, it is because people usually act on the assumption that they are not constrained by the choices of others so that, for example, small-scale entrepreneurs believe that they will make it even though it is objectively impossible in the economic structure of Latin America for all but a tiny fraction to be successful.

property in the homeland, and these were important to their chances of marriage. They ploughed money back into the homelands, as well as into the maintenance of Frafra associational activity in the towns. The Frafra, Hart pointed out, did not come to town to become proletarians. They come to earn money to maintain their way of life. Consequently, the urban economic activities of the Frafra were designed less to further individual consumption or advancement than to maintain the network of ties and obligations essential to Frafra conceptions of security and lifestyle. The informal sector provided diverse and flexible income opportunities suited to Frafra migrants whose ethnicity and lack of formal qualifications, in any case, barred them from stable job opportunities in the formal sector.

This kind of approach was commonly used to study the informal sector in Latin America in the 1970s and later (Bromley and Gerry 1979; Eckstein 1975; Roberts 1975; Peattie 1975). It built upon earlier studies of the urban poor which, themselves, were responses to Oscar Lewis's concept of the culture of poverty— particularly, the implication that the urban poor were fatalistic and relatively passive. Anthropologists such as Anthony Leeds (1972) and Lisa Peattie (1968) sought to demonstrate that the poor, though structurally denied the possibility of substantially improving their position, were astute and active in making the best of an economically difficult situation. This line of analysis emphasized the interconnections between formal and informal sectors. It was not isolation that accounted for the vitality of the informal sector, but a social organization that enabled those within it to provide and receive goods and services from the formal sector without becoming totally dependent on it.

The detailed case studies that come out of this tradition of analysis showed that the workings of the informal sector were part of the wider set of community relationships that enable the poor to survive in the cities of the developing world. The informal sector was both directly and indirectly a lynch pin of the system by which the poor obtained welfare in the absence of public provision. It created earning opportunities for the aged and for the young, enabling them to contribute to the domestic economy and supplement the inadequate incomes of the "breadwinner." Household and neighborhood cooperation in obtaining and building housing are other examples of the informal provision of welfare—as are the information networks that serve as sources of advice and enable people in the informal sector to obtain jobs or conduct their business as well as solicit caring and aid in emergency. In this way, the informal sector, based on locality and local labor markets, can reinforce community relationships and, in turn, be reinforced by them (though it is recognized, of course, that informal sector entrepreneurial activities also can be divisive of communities).

Community and the informal sector.

Focusing on the substantive rationality of the informal sector raises the issue of the fit between the economic activities of that sector and social relationships among those within it. Reliance on family labor is, for example, seen as a defining characteristic of the informal sector in both the PREALC and the political economy perspectives. As noted above, broadly defined the informal sector is the means whereby city people make out in the absence both of State provision of basic welfare services and of private mutual interest associations which defend their members and advance their interests. In the European countries, during the long period of their urbanization and industrialization, people came to cope with the economic and social uncertainties of urban life by developing associations such as trade unions or friendly societies and by securing State provision of basic welfare. Even in these societies, especially in the early period of urbanization, basic security was provided by urban social networks based on family, local community and, in the case of migrants, fellow villagers (Anderson 1971).

As Mingione (1987) points out, the informal sector in developing countries, and the social relationships involved in it, are protective of those who do not have the individual characteristics, such as education or income, to survive in the competitive and impersonal world of the large city. They are protected economically in two ways. First, they are sheltered from competition in the labor market since jobs in the informal sector are recruited through kinship and community networks and are not generally available to outsiders; in this restricted sense, the informal sector is not an easy-access sector because entry into depends on having certain skills and relationships. Secondly, they have some relief from broader market pressures since mutual aid within the informal sector and its low cost goods and services allow people substitutes for the same goods and services (e.g., housing, transport, child care) that are more expensive on the formal market.

The nature of family and community relationships and their affinity with the informal sector will vary culturally and in terms of such variables as size of city, urban economic structure and the degree of social and residential mobility within a particular city. Consequently, relationships will differ by country, by type of city and by time period, in terms of the opportunities they provide for urban populations. An example of this variation can be found in southern Italy where, it is argued, urban kinship and community relationships have been so weakened by the pattern of urbanization that, in the social as well as economic sense, the informal sector does not flourish (Mingione, 1987). In Latin America, there has been relatively little comparative research on this issue. There is a large number of carefully conducted case studies of the social and cultural organization of the informal sector but, to my knowledge, little that explicitly compares the strength, say, of kinship organization in different settings and relates it to the relative dynamism of the informal sector.

We can start with the pattern of urbanization and its timing. Most of the familiar Latin American case studies of the informal sector—in Mexico, in Ecuador, in Brazil, and in Peru—have been carried out in countries and cities experiencing rapid urban growth based, to a great extent, on rural out-migration. There are two interesting dimensions of contrast here, one based on stage of urbanization, the other on rural social organization. In the early period of urbanization, the way people coped in the cities of Latin America inevitably was influenced by the fact of an intensified competition for jobs and living accommodation resulting from the large numbers of young adults entering the urban labor and housing market. The intensity of this competition, and the circumstance that the only relevant social and economic capital of many migrants was their social networks, meant that kinship and community relationships were likely to be unusually important in coping with urban life.

We are now entering a period in which the predominant migration patterns are no longer rural to urban, but urban-to-urban, and international. This implies that competition over jobs and space is likely to assume a different character when compared with the earlier period. For a start, those entering the urban labor market are now more likely to have been socialized into its practices either in the city of residence or in one of previous residence. In our sample of workers in formal industry in Guadalajara, we found that most were born in the city and had previously worked in informal workshops where they gained their skills. Migrants in our study were concentrated in construction. I am suggesting that changes in labor supply in the city, and in their social networks, are likely to provide a different pattern of opportunities for informal sector activities. Predominantly urban-entry cohorts (and, usually young, single urban recruits) provide the basis for an increasing differentiation within the informal sector as manufacturing and service enterprises base themselves on cheap, unprotected labor either in informally organized firms or as out-workers.

Countries have differed in the extent rural structures allowed migrants to capitalize on these. In a comparison of Peru and Guatemala (Roberts 1974), I have noted that migrants to Lima had more reason to maintain on-going relationships with their villages of origin than did migrants to Guatemala City. The salience of their relationships with places of origin to the Peruvian migrants meant that they provided receptive bridgeheads for further migrants who were incorporated into established city colonies and used in the informal sector enterprises of their fellow-villagers (Alderson-Smith 1984). In Guatemala in the 1960s, there was some evidence of fellow-villagers living close to each other and working in the same enterprise, but my impression remains that the extent to which kinship and community helped people to cope in Guatemala was much less than in Peru.

There is a striking contrast between my (1973) report of community organization in a squatter settlement in Guatemala City and Lomnitz's (1977) account for a similar settlement in Mexico City. Relative to the case data, there is more internal competition and "disorganization" in Guatemala while, evidently, those in Mexico City are more cooperative and communitarian. This contrast is due to major differences between the two settings: To a considerable extent, the Mexican settlement consisted of migrants from the same rural area who had found each other jobs in a nearby factory; the Guatemalan settlement, however, contained people from many different parts of the country, who worked all over the city, and who had few ties with their villages of origin.

A note of caution is needed at this point: Whether in the informal or the formal sector, local networks are important in obtaining work—but I suspect that they serve as much to facilitate economic exploitation as economic independence, enabling the young, women, and the old to gain access to a low income but not providing them with the means to accumulate capital or earn enough to maintain a family. Kinship and community remain the essential bases of social welfare in Latin America's cities because of a generalized poverty and the lack of public provision. The increasing importance of informal employment for the survival of urban households emphasizes the significance of these local relationships. The employment of women outside the home (usually obtained through local networks) is mainly in the informal sector is likely to emphasize the importance of the informal caring provided by household and community since it is likely that these workers receive no coverage from such entitlement programs as social security.

The informal sector, then, emphasizes local relationships and localism, but its effect on community are likely to be varied. Informal sector activities are likely to be competitive and exploitative, often weakening community solidarity, but common needs and exchanges in the absence of welfare provision by State or private agencies will tend to strengthen community bonds. In some cases, such as that of Santiago, Chile, reports suggest that this localism has weakened community solidarity and collective action (Tironi 1987). Previously, the impulse for community action had come from workers' organizations, but with the closing of many industries, *pobladores* must increasingly find work in casual activities in or around their neighborhood.

One factor in the changing significance of kinship and community is the increasing salience of the household as the means of coping with urban life. In several recent reports, it is clear that people have confronted the current economic crisis through household relationships, e.g., in order that more members of the household may work and contribute to the common pot, children delay leaving the household (whether to marry or set up independently). The importance of the household can often be at the expense of wider kinship or community relationships. Household members concentrate resources and time in household-related activities (including paid work outside), frequently at the expense of their relationships with other kin, neighbors, or friends. This, of course, is far from the privatization based on home and family noted in the European countries and contrasted with previously more communitarian patterns of public participation and urban community life. It does make clear, however, one of the contradictions of the informal sector in its broader sense: The sector makes available a broad and flexible set of income opportunities that enable the poor to survive, but the money gained is so low that the expenditure of considerable time and effort is required to earn enough for subsistence, diminishing the time available for investing in social networks and thus limiting their welfare potential.

The culture of informality.

The final issue which I will take up is that of the affinity of informal sector economic activities with practices and beliefs in other spheres of urban life in Latin America. The issue here is whether there is a more general socioculture developing, of which the informal sector is a part. This altered socioculture would emphasize the importance of chance, the unpredictable and the opportunistic, while downplaying work as a source of identity and social mobility. Peter Fry (1978) noted, for example, the affinity of *Umbanda* (a syncretic religion) with more general features of Brazilian socioculture, including the informal sector.

The issue has acquired a certain notoriety because of the increasing importance of the drug trade to the economies of Latin America. The drug economy is, in certain respects, the informal sector *par excellence* —in some locales, e.g., Bolivia, even replacing the formal economy in economic importance (Blanes 1989). It is not formally regulated by government; it depends heavily on informal social networks to conduct its business; and it generates a great deal of small-scale employment. It evidently contributes to the informalization of other spheres of life through the bribing of government officials and the corruption of justice.

In Brazil, it has become part of the fabric of social and economic life in low-income urban areas, providing employment, becoming involved in local politics and, by the conspicuous life styles of the traffickers, provided an alternative set of role models and career opportunities to the local inhabitants. I will use a detailed community study for Rio de Janeiro to take up the issue of the values of those involved in informal employment as contrasted with those in the drug economy (Zaluar 1986, 1987). Zaluar's informants are mainly involved in informal economic activities—casual workers in construction, street sellers, and the like. In this respect, the economic position of such workers is as unstable and unregulated by the State as is that of those involved in the neighborhood's drug trade. She notes, however, important differences in attitudes to work: Those not involved in drugs take a certain pride in emphasizing that they, unlike the drug traders, "work" for a living. They stress the virtue of hard work as bringing real material gains and contrast such gains with the flashy but ephemeral consumption of those in the drug trade since, they say, such efforts do not lead to lasting gains. The equation they draw is that poverty leads to work while wealth leads to idleness. Those involved in the drug trade (including the participants' children and relatives), are viewed as having money but as not working for it. While their wealth may be envied, the drug traffickers are also depreciated because they are not seen as workers. Zaluar stresses that, in the community in which she has worked, people treat drug traffickers as a normal part of neighborhood life, seeking favors and even contributions to community projects from them. But, while there is no great hostility towards the drug traffickers, neither is there admiration.

What Zaluar's analysis suggests is the need to discriminate carefully when relating participation in the varied activities of the informal sector to broader identities. There are few types of informal employment that are likely to convince their workers of the virtues of entrepreneurship or of the ease by which one can get something for nothing. The reality of most work in the informal sector is that it is only by hard and persistent work that an adequate subsistence is to be gained. The other reality of the informal sector is that whatever benefits are gained for the individual or the family come from their direct effort, not through State beneficence or company protection. These realities are likely to have contradictory implications for identity and aspirations. There is little in the nature of informal economic activities that is likely to persuade people of the virtues of collective action or the prospect of social mobility. They also appear to keep alive the belief in material progress both for themselves and for their children. Yet, it is clear that they do engender a strong sense of being workers in contrast to the affluent or non-workers.

An important reason for suggesting that the working culture of informal and formal sectors is not all that distinct is that the boundaries of the two sectors are not likely to be clear-cut to the urban population of Latin America. In their working careers, individuals will often pass from one sector to the other, beginning in the informal sector, passing to the formal and, in later middle age, returning to the informal sector. As suggested above, these movements are based partly on choice and partly on constraint. At times, informal sector employment offers higher and more flexible forms of income than could be gained in the formal given age and qualifications. These times will vary depending on economic circumstances, but there are also the constraints on choice resulting from the limited number of jobs in the formal sector and the qualifications needed for entry. At the level of the household, the situation is more fluid since it is common for different members to work in different sectors. Since it is the household rather than an individual's income that determines the welfare of its members, the particular type of job, whether formal or informal, is likely to be less important for the occupational culture of household members than the fact of having work and contributing to the common pot.

Conclusion.

The types of economic activity that are classed in the informal sector provide a substantial part of the employment in Latin American cities. This proportion, often as much as half the labor force, is not likely to diminish. Earlier expectations that economic growth would eliminate informality have been confounded not simply because of the economic conjuncture of the debt crisis but because of general economic trends, e.g., the restructuring of the international economy. In the developed world, industrialization and urbanization has produced a modern economic environment in which State provision and the development of an extensive formal service economy resolves the employment issue either by paying people not to work or by incorporating them flexibly into the new economic roles. In Latin America, which never became economically modern in the European sense, the post-modern urban economy has made use of, and fostered, the informal sector.

The informal sector in Latin America does not involve simply a question of economic activities; it is linked inextricably to community organization and welfare provision. The practices of the informal sector in this broader sense, including its community and household welfare aspects, contrast with the sphere of State action, based on a limited public provision of welfare and the formal sector of the economy. This latter sector has become an increasingly irrelevant source of income and protection for the Latin American working classes. Thus, the interesting relations to explore are those between State and local community, relations structured by the State's circumscribed set of administrative and economic practices that only tangentially affect the bulk of the urban population that, all the while, continues actively to secure its own livelihood within a community economically integrated in the informal sphere but not well articulated politically or culturally.

References.

Alderson-Smith, G.
1984   Confederations of Households: Extended Domestic Enterprises. In N. Long and B. Roberts, eds., City and Country: Miners, Peasants and Entrepreneurs. Cambridge: Cambridge University Press, pp.217-234.

Anderson, M.
1971   Family Structure in Nineteenth Century Lancashire. Cambridge: Cambridge University Press.

Arias, P. and B. R. Roberts
1985   The City in Permanent Transition: The Consequences of a National System of Industrial Specialization. In J. Walton, ed., Capital and Labor in the Urbanized World. Beverly Hills CA: Sage Publications, pp. 149-175.

Benaria, L. and M. Roldan
1977   The Crossroads of Class and Gender. Chicago: University of Chicago Press.

Blanes, J.
1989   Cocaine, Informality and the Urban Economy in La Paz, Bolivia. In A. Portes, M. Castells and L. Benton, eds., The Informal Economy. Baltimore: John Hopkins Press, pp.135-149.

Boeke, J. H.
1942   The Structure of the Netherlands Indian Economy. New York: International Secretariat, Institute of Pacific Relations.
1953   Economics and Economic Policy of Dual Societies as Exemplified by Indonesia. New York: International Secretariat of Pacific Relations.

Breman, J.
    1985   A   Dualistic   Labor   System?   A   Critique   of   the
            "Informal Sector" Concept.   In R. Bromley, ed.,
            Planning for Small Enterprises in Third World Cities.
            Oxford: Pergamon Press, pp. 43-64.

Bromley, R. and C. Gerry, eds.
    1979   Casual Work and Poverty in Third World Cities.
            Chichester: John Wiley and Sons.

De Soto, H.
    1986   El Otro Sendero.   Lima: Editorial El Barranco.

Eckstein, S.
    1975   The   Political   Economy   of   Lower   Class   Areas   in
            Mexico City: Societal Constraints on Local Business
            Prospects.   In W. Cornelius and F. Trueblood, eds.,
            Latin American Urban Research 5.   Beverly Hills CA:
            Sage: Beverly Hills, pp. 125-146.

Escobar, A.
    1986   Con el sudor de tu frente: mercado de trabajo y clase
            obrera en Guadalajara.   Guadalajara: El Colegio de
            Jalisco.

Fry, P.
    1978   Two   Religious   Movements: Protestantism   and
            Umbanda.   In J. Wirth, ed., Manchester and São Paulo.
            Stanford: Stanford University Press, pp. 177-202.

Geertz, C.
    1963   Peddlers   and   Princes: Social   Development   and
            Economic   Change   in   Two   Indonesian   Towns.
            Chicago: University of Chicago Press.

Hart, K.
    1973   Informal   Income   Opportunities   and   Urban
            Employment in Ghana.   Journal of Modern African
            Studies 11: 61-89.

1975   Rural-Urban Migration and the Proletarianization of the Peasantry in West Africa. Discussion Paper, Center of International and Area Studies, University of London.

International Labor Office.
1972   Employment, Incomes and Equality: A Strategy for Increasing Productive Employment in Kenya. Geneva: International Labor Office.

Leeds, A.
1971   The Culture of Poverty Concept: Conceptual, Logical and Empirical Problems, with Perspectives from Brazil and Peru. In E. Leacock, ed., The Culture of Poverty: A Critique. New York: Simon and Schuster, pp.226-284.

Lomnitz, L.
1977   Networks and Marginality: Life in a Mexican Shanty Town. New York: Academic Press.

Malloy, J.
1985   Politics, Fiscal Crisis and Social Security Reform in Brazil. Meadville PA: Allegheny College.

Marshall, A.
1987   Non-Standard Employment Practices in Latin America. ILO Discussion Papers, Labor Market Program. Geneva: IILS.

Mingione, E.
1987   Economic Development, Social Factors and Social Context. Paper presented at the annual meeting of the American Sociological Association, Chicago.

Moser, C.
1978   Informal Sector or Petty Commodity Production: Dualism or Dependence in Urban Development? World Development 6: 1041-1064.

Peattie, L.
1968   The View from the Barrio. Ann Arbor: University of Michigan Press.
1975   "Tertiarization" and Urban Poverty in Latin America In W. Cornelius and F. Trueblood, eds., Latin American Urban Research 5. Beverly Hills CA: Sage Publications, pp. 109-124.

Portes, A.
1985   Latin American Class Structures. Latin American Research Review XX: 7-39.

Portes, A.,and J. Walton, eds.
1981   Labor, Class and the International System. New York: Academic Press.

Portes, A., S. Blitzer, and J. Curtis
1986   The Urban Informal Sector in Uruguay: Its Internal Structure, Characteristics, and Effects. World Development 14: 727-741.

Portes, A., and S. Sassen-Koob
1987   Making it Underground: Comparative Material on the Informal Sector in Western Market Economies. American Journal of Sociology 93: 30-61.

PREALC
1976   The Employment Problem in Latin America. Santiago: PREALC.
1987   Ajuste y Deuda Social: Un Enfoque Estructural. Santiago: PREALC 1978 Sector Informal: Funcionamiento y Políticas. Santiago: PREALC.

Przeworski, A.
1982   Teoría sociológica y el estudio de la población: reflexiones sobre el trabajo de la Comisión de Población y Desarrollo de CLACSO. In W. Mertens, et al., Reflexiones teórico-metodológicas sobre

investigaciones en población.   México, D.F.: El
Colegio de México, pp. 59-100.

Roberts, B.
1973   Organizing Strangers: Poor Families in Guatemala
City. Austin: University of Texas Press.
1974   The Interrelationships of City and Provinces in Peru
and Guatemala. In W. Cornelius and F. Trueblood,
eds., Latin American Research 4. Beverly Hills CA:
Sage Publications, pp. 207-236.
1975   Center and Periphery in the Development Process: The
Case of Peru. In W. Cornelius and F. Trueblood, eds.,
Latin American Urban Research 5.   Beverly Hills
CA:Sage Publications, pp. 77-106.
1987   The Other Working Class: Uncommitted Labor in
Britain, Spain and Mexico.   Paper presented to the
annual meeting of the American Sociological
Association, Chicago.
1989a   Employment Structure, Life Cycle, and Life Chances:
Formal and Informal Sectors in Guadalajara. In A.
Portes, M. Castells, and L. Benton, eds., The Informal
Economy: Comparative Studies in Advanced and Third
World Countries.   Baltimore: Johns Hopkins Press,
pp. 41-59.
1989b   The Other Working Class: Uncommitted Labor in
Britain, Spain and Mexico. In M. Kohn, ed., Cross-
National Research in Sociology. Beverly Hills CA:
Sage Publications, pp. 352-372.

Tironi, E.
1987   Pobladores e integración social. Proposiciones 14: 64-
84.

Tokman, V.
1986   The Informal Sector: Fifteen Years Later. Paper presented to Conference on the Comparative Study of the
Informal Sector, Harper's Ferry WV, October.

Zaluar, A.
1985   A máquina e a revolta: As organizaçoes populares e o significado da pobreza. Editora Brasiliense: São Paulo.
1987   Crime e criminalidade nas classes populares do Rio de Janeiro. Paper presented to Quarto deminario do grupo de trabalho direito e sociede de Clacso, Belo Horizonte, Setembro.

THE INFORMAL ECONOMY AND
THE STATE IN TANZANIA

Aili Mari Tripp
Department of Political Science
Northwestern University

Introduction.

The informal economy has grown and taken on many new dimensions in recent years in Tanzania as a result of the economic crisis of the late 1970s and 1980s. This growth is part of a whole series of survival strategies people have adopted to weather the crisis. There has, for example, been a dramatic growth in informal income-generating activities of urban wage earners and their household members as a result of declining real incomes. Large numbers of people have started farming on the outskirts of the city. Some have left their urban jobs altogether to move back to the countryside to farm. Frequently, the husband will remain in the city, keeping his job, while his wife and children return to the countryside to farm. Once the wife's situation is sufficiently secure, the husband will leave his job and join the rest of his family. Those who cannot initiate a base in the countryside often start sideline enterprises, eventually leaving wage work to become self-employed on a full-time basis.

These phenomena are by no means peculiar to Tanzania. However, of all African countries, Tanzania has experienced one of the sharpest declines in real income in the past ten years. Tanzanian wage earners in general suffered a 65% decline in real wages 1979-1984, consumer prices increased tenfold from 1976-1986 and, in the same period, the ratio of minimum wage earnings to agricultural value added per worker declined by 60%. Thus, workers suffered a much steeper decline in income than agricultural producers (Helleiner 1985: 25; Ghai 1987).

49

While there are many interesting and relevant dimensions to this expansion of the informal economy in Tanzania, this paper will stress how this particular sector of the economy has been a catalyst for political and economic change, forcing a redefinition of the boundaries of State control as seen in the recent liberalizing, privatizing and State-shrinking trends in the country. While external stresses such as the International Monetary Fund (IMF) have played a role in the liberalization process, there have also been internal forces pressuring the State from below. These internal strains have come about where societal preferences and choices are not always consonant with the State's notions of how people should go about making a living. One mechanism of such internal societal pressure is the constant day-to-day non-compliance with State policy. The informal economy could, in many ways, be considered in terms of these "everyday forms of resistance"—a phrase popularized by James Scott (1986). This paper shows how the exercise of such non-compliance via the informal economy is quietly and effectively changing the predicates of politics from within society without openly confronting the State.

Brief mention must be made concerning the field work upon which the data and analysis are based. Research was conducted between 1987 and 1988 in Dar es Salaam, the largest city in Tanzania. Dar es Salaam has a population of nearly 1.4 million while Tanzania's population as a whole is around 23 million. Altogether my assistant and I conducted over 1000 interviews. The study was concentrated in two of the most heavily populated parts of the city employing a cluster sample survey and in-depth interviews. One of the areas is Buguruni, an older part of Dar es Salaam, and the other is Manzese, a relatively recently developed area. Both are primarily working class neighborhoods whose residents depend heavily on income from the informal sector. We interviewed local Party leaders, teachers and religious leaders as well as ordinary citizens. We also conducted a smaller, city-wide survey of middle-income civil servants and their sideline incomes, expanding our network of informants as we went by using current contacts to collect new ones. Finally, since Tanzania has a one-party system, with Chama Cha Mapinduzi as the ruling party, top Party and government leaders, including several Cabinet members and Party

Central Committee members, were also interviewed. The basic focus of the research to investigate: (1) How are people in the city, and in particular wage earners, surviving today amidst unprecedented hardship; (2) how are their survival strategies shaped by State policy; (3) how do these same strategies in turn affect State policy? A decade ago the wages of an average worker would not only support a family but could even provide for additional relatives. Further, at that time few urban women were wage workers or self-employed. In contrast, today, everyone in Tanzania knows that no one is simply living off official wages. Survival requires that household heads have sidelines and that other household members—especially women, children, and retired/senior citizens—also practice income generating activities. The latter are as diverse as agriculture, animal husbandry, sewing, food vending, shoemaking, carpentry, and hairdressing; in short, anything that produces income.

The study showed that these sideline income-generating activities can easily bring in ten to fifteen times the income of formal wages—which generally cover expenses for only three days of the month for a family of six. These sideline activities are usually untaxed, unlicensed and outside of State controls and supports, clearly making them part of the informal economy. Virtually all employed people engage in these sideline activities, but the kinds of strategies that people choose depend on their class, occupation, education, gender, age and ethnic group. The sideline activities of some may be related to their job, e.g., teachers often hold tutorial sessions after hours; others perform work completely unrelated to jobs held in the formal sector, e.g., an office clerk may run a food stall or repair radios.

Everyday forms of resistance.

Within the conflict literature on "everyday forms of resistance," the focus has generally been on peasant strategies to resist pressure to extract labor, food, taxes, rents and interest. The strategies include: malicious gossip and slander, foot dragging, calculated error, feigned incompetence, pilfering, arson, banditry, vandalism, crop destruction, or denial of labor or resources from a landlord, patron or the State (Scott 1985, 1986; Adas 1981, 1986).

51

These are generally individual acts of resistance and they are characterized by the fact that they "avoid any direct symbolic confrontation with authority or with elite norms" (Scott 1985: 29).

The emphasis in this literature has been on everyday forms of resistance as attempts to preserve the *status quo* in the face of external pressures to change. The strategies are seen primarily as defensive measures that derive from the risk-aversive character of subsistence production where the prerequisite to survival is placing a protective perimeter around subsistence routines within which risks are avoided (Scott 1976). Although this body of literature is primarily concerned with peasant strategies, many of the same principles could be extended to the urban context. Similar strategies are clearly visible in the urban informal sector's attempts to evade State control. Both the rural and urban informal sectors of Tanzania exhibit this conservative form of non-compliance.

However, the Tanzanian case (and probably many others) also demonstrates another more active side to these forms of protest which suggests that Scott's characterization of these strategies may be too limited. While the choice of strategy for resistance may derive from Scott's notion of a subsistence ethic or risk aversion, non-compliance is not simply a defense mechanism or an attempt to preserve the *status quo* in the face of pressures to change. It can, in point of fact, be an important impetus and pressure point for policy change as my paper will show with respect to urban survival strategies.

In addition, the emphasis on the individual nature of these acts of non-compliance underestimates the collective impact that these efforts have in bringing about change. When one examines the rationales behind individual acts of non-compliance one often finds far greater collective consciousness than the individualistic nature of acts of non-compliance might reflect. Moreover, the pervasiveness and spread of individual strategies of non-compliance may have important collective impact in changing policy on the part of the powers that be.

This is what happened in no small measure to Tanzania's collectivization program in the 1960s and 1970s. Goran Hyden (1980) has shown how peasants tried every step of the way to extract all they could from the State in terms of public goods and services, while evading government pressures to collectivize farming and regulate their production. I would add to this that the effect of peasants' "evasion of the State" was the State's retreat from "village-ization" in the 1980s, and even an admission on the part of some top government and party leaders in recent years that the policy was ill-conceived and poorly carried out.

Similarly, throughout the 1970s, monopsonic crop authorities paid poor prices to peasants producing cash crops, sometimes two-thirds below world market prices. This resulted in a series of individual strategies that had collective impact. Most significantly, peasants sold the majority of their crops on parallel markets to obtain better prices, thereby depriving the government of badly needed foreign exchange and revenue. Peasants also shifted to the production of food and other more lucrative cash crops, or left agricultural production altogether and moved to the city, seeking self-employment. As a result of this "collective action," the level of officially marketed crops dropped so low that it necessitated a change in policy on the part of the government which, since 1986, has increased producer prices, from 30% for cotton and tobacco to 80% for coffee.

The study of the rural/urban informal economy in Tanzania challenges the emphasis in the non-compliance literature of the defensive, passive nature of these strategies, showing that the desire to bring about change in State policy can also generate active measures. Moreover, although the resistance may initially start out in the form of a simple defensive reaction to change, the strategies often involve a collective consciousness that goes beyond isolated individual acts of non-compliance, leading to changes in State policy that could only be brought about through collective pressure.

Contracting boundaries of state control.

The change to which I refer is the retreat of the boundaries of State control in the economy, i.e., the recent liberalizing trends within the country. These trends include such measures as the liberalization of internal and external trade, cuts in government expenditure, streamlining and elimination of inefficient State companies, reduction of price controls on goods, raising of producer prices, and encouraging private and foreign investment ventures. The crisis that necessitated these measures had its origins in both external and internal factors. External factors include the declining terms of trade after 1977, especially for coffee, Tanzania's largest export commodity. Another factor was the rise in import prices, especially Tanzania's oil bill, which trebled after the 1978 oil price increase. In addition, several internal factors contributed to the State's retreat. Many of these internal factors had their origins in the excessive State intervention and monopoly in the economy.

State intervention in the economy expanded dramatically after the Party's 1967 Arusha Declaration, which resulted in the nationalization of major financial, commercial and manufacturing institutions. In the years following the Arusha Declaration, hundreds of new public institutions and state companies, "parastatals," sprung up in virtually every sector. The State exerted a growing influence in virtually every area of social life. From 1972 to 1975 the State carried out a massive campaign to resettle rural people in villages. After 1975 it emphasized industrial investment at the expense of agriculture. In 1976, it launched a Universal Primary Education campaign; expanded health and water services; and abolished cooperatives, replacing them with crop authorities under the direct control of the government. Hiring in government agencies increased as did government expenditure. The State exerted greater control over small-scale enterprises, including agricultural smallholders. The bottom line was that, in the face of external pressures (particularly the decline in the terms of trade), the economy simply could not sustain this kind of government expansion. As a consequence, Tanzania became even more dependent on foreign aid and loans (Boesen et al. 1986).

Some of these policies had a direct effect on the expansion of the informal economy. As mentioned earlier, low producer prices led to an increase in parallel markets and many peasants left agriculture to work in small-scale enterprises. The Villages and *Ujamaa* Villages Act of 1975 had a prohibitive affect on individually owned small-scale enterprises in the villages since it decreed that all small industrial units were to be owned by the village, which itself would function as a multi-purpose cooperative society (Havnevik 1986: 280).

As the crisis deepened and shortages became more pervasive, hoarding, price hiking and sales of scarce commodities took place in parallel markets. Official pricing and government rationing of foods, evolved to deal with the shortages, had the opposite result and pushed even more commodities into the parallel market (Boesen, et al. 1986: 27). An Economic Sabotage Act was passed in 1983 and revised in 1984; a National Anti-Economic Sabotage Tribunal was set up to investigate and try offenders of economic crimes like price hiking, hoarding and smuggling. Initially, the efforts of this tribunal were welcomed. But it quickly lost support when it started harassing and turning against "ordinary people," most of whom participated to one degree or another in these parallel markets. Compounding the frustration, was the knowledge that the anti-corruption campaign left unscathed the largest operators—who continued to take advantage of the crisis to make large profits.

The severe commodity shortage also led to a growth of informal activities to meet people's basic needs. The early 1980s saw an increase in the small-scale manufacture of such products as soap, tie-and-dye material (cloth was virtually unobtainable until 1984), furniture varnish, mattresses, kerosene lamps, and a myriad of other common household and personal items. From this perspective, the informal economy can be seen to have served a safety valve function for the State, defusing an open legitimacy crisis at a time when economic calamity threatened its credibility. The informal economy emerged to meet people's needs where State decline had most affected their livelihood. For example, people attempted to make up the difference with informal, sideline jobs where the government could not ensure sufficient supplies of commodities, adequate wages and jobs.

In the early 1980s, however, the State was forced to pull back the boundaries of its control in the face of near economic collapse. Its plans had gone awry because, coupled with the fact that the government had over-extended itself and was simply unable to enforce many of its key policies, many factors had interfered, including the impact of the world economy. Moreover, politicians themselves had constituencies to appease and please, and the continuation of various policies began to threaten their own political futures. Lastly, as the rest of the paper will show, popular non-compliance with state regulations had no small role in this retreat. The retreat began with various stabilization and adjustment programs in the early 1980s and became even more visible after 1984 when a new emphasis was placed on the shrinking of government expenditure, privatization, liberalizing internal and external trade, decentralizing political structures in the countryside and opening the country to various foreign ventures.

It should be pointed out that although liberalization of the economy was initiated by former President Julius Nyerere, the question of how far these measures should go has been a matter of contention under the administration of the new President Ali Hassan Mwinyi. It has been a continuing source of conflict between the leadership of the government and that of the Party (presently headed by Nyerere), which would like to see more restraint in the reforms.

The following sections outline the shifts in State policy toward the urban informal economy in the 1980s. The changes demonstrate that people have not been complacent in seeking new sources of livelihood amidst economic hardship which has often been compounded by inflexible government policy. People have instead played an active role in bringing about changes to legitimate their survival strategies.

Changing the rules of the game.

With the onset of the economic crisis and the broadening of the country's structural problems, the beleaguered leadership needed to assert its strength and show that it was in control. Indeed, this had been one reason behind the government's first attempted resettlement of "unemployed" (mostly self-employed) residents of Dar es Salaam into neighboring villages as early as 1976. It did not take long before the majority of them had returned to the city—some only a few hours after being moved out! As the crisis intensified, the government enacted a Penal Code amendment in 1983 which banned from the cities "idle and disorderly persons" involved in so-called "unproductive" activities (Shaidi 1987).

A year later the Human Resources Deployment Act was passed, requiring all Tanzanians to be registered and provided with labor identification cards. Those who could not meet these requirements (including the self-employed) were to be resettled in the countryside. In the Dar es Salaam region all unlicensed self-employed people, whether they were shoeshiners, peanut vendors, bicycle repairmen or tailors, were lumped into this "idle and disorderly category" and treated as "loiterers." President Nyerere depicted this campaign as a strong vehicle for promoting economic production and ordered the Prime Minister to be "bold" in implementing this act, saying: "If we don't disturb loiterers, they will disturb us." The so-called loiterers were compared with economic saboteurs and racketeers "whom the nation has declared war on" (*Daily News* 9/26/1983: 1). Immediately following the enactment of the Deployment Act, the national service soldiers and people's militia started rounding up thousands of suspected loiterers on a random basis. However, the campaign was short-lived and by 1984, when the crisis began to subside, the mass arrests were curtailed significantly.

The State was, in effect, targeting most urban dwellers in Dar es Salaam, the majority of whom were engaged in these small income-generating activities. Not surprisingly, the task proved to be far beyond the capacity of the State. Moreover, it merely served to antagonize the majority of the population who simply could not see the point of this policy. It was implemented at a time when there were virtually no new jobs, and even more affluent middle income workers were being forced to seek informal sideline incomes. The campaign failed because people went on with their daily income-generating activities as they always had, ignoring the new policy because survival was contingent on continuance of these activities.

The absurdity of the policy was underscored by reports such as that giving an account of 22 shoeshiners who were arrested on the grounds of being unproductive. It was discovered that several of them were physically handicapped and half of them were students at a nearby vocational school who were trying to supplement their income through this sideline activity. A city official warned them against turning to shoeshining and told them to find jobs (at a time when virtually no jobs were available). He announced that people with leather shoes needing regular polishing should learn to do it themselves. "Otherwise you have to buy safari boots or canvass [sic] shoes" (*Daily News* 11/17/1983: 3).

Public response to this campaign was by no means neutral. The notion that these activities were not "productive" made little sense to most people. What the campaign did accomplish was to expose the depth of the chasm separating the state and society and their respective notions of self-reliance and economic justice. The *Tanzanian Daily News* (10/2/1983: 5) carried a series of interviews with self-employed people and asked them about the illegality and "unproductive" nature of their activities. One fishmonger said:

> I regard this activity as being gainful. Everyday I make a profit of at least 100 and 200 shillings or more at best. I have a wife and five children who are dependent on me. It is a good thing that people should be involved in some gainful activity or other. But there are people who have their businesses who will be harassed for no good reason. I don't see how you will convince me that a certain job is better than what I am doing now. Even if you give me employment in your company, I won't accept it. I just couldn't survive on a monthly salary.

A peanut vendor responded:

> I tell you I have been able to keep a wife and four children by doing nothing but selling groundnuts. My children are now in school and I rent a house. I have saved 3000 shillings in a bank. I have even helped people who are employed in offices who came to me to borrow money when in financial trouble.

A knife sharpener answered:

> It would not be fair to dismiss this as a useless activity since very many people depend on us. Shopkeepers, hoteliers, butchers and even other individuals bring their knives and *pangas* [machetes] for sharpening. The government should instead give us licenses and a place where we can conduct our activities.

Around the time the new President Ali Hassan Mwinyi came to power in 1985, the policy began to soften and the government gave official recognition to them by commencing the licensing of these small micro-enterprises. People's insistence on going about their own affairs and completely disregarding official policy finally pressured State policy into recognizing their right to be self-employed in jobs of their own choosing.

Referring to this change in policy, one young man we interviewed said:

> Up to now the government has failed because it wants people to work, but it fails to provide work. They arrested people and sent them to the villages without capital. Even in the past we were not loiterers, we were doing *shughuli ndogo ndogo* [micro-enterprises] but the government did not want to recognize what we were doing. Now, at least, they have considered that.

While many appreciate that they no longer have to run from the City Council militia for engaging in "unproductive activities," the whole question of licensing has posed a new set of problems. In a country where there are few government welfare provisions and the people themselves have to care for their own sick, elderly, disabled and unemployed, and in a situation where wages are not adequate, licensing regulations are often seen as a violation of popular notions of redistributive justice. Moreover, in order to pay the license one has to go through the bureaucracy and pay bribes three to four times the cost of the license itself. As one woman pastry seller told me:

> I went to the legal councillor in our local Party branch to try to get out of paying the license. I have an old mother and father to support. My husband is blind. I have my own children to support and my sister died so I am taking care of her children. I have to support them off my pastry sales. All the councillor said to me was, "Tough. That is not my problem. That is your problem." I left his office and thought to myself, what can I do? All I have left to do is swallow stones!

The license fee is not large even by people's own standards, but it is the whole idea of State regulation of a part of life that is considered their own, the area of life that has to do with sustaining themselves, that they reject. In contrast, people express little concern about the heavy taxation of their formal wages, since this income is only a small fraction of their informal income, which is their primary source of livelihood.

Much of the informal economy in Tanzania operates along the lines of Karl Polanyi's "human economy," i.e., an economy where reciprocity and mutuality are paramount. Those who are advantaged help those less advantaged and survival strategies are collective rather than individual endeavors. This is why the the City Council militia's harassment, mainly of youth and women, over licenses does not sit well with most people we interviewed. It challenges the most basic notions of what it is to be human. One man offered the following reflection on this harrying:

> There are three kinds of laws in this world. The first one is spiritual. These are God's laws. These can't be changed. The

second kind of law is of the government and these laws can be changed since they are man-made. The third kind of law is that of *utu,* humanity. These laws are obviously lacking when you see this kind of behavior.

Nevertheless, there has been a marked change from 1983 when virtually all the self-employed were threatened with arrest. In November of 1987 President Mwinyi directed the Dar es Salaam City Council to stop harassing women and youth food vendors and let them continue their activities. (The City Council for reasons of its own did not heed this directive, indicating rival interests between different levels of the government itself.)

The change from 1983 was also evident in the remarks of the Director of the National Vocational Training Program Morgan Manyanga, who said in a speech to Parliament that the "informal sector" is a "hidden sector." Services, he said, are provided without valid training licenses, working contracts or taxation. He urged that such groups come out of "hiding" so that they could greatly help the nation by undertaking productive ventures. Although there is an element of absurdity in the notion that 95% of Dar es Salaam's population should "come out of hiding," the stance of this official is different from the tone exhibited in 1983, indicating a greater legitimation of these informal activities (*Daily News* 9/6/1986: 4).

Another indication of policy change toward the informal economy is the privatization of sectors that were previously controlled by state monopolies, e.g., the privatization of bus services. Up until 1983, the only buses that could legally operate were government-owned. The transport needs of the population, however, far exceeded the available services and, as the transport problem began to reach crisis proportions, informal buses called *daladala* came into greater use. Individuals also began to give people rides for a small fee, using a private vehicle as an illegal *taxibubu*. Both the drivers of these vehicles as well as the passengers were liable for a penalty if caught. One tactic people employed to evade police harassment was to pretend they were all part of one big family going to a wedding. On one occasion, when stopped by police, an entire group of 40 passengers— who, up to that moment, had been perfect strangers—instantaneously transformed themselves into a wedding party and started singing, clapping and ululating. They told the police that they had just rented the bus to take them to the wedding. As is often the case in such situations, the identification of common interests was unambiguous and unanimous; all the passengers had to get to work. Hard times, people often remarked to me, mean that you have to use your *ubongo* (brains, ingenuity) to survive. In such situations a broader collective identity is created among "us people at the bottom," as individuals frequently refer to themselves.

Nyerere had been adamant that the government-owned buses retain their monopoly status, but the desperation of the situation and the existence of the informal sources of transport resulted in the eventual legalization of the *daladalas* in 1983. Three hundred buses were registered and had to pay a fee to the government bus company.

Today, only 100 government buses are operating, while, due to the high agency fee they are required to pay, the *daladalas* have dwindled down to 183. According to experts, the city needs a minimum of 750 buses (*Daily News* , 3/8/1988: 3). Nevertheless, the very fact that the State moved away from its refusal to allow competition shows that it is not immune from societal pressure.

Dispute over sideline incomes.

An even further softening of the State came in May 1987 when Mwinyi said that, since the government could not afford to pay people adequate salaries, individuals should be free to do various income-generating activities to support themselves. A recent session of the Parliament also discussed the possibility of changing from the work week from the present six to five days so that workers could undertake activities to supplement their incomes (*Daily News* 7/22/1987: 3). Once again, these are examples of the State acknowledging the *de facto* situation in which the majority of wage earners are pursuing informal sideline incomes.

There has been, however, an ongoing conflict between the Party and government leadership over the sideline incomes of Party members and civil servants (who are generally supposed to be Party members). This conflict is a small part of a much larger conflict between the Party and government leadership over the whole direction of liberalization. While the government is moving toward softening its stance, the Party leadership officially adheres firmly to the 1967 Arusha Declaration and the Party Leadership Code, which declares that Party leaders and civil servants can have only one income. I talked to a member of the Central Committee about this and asked if the policy was not unrealistic given the present situation. He said:

> There is nothing wrong with the policy. It is just the people who aren't implementing the policy correctly. If one has two jobs, one's formal job suffers and you end up cheating the State....If you employ someone to do your sideline job, then you are violating the Leadership Code because you are making money off the sweat of another person and that is exploitation.

Other Party leaders have been reported saying that people who do small projects—such as poultry keeping—are "enemies of our socialist policies." In a recent interview, the Chairman of the Commission for the Enforcement of the Leadership Code, Selemani Kitundu, said that public leaders (which includes civil servants) are prohibited from having secret incomes and engaging in business which condone exploitation of man by man. Since many people who work use relatives, close and distant, in these projects, Kitundu criticized leaders who used kin or friends who were Party members to run huge businesses on their behalf (*Daily News* 7/29/1987: 3).

The old guard Party leaders have too much at stake to back down from this ideologically determined line. Their whole careers were built on advocating the Arusha Declaration and Leadership Code; to revise their positions now would be to undermine the basis of their power, i.e., other old guard Party leaders who can make or break them. For government leaders, who have to keep their constituencies happy, promoting unpopular policies can be political suicide and they are more likely to opt for pragmatic solutions, rather than ideologically inspired policies.

The average citizen does not see why two (or more) incomes should be such a big issue. People often express doubts that the country's leaders have any conception at all of how difficult life is and what a struggle it is to survive from day to day. They see no conflict between engaging in sideline activities and their loyalties to the nation as the following two examples illustrate.

I talked to one plumber who works at a government hospital but also does sideline plumbing to support his wife and children. He makes the minimum wage even though he has worked there 15 years. When I asked why he continues to work when he could make so much more in his private sideline business if he did that full time, he answered indignantly:

> But I have to work at the hospital! How would this country develop if everyone left their jobs? My work at the hospital is my contribution to the nation and my *miradi* [sideline project] is how I feed my family.

When I went to the government map office to purchase a map of the city I was told there were none available and that they had not had any in print for years. Then the map salesman there said that, if it was all right with me, he could sell me a print of the map he had made himself in his own private duplicating service. In the course of what became a rather lengthy discussion, the map salesman told me that he had worked in the government map office for six years and still made only the minimum wage. By reproducing and selling these maps he matched, every two days, his formal income for the entire month. And, since the map office had been unable to provide such materials, he saw such supplementary labor as both a private good and a public service: "This way I can help myself and the government too."

One typical response to our question concerning what people thought of the Party policy on two incomes was that of an individual who worked as a messenger at the Tanzania Harbor Authority but also made soap as a sideline activity. "Our Party should change its policy on that point," he said. "We have to survive and our wages are not enough. We don't want to offend the Party, but we have no option." The messenger still makes the old minimum wage of 810 shillings a month even though the wages were supposed to have been raised by 450 shillings in 1987.

These examples highlight the vast gap that exists between the State policy and the perceptions of people—even those who are highly sympathetic with the State. However, not all responses are as deferential to the State as these comments of the plumber, map seller and messenger might suggest. A more critical but equally typical response to our question was made by a local college administrator who said: "Men of politics are cheats. The big shots in the Party have three incomes themselves and they are telling us not to have projects." The administrator, who himself has a kiosk, chicken business and piggery, pointed out:

> With the first phase government [under Nyerere] there were many problems, especially with supplies. At that time *miradi* [projects] had to be hidden. The Arusha Declaration said that leaders were not permitted to do *miradi*. If they did this, they were violating the Leadership Code. With the second phase government [under Mwinyi] one can support oneself with one's income by doing *miradi*. Mwinyi says that the government doesn't have the resources to provide adequate wages and people should supplement their incomes with other means.

As far back as 1981, a Dar es Salaam resident wrote a telling letter that appeared in the People's Forum column of the *Daily News*. It laid the issues regarding sideline incomes squarely on the table. The writer was responding to the suspension of 102 Zanzibari workers for carrying out sideline activities:

> The practice of indulging in personal *miradis* has become very common these days. We therefore need to ask the question why? Is it because our workers have suddenly become so greedy, bent on making as much money and as fast as possible?

65

It is true that there are some workers especially the top bureaucrats, who are in a position to accumulate money rapidly through corrupt practices....Most of the government workers in the middle and lower levels, however, are hardly in a position to accumulate much...the cost of living of the middle and lower income workers has increased nearly twice as fast as their wages since 1969. This is not taking into consideration the fact that many of the essentials can now be obtained only at "black market prices." [They] have to choose either to reduce their consumption below the minimum necessary for survival, return their families to the rural areas, or find other means of supplementing their incomes through petty corruption or petty personal businesses (*Daily News* 2/9/1981: 4).

The biggest change in recent years with respect to sideline incomes is that workers with such incomes are no longer harassed, questioned, spied on, or even, as in the aforementioned case, suspended. Nevertheless, in spite of Mwinyi's statements, there is still apprehension about these sideline jobs because the Party's position remains so ambiguous. Workers with whom I spoke still feared being discovered with a sideline job, not so much because they were untaxed or unlicensed (although this is a growing concern) but because such a revelation might jeopardize their formal job. Even though middle income people make considerable amounts of money through these sideline activities, they can not register them because this would be an admission that they have two incomes. They do not want to lose their formal job because it is important as a source of capital if their sideline enterprise fails. It provides numerous benefits, e.g., some obtain housing, which is scarce, through their jobs. Further, the formal job is, in spite of its low pay, a source of prestige, especially for professionals. Finally, such jobs mean being situated in locales where one comes in contact with people with whom one can exchange information, resources or favors, thus enhancing one's sideline business.

The debate over sideline incomes has been especially heated in the field of medicine. The low wages of health workers (which includes doctors, nurses and laboratory technicians) has forced them to seek informal sources of income, both on the job and outside of work. In one hospital, the lab technicians make a minimum of 200 shillings a day from patients who pay 50 shillings to have their blood tests analyzed quickly. They call it *chakula cha daktari* or "food for the doctor" (laboratory technicians are often called "doctor" by patients). Most physicians engage in agricultural production or animal husbandry on the outskirts of the city to supplement their formal income. They often hire local villagers to tend their farms but, even doing this, a large part of their time is taken up in their sideline activities. As one woman told me: "When I studied to be a doctor, I never thought I'd learn so much about chickens or end up doing so many other things."

The debate centers around the question of privatization. The movement for privatization has been spearheaded by the Medical Association of Tanzania (MAT) and it appears that the consensus among doctors and hospital workers is to privatize. However, the Minister of Health and Social Welfare, Dr. Aaron Chiduo, opposes the move on political grounds, saying that the poor will not have access to health provisions and will suffer.

The MAT counters that their intention is not to do away with public service. They maintain that time in private practice would provide badly needed medical services as well as free physicians from the current necessity to spend that same time in their fields planting banana trees in order to supplement their income. The President of the MAT, Dr. Philemon Sarungi, said at a recent conference of the association that, to prevent doctors employed in the public service from having private practices during their free time, is to force them to deviate their energy and professional knowledge to non-medical pastimes such as rearing chickens or pigs (*Daily News* 9/18/1986: 1).

Because of the shortages of medical staff, medicines and other equipment, bribes and favoritism are the order of the day for anyone who has ventured inside the medical system. As one doctor told me: "As it is, the medical system only benefits the wealthy anyway."

The debate has made it into Parliament where Member of Parliament Dr. Zainab Amir Gama argued forcefully that the Ministry would "do justice to both the doctors and to the profession if it allowed doctors to practice on part-time basis instead of going for poultry keeping." She said it was

> ...an open secret that some doctors were working with private clinics and hospitals on a part-time basis, although it was illegal. Others engaged in poultry projects so as to augment their 'meager' salaries" (*Daily News* 7/29/1987: 3).

The very fact that the issue of privatization has come into debate in the Parliament and the ministry and is now the focus of a study by the MAT shows once again the impact of the informal economy on changing policy.

Conclusion.

The Tanzanian policy was based on principles of self-reliance, cooperation and communalism as formulated by the former President Nyerere. Yet, more than ever before, in recent years people have had to become more self-reliant, not because of the Party's self-reliance policy but, often, in spite of it. "You scratch your back where your arm reaches," exclaimed one local beer maker in explaining how in hard times you do what you can, what is within your means, to survive. One woman hairdresser put it even more explicitly when she said:

> I sincerely thank Mwalimu [Nyerere] for putting Tanzanians through so much hardship because without these years we would not have learned to be so self-reliant and to depend on our own efforts. Women would not have been able to get into business the way we have now.

However, there is a certain irony to the present situation where the government's attempts to impose self-reliance from above have often come into conflict with people's own ideas of what self-reliance means in the situations they find themselves in.

The results of my study in many ways confirm an observation made by Ferman, Henry and Hoyman (1987: 172) in an article on conceptualizing informal economies. They wrote:

What seems to be emerging from the last ten years of work is certain evidence that people can make a difference to the structures that shape their lives, that many more people are involved in [informal economies] than their peripheral status would suggest, and that the rewards of participation are often as much social as material.

The experience of the informal economy in Tanzania in the past decade has shown that even in a situation where the government attempts to exert control over virtually every sphere of economic life, people can create a space for themselves and effectively assert their preferences. They are by no means victims of an overly protective or paternalistic state. On the surface the State looks formidable and dominant but, in the final analysis, the ultimate strength lies with the weaker side—society. Through society's non-compliance strategies it has the last word and in this way has brought about significant changes in the political and economic structures of the country.

References.

Adas, M.
1981   From Avoidance to Confrontation: Peasant Protest in Precolonial and Colonial Southeast Asia. Comparative Studies in Society and History XXIII: 217-247.
1986   From Foot dragging to Flight: The Evasive History of Peasant Avoidance Protest in South and Southeast Asia. Journal of Peasant Studies XIII: 64-86.

Boesen, J., K. Havnevik, J. Koponen, and R. Odgaard, eds.
1986   Tanzania: Crisis and Struggle for Survival. Uppsala: Scandinavian Institute of African Studies.

Ferman, L. A., S. Henry, and M. Hoyman, eds.
1987   Issues and Prospects for the Study of Informal Economies: Concepts, Research Strategies and Policy. In L.A. Ferman, S. Henry, and M. Hoyman, eds., The Informal Economy. Annals of the American Academy of Political and Social Science 493, pp. 154-172.

Ghai, D.
1987   Economic Growth, Structural Change and Labor Absorption in Africa: 1960-85. Discussion Paper No. 1. New York: United Nations Research Institute for Social Development.

Havnevik, K. J.
1986   A Resource Overlooked: Crafts and Small-Scale Industries. In J. Boesen, K. J. Havnevik, J. Koponen, R. Odgaard, eds., Tanzania: Crisis and Struggle for Survival. Uppsala: Scandinavian Institute of African Studies.

Helleiner, G. K.
1985   Stabilization Policies and the Poor. Working Paper No. B.9. Department of Economics, University of Toronto.

Hyden, G.
    1980   Beyond Ujamaa in Tanzania: Underdevelopment and an Uncaptured Peasantry. London: Heinemann Educational Books Ltd.
    1986   No Shortcuts to Progress. Berkeley: University of California Press.

Polanyi, K.
    1944   The Great Transformation: The Political and Economic Origins of Our Time. Boston: Beacon Hill Press.

Scott, J. C.
    1976   The Moral Economy of the Peasant: Rebellion and Subsistence in Southeast Asia. New Haven CT: Yale University Press.
    1985   Weapons of the Weak: Everyday Forms of Peasant Resistance. New Haven CT: Yale University Press.
    1986   Everyday Forms of Peasant Resistance. Journal of Peasant Studies XIII: 4-35.

Shaidi, L. P.
    1987   Legal Control of Surplus Labor in Tanzania's Urban Centers. Paper presented at the Workshop on Social Problems in Eastern Africa, Arusha, August 9-14.

INFORMAL SECTOR HOUSING:
SOCIAL STRUCTURE AND THE STATE IN BRAZIL

William P. Norris
Department of Sociology
Oberlin College

Introduction.

Originally formulated by Hart (1973) in reference to African urbanization, the informal sector concept has become widely used in labor market studies in developing countries. Recent works on the informal sector in labor markets (Portes and Sassen-Koob 1987) and on informal practices in government bureaucracies (Lomnitz 1988) have demonstrated that the informal sector is much more pervasive than previously realized. However, it has been less frequently considered in relationship to housing (cf. Peattie 1974). This paper investigates the relationship of informal sector housing to urbanization and development processes in Brazil. My specific purpose is to explore certain questions about which social groups participate in informal sector housing, the benefits to them, and the larger implications for the urbanization process.

The informal sector has been defined comprehensively by Portes and Sassen-Koob (1987; 31) as "the sum total of income-earning activities with the exclusion of those that involve contractual and legally-regulated employment." By extension, informal sector housing can be defined as relationships of purchase, occupation, production and exchange which focus on the provision of residence and exist outside of the modern and State-regulated economy. These residential areas are referred to generically as irregular settlements, and they include housing which is built on land, not owned or rented by residents, does not meet municipal or national housing standards, or is not officially eligible for urban services.[1]

Research on irregular or informal sector housing has tended to ignore or downplay the participation of middle or bourgeois class segments. The analysis of housing requires the consideration of land used for housing, or, as Gottdiener (1985) conceptualized it, housing is part of the "production of urban space." He identified several different producers of space, four of which are relevant to the present analysis: speculators, developers, builders, and owners of developed land. It is necessary to investigate the extent of activity by these kinds of entrepreneurs in informal sector housing.

Another class segment are State bureaucrats. The State is involved in the control and regulation of urban space property relations. Informal sector housing is control, but not State-recognized ownership of urban space. Thus, there is the potential for great conflict over the control and ownership of urban space underlying the relationship between State bureaucrats and irregular settlement residents.

The third segment are those middle class actors involved in supporting or organizing the residents as part of the struggle for control of urban space and as part of larger political processes. Thus, in addition to the residents of irregular settlements, other groups of concern in this analysis are entrepreneurs, State bureaucrats, and middle class actors.

---

[1]In Brazil, and Latin America in general, there now exists a substantial literature on irregular settlements, i.e., informal sector housing. Scholars have demonstrated that informal sector housing plays an important role in providing residences for a variety of people, preponderantly low-income, and that this is a survival strategy, a rational adaptation which allows for saving money and time, a cheap way for governments to cope with housing shortages, and a means of cheapening the cost of labor reproduction for employers (Evers 1984; Faria 1976; Kowarick 1977, 1979; A. Leeds 1977, 1974; Leeds and Leeds 1976; Lomnitz 1977; Oliveira 1972; Peattie 1974; Perlman 1976; Roberts 1973; Valladares 1978). In addition, scholars have shown that the housing informal sector is a political resource for politicians seeking to organize and gain support for themselves or their policies (Collier 1976; Eckstein 1977; Leeds and Leeds 1976; Valladares 1978).

The composition and functions of the informal sector in housing.

Earlier analyses of the housing informal sector ostensibly paralleled the labor market analysis of the period. The analysis of the functions of this housing suggested that it provided for the survival of the low-income population, that it probably was a temporary phenomenon of transition to a more modern economy, and that the sector was separate from, or marginal to, the general housing market and society. The debate focused on squatter settlements and concerned two questions—what is the relationship to urban areas, and what is the contribution to urban areas of the informal sector? The two opposing perspectives on these questions were the dualist and what Peattie and Aldrete-Haas (1981) have called "integrationist." The dualists saw the settlements and their residents as economically, socially and politically separate from their urban areas and not contributing to development processes, hence the name of marginality theory for this position. The dualist perspective has been largely superceded by the integrationist perspective. The integrationists argue that the housing areas and their residents are highly integrated into their urban areas, are heterogeneous in composition and multi-functional for society. They contribute to and are affected by development processes.[2]

The integrationist studies are quite varied. They range from Marxist historical structural to ecological system analyses to urban community to a focus on rational actors among the low-income. There exist several excellent reviews of the research and debates over the irregular settlements (Peattie and Aldrete-Haas 1981; Roberts 1978; Valladares 1983) and it is not my intention to replicate them but to focus on representative or particularly noteworthy studies emphasizing Brazil.

---

[2]If squatter settlements are transitional phenomena, they should be easily linked to a given developmental stage. However, the settlements have been present in Brazil at least since the period immediately after emancipation (the 1890s, the beginning of the Old Republic) when Brazil had only begun to industrialize and was basically a peripheral country dependent on agriculture. In recent years Brazil, now frequently grouped among the new industrial countries (NICs) has seen a veritable flood of squatting in and around São Paulo, the center of Brazilian industrialization.

An early analytical framework for analysis of settlement and settler integration was provided by A. Leeds (1969) who subsequently demonstrated that some middle class people lived in the settlements, that a variety of reasons led people to live in them, and that the settlements were a means of capital accumulation and social mobility for low-income people (1974, 1977). Peattie (1974), in her research in Colombia, showed the ways that the informal sector contributed directly to the national economy through the creation of use value in housing and potential exchange value worth many millions of dollars. Roberts (1973) and Lomnitz (1977) demonstrated the nature and extent of their social organization through detailed network analyses of low-income people and squatter settlements in Guatemala City and Mexico City respectively, and Perlman (1976) confirmed this interpretation in her economic, political and cultural study of marginality.

Irregular settlements are analyzed by Santos (1979) through his use of a theory of two circuits in urban economies of developing countries. The circuits interpenetrate, as in the informal housing construction materials industry, which ranges from recycling basic found materials (shipping and construction materials such as cardboard boxes and plywood forms) to bricks, poles and boards produced in traditional ways, to mass produced electrical materials.

This kind of housing cheapens the cost of reproduction of labor and therefore supports the very low wage structure in Brazil (Oliveira 1972; Kowarick 1977, 1979). The costs of shelter are borne by the worker, allowing the bourgeoisie to continue to extract a surplus profit. Evers (1984) in his discussion of irregular subdivisions (described below) took the economic argument one step further. Not only does this housing afford a savings by producing needed use values and avoiding spending limited funds, it is also the means whereby a fraction of the bourgeoisie can tap the household reproduction process of the low-income through the monthly payment for the plot.

The strategic political games played by settlers, politicians and others are very complex (E. Leeds 1972) and include forming coalitions with various elite groups (A. Leeds 1974). A similar variety of linkages were found among irregular settlements, politicians and the PRI in Mexico City (Eckstein 1977; Velez-Ibanez 1983).

Valladares (1978) extended this political analysis by documenting the complicated exchanges among residents, politicians and bureaucrats during the squatter settlement eradication program in Rio. She indicated, but did not analyze in depth, the involvement of State agencies in controlling the location and nature of the squatter settlement housing market. Dietz (1980) demonstrated the way that the Peruvian military government directly intervened in squatter settlement politics and social organization.

Collier (1976) and Leeds and Leeds (1976) provide a comparative political and structural analysis of the political process. Collier's (1976) landmark study of settlement policies of four Peruvian regimes demonstrates clearly that they are linked to general housing policies, i.e., they are an aspect of overall policy, ranging from Odria's paternalism to Velasco's corporatism. Leeds and Leeds (1976) analyze the underlying political structure, especially the articulation of popular interests through political parties as a means of understanding differences in settlement resident political behavior.

Informal activities are found within the State bureaucracies (Lomnitz 1988). The State has various kinds of impacts on the informal sector through the setting of various codes and standards (Valladares 1983), through the actions of specific agencies, such as the National Housing Bank (BNH) (Batley 1983), through the construction of infrastructure and the control of housing oriented social movements which usually focus on the lack of urban services (Kowarick 1979).

Why does the State allow these (frequently) illegal informal processes to proceed? Evers (1984) argues that the authoritarian State focuses on private appropriation of capital. In his words, "if the system of tiny lots guarantees the reproduction of the labor force and is lucrative, the State can do no better that to leave it to continue" (Evers 1984: 48, my translation). The State performs its function by not acting. In addition, the State maintains an unlimited labor force and pacifies that labor force by making the latter a property owner.

The above review suggests several hypotheses with which to organize this study. If irregular subdivisions are created, economic entrepreneurs will be involved as developers. If there is a change in status of irregular subdivisions or squatter settlements, State bureaucrats and agencies will be involved in that change. Furthermore, economic entrepreneurs will be found in land speculation or building in the informal sector, as will entrepreneurial residents of the actual informal housing areas. Economic entrepreneurs and State bureaucracies will be found to work with each other and in conflict with residents. Middle class actors such as lawyers, priests, academicians/consultants, and reporters will be found in the social movements to redress problems of the informal sector residents.

In order to explore these hypotheses, I have chosen four cases of informal sector housing for discussion. They represent the two most common forms of low-income urban housing in Brazil. They appear to represent regime involvement in informal sector housing, or provide information on the heterogeneity of the population involved in or taking advantage of the informal sector. They also represent significant moments in the evolution of the relationship between the regional and national governments and squatter settlements and irregular subdivisions. The presentation of the cases focuses on description of the processes involved, with particular emphasis given to who participates in the housing process and the various political aspects. Information is presented on the benefits to various kinds of actors. The two cases on squatter settlements are drawn from my larger research project on such settlements. The information on Vila Rui Barbosa was collected during four periods of residence between 1967-1987 and relies on interviews with area leaders and residents, a small survey of households, secondary data and my observations. Research on *Filhos da Terra* was conducted in 1987 and was based on interviews with area leaders, a local history, outside consultants connected with the Human Rights Commission, academic researchers and newspaper accounts. The information for the other two cases is drawn from other studies supplemented in the irregular subdivision case by interviews in 1987 with some participants and researchers.

This reliance on cases means that questions are raised about the nature of the housing market; however, more definitive answers await further research. Any generalizations from these findings should be undertaken carefully.

Case studies.

Case 1: The Vila Rui Barbosa squatter settlement. In 1948 a famous squatter settlement formed by a land invasion (*invasão*)[3] occurred in the Alagados region of Salvador, Bahia. The invasion was planned and conducted by construction workers, the dockworkers union and others. The Alagados are the salt marshes and adjacent land surrounding an inlet of the bay which Salvador overlooks. They are close to the industrial, commercial and port areas of the lower city. The target of the invasion was a *fazenda,* an abandoned sugar cane farm which was chosen by the construction workers who were employed nearby. During their lunch breaks they laid out streets and plots. An executive committee was set up to plan the invasion. Organization included arranging transportation for building materials and belongings for houses, contacting sympathetic press and city councilmen, choosing a day and a name, and assembling everyone. After the initial invasion, word spread, and others joined the squatters. A few Brazilian Communist Party (PCB) organizers helped them with contacts and press relations.

The municipal authorities decided to expel the squatters and the police appeared for that purpose early one morning. The squatters were ready for the police and fought back. The police retreated. The squatters delighted in recounting their victory, and the way that various people had become heroes and heroines—as when *Doña* Santa clouted one policeman with a pole. From 1948 until the early 1980s, the land remained in the hands of the State, and the residents remained in the ambiguous status of squatters. During

---

[3]My translation of key Portuguese terms are indicated in this manner thoughout the paper.

this entire period the residents engaged in a protracted struggle—negotiations, demonstrations, petitions—with the mayor, the State and individual politicians.

In the late 1970s the Alagados, by then with a population approaching 150,000, were "urbanized" which meant the inlet was partially filled, sewer, water, and electricity lines installed, some houses reconstructed, streets paved, and schools built. In the early 1980s the people received title to the land (Norris 1987).

Case 2: Filhos da Terra Squatter settlement. In April, 1983, economic conditions were difficult in São Paulo, and many people were having trouble paying rent, or finding suitable housing. In Vila Paulistana in the North Zone, an hour-long bus ride from downtown, a rumor circulated that the local Center for Human Rights had access to land, and people came to see if it was true. They were invited to attend meetings to see if something could be done about the housing problem. Each meeting attracted more people, and they organized themselves into a group named *Filhos da Terra* (Children of the Earth) which met regularly in assemblies with the purpose of educating themselves about the situation and how other groups without housing had coped with the situation. One of the first things they determined was that the problem was not lack of housing, but lack of land. A chant they wrote expressed it well:[4]

We have the right to live with dignity.
The land belongs to everyone.
The land belongs to God.
United we are strong.

---

[4]This is my translation. Of particular interest is the use of religious themes, which refle the strong religious tone present at times in the movement. For instance, the local histo used began in the following way (my paraphrasing): The newspaper headline read "The Sacred Right to Shelter," and the article described how, in the same way that Mary had been able to find room at the inn in Bethlehem, many Marys were searching for shelter São Paulo. One, Maria Aparecida, with the help of the Center for Human Rights of Vil Paulistana (a São Paulo neighborhood), was able to build a shack on public land alongs a small creek. From this small beginning grew the famous São Paulo squatter land occupation, Children of the Earth (*Filhos da Terra*). I suspect, but do not have clear evidence, that this also reflects the presence of base community activists in the moveme

Loving our companions and maintaining faith in God, we will
    win.
United and organized we will win.
Land is not earned, it is won.

By October, 200 families were participating in the assemblies,
a registry of participants had been established (*cadastramento*) and
attendance was recorded. Initial contacts were made with a
municipal agency (Family and Social Welfare). The people
developed a plan (backed up with a supporting petition) that called
for the municipality to use the power of eminent domain, first, to
purchase a large, nearby plot of land from Santa Casa de
Misericórdia (a Church-related charitable organization) and then
lease the land[5] to *Filhos da Terra* for residential use for an
indeterminate period of time. In late November, when they
presented the petition to Mayor Mario Covas. He responded
negatively but did refer them to another bureaucracy. That
bureaucracy explored in several meetings the remote possibility of
the purchase and resale of the land to the group. For two months the
people waited and planned alternative courses of action, specifically
an occupation of the Santa Casa land. Planning proceeded within the
executive committee, in secrecy to prevent municipal authorities
from discovering it. By then, the group contained experienced
organizers and received advice and support from lawyers, Worker
Party politicians and organizers, priests, as well as North Zone
neighborhood groups and their lawyers. In early February, 1984,
having given up hope of action from the mayor, they organized the
occupation, focusing on basic questions of organization, of lot
distribution and occupation, food, shelter for the children, and
security.

Filhos da Terra invaded the Santa Casa land in the evening of
February 11, 1984. They first constructed the communal building to
shelter the children and then turned to dividing up the land into lots
and assigning them to people, focusing on establishing the first lots

---

[5]This is a very long term lease arrangement (*direito real de uso*) which the
municipality had utilized in the case of some commercial and entertainment ventures
located on public land.

81

around the perimeters of the property. Everyone immediately began to build some kind of structure on their plot because the law stipulated that a claim for the land required the claimant physically and continuously to occupy the land on which a structure with a roof had been built. If they held the land in that manner, then the owners had to get a legal order to remove them. And they had occupied the land on Friday evening, which gave them the entire weekend to consolidate control.

After some legal maneuvering, the Santa Casa got an order to expel the occupiers, and the police were instructed to begin the process of removal. However, during this period, the Children of the Earth had consolidated their control of the land with hundreds of makeshift houses. They also made it clear that they would physically resist removal. They stacked rocks and staves near the only viable entrances into the area. If confronted by the police, they planned to keep the men in the rear, placing women and children in front and resisting only if provoked. During this period they had also publicized their situation; reporters from the major São Paulo papers, and even one from Rio, were constantly present. Some moved into the area for the duration. As a consequence, the newspapers were full of reports on the progress of the land occupation.

A stand-off resulted as the police made intimidating moves and the occupiers maintained a constant state of readiness. This continued for 40 days and was extremely stressful. Some gave up and left. Others lost their jobs because of the need to maintain someone constantly on their land. After 40 days, another assembly was held during which lawyers and supporting politicians told them that the point had been reached where the police had to act. The executive committee returned to the Housing Secretary and agreed to *consider* leaving the area if other land could be found. Their delaying strategy was successful—the Housing Secretary spent three fruitless months in the search for other vacant land and then decided to negotiate with the Santa Casa. After long negotiations, as well as increasing and sometimes tragic problems for the occupiers in arranging potable water, the Santa Casa decided to sell the land to the municipality to be resold to the occupiers in March, 1985.

Children of the Earth formed an association and bought the land as a unit. Subsequently, they have decided to subdivide the land into individual lots so that they can meet the other provisions of the housing laws. In spite of their allegiance to collective ownership, the association leaders and members agreed that, in order to protect their individual (and, therefore, collective situation) and to avoid attempts to confiscate or in some other way undermine their ownership, the land had to be subdivided into individual parcels. They are now in the process of completing this process—after which the remaining land will be ceded to the municipality for streets and parks. They believe that this will finally qualify them for full urban services and full protection before the law.

Case 3: Irregular subdivisions in São Paulo. Irregular subdivisions (*loteamentos clandestinos*) represent a different kind of informal sector housing. They are land subdivisions marketed by developers, aimed at low-income people, and located on the urban periphery. They become irregular because of lack of clear title, failure to adhere to subdivision codes, lack of access to urban services, or both. This was the dominant form of housing for the working poor of São Paulo from the late 1950s until 1979 when a new law[6] made the process less lucrative for developers. Precise information does not exist about the number of irregular subdivisions: Evers (1984) calculated that, in the São Paulo metropolitan region in the mid-1970s, there existed about 5000 irregular subdivisions containing about 1,000,000 building lots. In other words, about 5,000,000 people— constituting one-third to one-half the total urban population—probably lived in the subdivisions.

As described in Evers (1984), the subdivision process typically began when land developers purchased an area of vacant land on the São Paulo municipality periphery.[7] The developers subdivided the land into small lots to offer for sale. São Paulo housing law at the

---

[6]In 1979 a national law (Lei No. 6.766) was passed regulating irregular settlements and assessing penalties.
[7]"Periphery" has two meanings—a geographic one referring to location and an institutional referent relative to the extent of urban services, indicating the land is beyond the end of the bus line, water line, electricity lines, etc.

time established procedures and standards—lot sizes, street widths, amount of land left for open spaces, and certain infrastructural improvements. However, in order to maintain the price as low as possible so as to be able to sell the lots to low-income people, the standards and procedures were not observed. Instead, the land was cleared, rudimentary roads dug, and the lots sold.

Buyers faithfully made monthly payments for the usual ten-year period—only to find at the end that, because of the failure of the developer to follow procedures or meet development standards, their land could not be registered as their property. Instead, it remained the property of the developer. The developer had a claim on the property or on indemnification. Therefore, the lot could not be sold by the buyer, nor could it be inherited. Furthermore, in the event of expropriation for roads or subways, the buyer was in danger of losing everything. Because the neighborhood did not legally exist, the municipality was not required to install electrical, water or sewer lines, build schools, pave the streets or even provide police. At the same time, buyers were charged a building tax for their houses. Despite their failure to observe procedures, developers were not penalized. The consequence of all this was that residents had to battle on two fronts—against the municipality and the developers—if they were to hope to legalize their situation and gain improvements.

This process of subdivision buying and selling did not really begin until the 1950s and is part of the process of rapid and concentrated industrialization in Brazil. Most of the subdivisions were not organized until the late 1960s; consequently, the vastness of the problem was not evident until the 1970s when the buyers had completed their ten-year payment period (Evers 1984).

The developers manipulate the situation by selling those lots in a subdivision which are furthermost from the built-up limits of the city. New residents engage in struggles with the municipal government to have city services extended to them. The extension of these services greatly increases the value of the unsold lots of land between the new neighborhood and the old city limits. Consequently, the developer can sell them for more money. Santos

(1981) puts a somewhat different twist on his account of a similar process in Rio. His argument is that the irregular subdivisions are much better than the State sector housing offered by the National Housing Bank (BNH). He indicates that the developers range in size from big to small, and that buyers are attracted by the cheap lots, the personal relationship and attention provided by developer agents (*corretores*) present in every subdivision, and the set monthly payments. While recognizing that the residents must pressure the State for services, Santos notes that, if successful, the developers' unsold lots as well as the residents' lots also increase in value. He found that small construction firms were engaged in building some houses. And some residents subsequently engage in practices similar to developers, i.e., renting their lots or houses, subdividing their lots for sale or rental, or realizing the increased value through sale. He concludes that, while theoretically in conflict, in practice the residents and developers have mutual or at least compatible interests.

Most scholars agree that the irregular subdivisions would not be possible without at least the acquiescence of the State. Some (Evers 1984; cf. Valladares 1983) argue that bureaucrats or politicians actively aid the developers, e.g., one developer had personal ties to former Mayor Maluf.

The social movements which grew up to deal with the problems of the irregular subdivisions in São Paulo were first organized under the aegis of the Church with the aid of local academicians (Singer 1983) and lawyers from the Human Rights Commission. Others who became involved were Workers Party (PT) organizers, neighborhood groups affiliated with the Friends of the Neighborhood Societies (SAB), as well as opportunistic lawyers who claimed to have contacts with friendly bureaucrats who, for a price, could fix things. The social movements were successful in gaining title for at least some of the subdivisions and urban services for others.

Case 4: Informal sector impact of policies of the National Housing Bank. Between 1968-1972, the squatter settlement removal program in Rio de Janeiro, coordinated by the National Housing Bank (BNH), had a direct impact on the informal sector housing market. Details of the removal process also indicate the many ways that the squatters engaged in mini-land speculation. The ostensible purpose of the program was to remove unsightly buildings inhabited by presumably dangerous people who were living on valuable land, or (as some politicians put it) to "clean the city." The land in question was in Rio's South Zone, which includes such famous middle class residential, commercial, and tourist areas as Copacabana and Ipanema. However, it also included some spectacular squatter settlements (*favelas*) located on high volcanic ridges and around a large lake. By 1972, when the eradication program was halted, 16,647 *favela* residences had been destroyed (Portes 1979); ostensibly, residents were relocated, to new peripheral housing developments (*conjuntos*). As Valladares (1978) explains, however, the process actually expanded existing informal sector activities as well as creating new ones. Residence in the settlements became more valuable since the government planned to remove the residents to other and better housing with clear title and most urban services. In addition, the new residences varied in size and cost, creating another source of manipulation. This "fiddling," as Valladares aptly terms it, occurred at every stage of the removal process. At the first sign that a *favela* was to be designated for removal, some would sell their shacks—suddenly appreciated in value—to outsiders, thus giving the new owner access to a *conjunto* house. Others built new shacks in the area, or added rooms for other families to create a claim on the new dwellings. The *favelas* experienced a population boom. When time for the pre-relocation census came, residents inflated the number of families in a house (for more or larger houses) and the income earned (to gain access to better housing).

The process continued in the housing developments. When actually relocated, the residents were able to manipulate a whole set of financial and legal arrangements having to do with the purchase of the *conjunto* dwelling. At several points in the process, the former *favelado* might attempt to rent or sell either the right to, or the actual dwelling. The bureaucrats in the responsible government agency were also fiddling the system, accepting fees and favors to allow the illegal renting and selling to occur. With time, more and more owners of dwellings began to default on payments. By 1974, the default rate had reached 93% (Valladares, 1978). In 1973, the process was officially halted and the policies reorganized. The population eligible for the housing development was redefined to include lower middle class people—the ones who, in point of fact, had been renting or buying the individual units from the ex-squatters. Thus, the beneficiaries of the policy were some of the squatters, bureaucrats, and lower middle class people.

More important for this analysis, this case also clarifies one way that a State bureaucracy enters the informal sector housing market. The BNH selected informal sector housing only in the middle class residential area in Rio. It moved the squatters off that land and made the land available to developers. It provided support for big capital and class segregated housing in Rio.

Discussion.

All scholars studying the irregular subdivisions and squatter settlements agree that the ultimate problem represented by them is the result of the Brazilian development process, in particular the low wages paid to workers. The relatively cheap lots in the subdivisions offered a way to buy land, on which to build their own houses themselves. The squatter settlements were relatively cost-free but tended to be in worse areas and were inherently unstable living situations. In both cases, the subdivision plot purchasers or the squatters must build their own houses.

The four cases indicate that (1) informal sector housing is quite heterogeneous and (2) various kinds of economic entrepreneurs, State bureaucracies, and middle class people are involved in many and complicated ways. Summarizing the findings briefly: It is clear that developers with various sized firms are actively engaged in irregular subdivisions. The developers make a profit from taking unused or rural land on the urban periphery, subdividing it, and putting the lots up for sale in the systematic fashion outlined above. This process suggests that either the developers are dealing with speculators or are themselves engaged in land speculation. Small scale construction firms, wholesalers and retailers of building materials—and entrepreneurial residents—are also involved.

State bureaucracies are directly involved in the removal of squatter settlements and change of control and ownership of land. The BNH-supported bureaucracy in Rio removed settlements in the South Zone to facilitate development favorable to entrepreneurial and middle class groups.

In São Paulo, municipal agencies mediated between land occupiers and land owners. In many other cases, the State expelled squatters as soon as they moved onto the land in question. Thus, the State also intervened to control and regularize informal processes, such as land occupations. In Salvador, the BNH condoned giving title to residents of the squatter settlement, apparently for political legitimation purposes. Inaction also appears to be an important tool of the bureaucracies. Given the extent of the irregular settlements in São Paulo, it is unlikely that neither the registries of deeds nor other agencies were aware of this process and its implications. This suggests that inaction was not a particularized strategy of individual bureaucrats but an institutional feature of the bureaucracy. Of course, by doing nothing, the bureaucracy facilitated the actions of the developers.

Another important group of actors are the lawyers, organizers, reporters, priests, politicians, etc., some of whom reside in the informal housing areas. Essentially middle class, they provide the information and skills which help the land occupiers and irregular subdivision residents to resist expulsion, to organize their claims, and to gain title as well as urban services. Even though they occurred some 35 years apart, when the two squatter cases discussed above are compared, it is apparent that some of the same kinds of actors were involved—i.e., middle class individuals connected with critical/oppositional groups. They are often, but not always, part of such organizations as the Workers Party (PT), the Communist Party of Brazil (PC do B), the Human Rights Commission, the Roman Catholic Church and the media, which have a critical if not oppositional stance towards the State, its policies, or both.

In sum, participants in informal sector housing are quite heterogeneous and include a variety of economic entrepreneurs, middle class people, as well as State bureaucracies. Another way of summarizing the meaning of their participation is to look at the various ways individuals and groups benefit from the process. Based on the cases presented, it appears that the State and State bureaucracies benefit from the housing informal sector in the following ways: Fewer funds are needed for housing; public sector land can be converted to private sector uses and often property; the housing process becomes a source of graft for bureaucrats through the manipulation of land ownership and bureaucratic rules; housing is a source of votes and other forms of support—i. e., power—for politicians who can provide services, contacts, etc. More generally, different regimes can manipulate informal housing to gain legitimacy from the poor or middle class. Note that the different regimes of the State emphasize different combinations of these benefits.

Subdivision developers benefit since they profit from the search for housing by lower-income groups. It is evident that these profits can be increased through manipulating the sale process and through contacts with State bureaucracies.

Various middle class people and opposition groups also benefit. The problems of housing, especially squatter settlement eradication, provision of urban services and lack of clear title for squatters or irregular settlement residents, create a reserve of discontent which delegitimizes the regime. This is both cause and effect of the actions of some of these individuals and groups. Of course, this situation also provides a set of clients for individual politicians and bureaucrats.

And the informal sector has other benefits besides survival for residents. It serves as a source of capital accumulation and mobility as well as the base for the creation of residential solidarity. Paradoxically, it is a means of gaining more resources from the State because of its illegality.

I hypothesized that the economic entrepreneurs and State bureaucracies would not have conflicts with each other, but with the residents of the housing areas. In point of fact, this relationship is more complicated than the one hypothesized. Given the variety of interests involved, conflicts occur, but not always in class terms. For instance, resolution of some of the collective consumption demands benefits all lot owners, whether individual residents or subdivision developers.

A way of clarifying the conditions under which different kinds of conflict occur is to look at how different groups utilize the informal sector as a resource. Conflicts occur when different groups compete to use the same resource in different ways. Purchasers of lots in irregular subdivisions know at the very least that their lot does not have the usual urban services and they probably know also that they must confront the state authorities in order to resolve their problem. On the other hand, purchasers of the lots do not know that the lack of registration of the land subdivision means that the developer has put them into the informal sector. This becomes a point of conflict between residents allied with middle class activists, developers, and State bureaucracies.

The occupiers of land are seizing control of it in order to gain housing. Part of their subsequent strategy is almost always to gain title, that is, to move back out of the informal sector by regularizing their ownership of the land and gaining urban services. However, while they remain in the informal sector, the residents provide a vote and graft resource for politicians and bureaucrats. As such, politicians may have little interest in resolving the land title question for the squatters or irregular subdivision residents. The conflict frequently divides along lines approximating class divisions when resource issues are focused on property ownership. Collective consumption issues, i.e., urban services, tend to result in more heterogeneous coalitions. Thus, the participation of the middle class in the conflict and the shifting locus of confrontation makes the class interpretation problematic.

Social movements tend to form at these points of conflict. The movements are an important tactic for those who are in some way outside of the system and are less advantaged than those within it.

The discussion of housing and residence has a spatial component which sets it apart from labor market analyses. Space or land provides another dimension which spawns phenomena such as land speculation. Theoretical work on these issues must confront the problem of whether to deal with land and control/ownership issues as contributing directly to capital accumulation (cf. Gottdiener 1985)— and, if so, how, as well as theories of urbanization and development.

Conclusion.

The housing informal sector is central to the urbanization process. Beyond that, the informal sector has a certain integrity of its own as well as being ineluctably tied to general economic and political processes. The individual squatter buys building materials, purchases the labor of others, contributes to the housing stock through his own labor, and to the stock in general if he sells or rents the house, and engages in political activities with politicians, political groups and State bureaucracies aimed at gaining title and urban services. The irregular subdivision resident purchases a lot and also engages in all of the activities listed for the squatter. The capital that each expends supports a whole range of production and land development. Real estate investment and development are important components of development processes. Furthermore, the location and consolidation of these areas affect not only the cityscape, but urban planning in general. State bureaucracies actively and passively promote the processes by creating and manipulating laws and procedures governing the creation, organization and sale of subdivisions, and the provision of urban services. All of the various actors utilize informal sector housing as a resource for such things as housing, production, commerce, provision of services, profits, votes and influence. Thus, it feeds the economic and political processes directly through cheapening labor, providing housing, and offering entrepreneurs a range of profit-making opportunities related to housing. In part, the informal sector is a creature of the State and, as such, provides a resource and a problem for bureaucracies and bureaucrats, political parties and politicians.

The extensive involvement of State bureaucracies, economic entrepreneurs and middle class groups in informal sector housing means that this is a much more complicated sector than previously understood. Further research is required to confirm and extend these findings. Theoretical work needs to link these additional groups to the general problematic of reproduction of labor power. This work on housing may also provide some suggestions on how the State is involved in the informal sector labor market. It is clear that the informal sector is more complicated and has a more central relationship to the general economy and society of Brazil than has been previously appreciated.

References.

Batley, Richard
1983 Política Urbana e Burocracia no Brasil. Espaço e Debates 8 (jan/abr): 5-29.

Collier, David
1976 Squatters and Oligarchs. Baltimore MD: The Johns Hopkins University Press.

Dietz, Henry A.
1980 Poverty and Problem-Solving under Military Rule. Austin: University of Texas Press.

Eckstein, Susan
1977 The Poverty of Revolution. Princeton NJ: Princeton University Press.

Evers, Tilman
1984 Reprodução da Forca de Trabalho e Movimento Populares: O Caso dos Loteamentos Clandestinos em São Paulo. In P. Krischke, org., Terra de Habitaçao/Terra de Espoliação. São Paulo: Cortez Editora pp. 31-56.

Faria, Vilmar
1976 Occupational Marginality, Employment and Poverty in Urban Brazil. Unpublished Ph.D. dissertation. Harvard University.

Gottdiener, M.
1985 The Social Production of Urban Space. Austin: University of Texas Press.

Hart, Keith
1973 Informal Income Opportunities and Urban Employment in Ghana. Journal of Modern African Studies 11: 61-89.

Jacobi, Pedro
1986   Movimentos Sociais Urbanos no Brasil. In BIB: O que se Deve Ler em Ciências Sociais no Brasil. E. Diniz, org. São Paulo: Cortez, pp. 221-236.

Kowarick, Lucio
1977   Capitalismo e Marginalidade na América Latina. 2a. ed. Rio de Janeiro: Paz e Terra.
1979   A Espoliação Urbana. Rio de Janeiro: Paz e Terra.

Leeds, Anthony
1969   The Significant Variables Determining the Character of Squatter Settlements. America Latina 12: 44-86.
1974   Housing Settlement Types, Arrangements for Living, Proletarianization, and the Social Structure of the City. In W. Cornelius and F. Trueblood, eds. Anthropological Perspectives on Latin American Urbanization. Beverly Hills CA: Sage, pp. 67-100.
1977   The Metropole, the Squatment and the Slum: Some Thoughts on Capitalism and Dependency. Paper delivered at the Burg Wartenstein Symposium No. 73. Wenner Gren Foundation for Anthropological Research.

Leeds, Anthony and Elizabeth Leeds
1976   Accounting for Behavioral Differences: Three Political Systems and the Responses of Squatters to Them in Brazil, Peru and Chile. In J. Walton and L. Masotti, eds., The City in Comparative Perspective. Beverly Hills CA: Sage, pp. 193-248.

Leeds, Elizabeth
1972   Forms of Squatment Political Organization: The Politics of Control in Brazil. Unpublished M.A. thesis. Austin: University of Texas.

Lomnitz, Larissa
1977   Networks and Marginality: Life in a Mexican Shantytown. San Francisco: Academic Press.

1988   Informal Exchange Networks in Formal Systems: A Theoretical Model. American Anthropologist 90: 42-55.

Norris, William
1986   The Impact of Brazilian State Housing Policies on Squatter Settlement Residents and Movements: Rio de Janeiro and Salvador during the Military Regime and the Democratic Transition. Paper presented at the International Sociological Association XI Congress. New Delhi.

Oliveira, Francisco de
1972   A Economia Brasileira: Crítica à Razão Dualista. Estudos CEBRAP 2.

Peattie, Lisa R.
1974   The Informal Sector: A Few Facts from Bogota, Some Comments and a List of Issues. Unpublished ms. Massachusetts Institute of Technology.

Peattie, Lisa R. and Jose A. Aldrete-Haas
1981   "Marginal" Settlements in Developing Countries: Research, Advocacy of Policy, and Evolution of Programs. Annual Review of Sociology 7: 157-175.

Perlman, Janet
1976   The Myth of Marginality. Berkeley: The University of California Press.

Portes, Alejandro
1979   Housing Policy, Urban Poverty, and the State: The "Favelas" of Rio de Janeiro, 1972-1976. Latin American Research Review XIV(2): 3-24.

Portes, Alejandro and Saskia Sassen-Koob
1987   Making it Underground: Comparative Material on the Informal Sector in Western Market Economies. American Journal of Sociology 93(1): 30-61.

Roberts, Bryan
  1973   Organizing Strangers. Austin: University of Texas Press.
  1978   Cities of Peasants: The Political Economy of Urbanization in the Third World. Beverly Hills CA: Sage Publications.

Santos, Carlos Nelson F. de
  1981   Velhas Novidades nos Modos de Urbanização Brasileiros. In L. Valladares, org., Habitação em Questão. Rio de Janeiro: Zahar, pp. 17-48.

Santos, Milton
  1979   The Shared Space. New York: Methuen.

Singer, Paul
  1983   Movimentos de Bairro. In P. Singer e V.C. Brant, orgs., São Paulo: O Povo em Movimento. Petrópolis: Editora, Vozes/CEBRAP, pp. 83-107.

Valladares, Licia
  1978   Passa-se Uma Casa. Rio de Janeiro: Zahar Editores.
  1983   Estudos Recentes sobre a Habitacao no Brasil: Resenha da Literatura. In L.Valladares, org., Repensando a Habitação no Brasil. Rio de Janeiro: Zahar Editores, pp. 21-78.

Vélez-Ibañez, Carlos
  1983 Rituals of Marginality. Berkeley: University of California Press.

MACROTHEORIES, MICROCONTEXTS, AND THE INFORMAL SECTOR: CASE STUDIES OF SELF-EMPLOYMENT IN THREE BRAZILIAN CITIES[1]

Leo A. Despres
Kellogg Institute of International Studies
University of Notre Dame

Introduction.

Caroline O.N. Moser (1984: 135), an economist, notes that since the informal sector concept was first introduced into academic anthropology by Keith Hart (1973) and then popularized by the International Labor Office, studies attempting to define, describe, and analyze it have been so numerous as to constitute what she calls a "growth industry." In general, the ILO's interest in the informal sector concerned its capacity to absorb surplus labor and thereby ameliorate some of the most negative conditions of urban poverty. Various studies motivated by this concern have sought to determine further whether or not the informal sector absorbed surplus labor in an involutionary manner, without increase in productive output, or if it contained autonomous dynamism for growth and, if so, how growth might best be stimulated by government policy. In any case, based on her rather extensive reviews of the literature, Moser (1978

---

[1]The data to be discussed were collected in the cities of Manaus, Juiz de Fora, and Joinville, located respectively in the Brazilian states of Amazonas, Minas Gerais, and Santa Catarina. Fieldwork in Manaus was conducted in 1984 in association with the Instituto Universitario de Pesquisas do Rio de Janeiro and with the support of a grant provided by the National Science Foundation (BNS 83, 17543). Fieldwork in Juiz de Fora and Joinville was done in 1986 under the terms of a Fulbright award made to the author and to Centro de Estudos de Cultura Contemporânea (São Paulo) by the U.S. Council for International Exchange of Scholars and the Commisão para o Intercâmbio Educacional entre Os Estados Unidos da América e O Brasil. I want to thank Drs. Regis S. de Castro Andrade, Paulo J. Krischke, and other colleagues at CEDEC in São Paulo as well as colleagues at the Kellogg Institute for International Studies (University of Notre Dame) for their helpful comments on various drafts of this paper.

1984) was driven to conclude that the informal sector remains an exceedingly fuzzy concept. Studies of it have embraced such an astonishing heterogeneity of economic activity that it is virtually impossible to draw firm conclusions from their comparison. In fact, such studies appear to have contributed more to the debate surrounding the dualist and nondualist conceptions of the economy than they have contributed to the empirical resolution of questions concerning economic institutions, the organization of firms, enterprises, labor markets, the economic strategies of workers, or the economic and social inequalities attaching to any or all of these.

More recently, Lisa Peattie (1987) has outlined how, with the same confusing results, the dualistic conception of the economy has been assimilated to various macrotheories of political economy. She argues (p.852) that in the tradition of Boeke (1953) and Geertz (1963), the informal/formal sector dichotomy is generally linked with the modernization paradigm. Modern enterprises enter into a backward economy and, in the process of their expanding influence, traditional sectors and populations are, for a time, marginalized and impoverished (see, e.g., Nun 1969; McGee 1973; Quijano 1974; Mingione 1984) In the Marxist or neo-Marxist traditions, theories of dependency, underdevelopment, or both shift the focus from marginalization to the structural linkages that exist between the informal and formal sectors. According to one's particular macrotheoretical orientation, dependent structural linkages between the informal and formal sectors are shaped by the commingling of petty commodity and capitalist modes of production (e.g., Hart 1973) or, alternatively, they result from the wage and labor strategies of capitalist enterprises which seek to lower costs by maintaining a reserve army of surplus labor (e.g., Frank 1970; Roberts 1978: 159-77; Souza and Tokman 1976; Portes and Walton 1981: 67-106; Richardson 1984; Nattrass 1987). Implicit in these structural linkages is a dualistic conception of the economy, and Peattie (pp. 857-858) concludes that this framework is much too muddled to be of heuristic value. Thus, in response to Moser's (1984) review, she (Peattie 1984: 180) suggests that we set aside the informal sector concept and begin instead by specifying the questions we really have in mind to explore.

Before setting aside the informal sector concept, however, it is instructive for purposes of the present paper to briefly consider Hart's (1973) use of it in his anthropological studies of Ghana's capital city of Accra. As introduced by Hart, the concept was employed simply to present an ethnographic description of the range of income opportunities available to the urban poor. "The distinction between formal and informal income opportunities," Hart emphasized, "is based essentially on that between wage-earning and self-employment" (p. 68). It was not Hart's purpose to present a macrostructural analysis of the whole economy. Nevertheless, by equating self-employment with the informal sector and then suggesting that self-employment constituted an effort primarily on the part of the "reserve army of urban unemployed and underemployed" to generate income, Hart unavoidably proffered a macrotheoretical explanation of what might very well have been a microtheoretical problem: i.e., the decision taken by individuals as to whether or not they will work for themselves or commoditize their labor. In effect, the microcontextual analysis of the productive work elected by different types of workers became entangled with the analysis of firms and enterprises, migratory flows, labor markets, and an urban economy conceived as having a dualistic macrostructure.

The present paper returns to this problematic. It seeks to explore whether or not wage-work and self-employment are best explained by macrotheories relating to the development of urban economies or by reference to the decision-making calculi of individual workers. In addressing this problem, we shall follow the advice of Peattie and put aside the informal sector concept. Self-employment is not considered as work performed in the informal sector. Rather, it is conceptualized as work performed by individuals who commoditize not their labor but what they produce with it.

The analysis proceeds on the basis of data collected in a comparative study of firms, workers, and working class families in three Brazilian cities: Manaus (in Amazonas), Juiz de Fora (in Minas Gerais), and Joinville (in Santa Catarina). In order to contextualize the analysis to follow, it will be useful to begin with a brief description of the patterns of urban-industrial development characteristic of each of these cities.[2]

Patterns of Urban-Industrial Development.

Manaus. The urban economy of Manaus is peculiar by virtue of the city's location and the character of its industrial development. Located in the Central Amazon near the confluence of the Rio Negro and Solimões rivers, this old port city had once been the prosperous center of Brazil's rubber boom.[3] Following the rubber boom, the city's economy remained largely dependent upon the extraction and trade in forest products and, as a consequence, it stagnated for well over a half century. In 1967, in conformity with the development policy of the federal government, Manaus was made a Free Trade Zone and designated a "pole" for industrial development in the Central and Western Amazon region. With infrastructural investments in excess of US$47 million (1982 prices) and a powerful program of fiscal incentives, SUFRAMA (Superintendency of the

---

[2]With reference to these data, a caveat is in order. The workers included in the study do not constitute a randomly selected sample drawn from a defined universe of wage- and self-employed workers. Rather, they comprise a purposive and diversified group of cases selected for the anthropological study of firms and sectors of employment. The fundamental question which the original research sought to address may be phrased as follows: In the context of different patterns of urban-industrial development, what kind of work must individuals perform in order to live and how must they and their families live in order to perform particular kinds of work? For purposes of the research, the selection of cases included self-employed workers and three categories of wage-workers. Of the latter, one category was selected with reference to employment by new industrial firms; a second included employees of older and more traditionally established industrial firms; and the third category included lower-eschelon employees performing white-collar work in the rapidly expanding, non-industrial sectors of the urban economy. For the most part, self-employed workers included artisans, street vendors, repairmen, small shopkeepers, taxi operators, truckers, and the like. Thus, unemployed workers looking for work were not included in the study except as they formed part of the households of the workers that were included. The rationale for selecting the cities in question was based upon their regional location, the different social and cultural origins of their working class populations, and the fact that each city revealed a somewhat different pattern of urban-industrial development and populational increase.

[3]For a more detailed description of developments in Manaus, see Despres (1988 passim; 1987: 67-88).

Free Trade Zone) attracted to the city 193 new industrial firms by 1982. These new firms contributed almost one-third to the total number of the city's industrial establishments and they employed approximately 60% of the economically active industrial workers. Most of these new firms were of the assemblage type, more labor than capital intensive, and almost 25% of them were tied to the production for export of electronic units, mainly television sets, stereophonic systems, tape decks, VCRs, video games, digital watches, pocket calculators, and the like.

In conjunction with these developments, between 1975 and 1980 the number of commercial establishments in the state of Amazonas increased from 6996 to 13,144. Of these, 7704 (58%) were located in Manaus. Retail outlets accounted for 96% of the commercial establishments, of which 926 specialized in the sale of watches, television sets, and other products assembled in Manaus. A major local market for these goods consisted of tourists from other regions of Brazil who come to Manaus, on the average of 1500/day, primarily to purchase high-cost consumer durables at prices considerably lower than those that prevail outside of the Free Trade Zone.

The overall impact of the government's development project in Manaus may be summarized as follows: First, in terms of work, between 1960-1980 the reported number of economically active persons in the urban population exploded from 39,000 to 216,000. This growth reflected a 400-500% increase in virtually all sectors of economic activity. However, while the number of self-employed workers increased from 9000 to 42,000 during this period, their proportion among the economically active actually declined from 33% to 21% of the total. In 1984, there certainly existed disguised unemployment in the city and many workers, particularly in the new industrial sector, were shunted from one firm to another as a consequence of production decisions taken in São Paulo. While a great many of these workers did not consider their employment secure, very few of them elected self-employment in favor of wage employment in the new industrial sector.

Secondly, the government's development project exacerbated a traditional migratory flow from the interior, which resulted in a rather massive explosion of the urban population. In 1960, Manaus contributed only 24.5% to the population of the state; in 1980, it contributed 44.4%. Despite this increase in population, there was little evidence to suggest that there existed in Manaus an unusual surplus of labor.[4]

Finally, as might be expected, this demographic shift substantially transformed the social and cultural character of the city. For example, near the end of the rubber boom in 1902, Manaus contained 50,000 people living in four or five *bairros* (neighborhoods that formed an area of approximately 20 square blocks at the river's margin. By 1984, it had become a metropolitan center of close to a million people living in 50 or more *bairros* sprawled over an area of almost 95 square kilometers. More than half of this spatial expansion and 79% of the growth in population occurred within a period of less than 20 years. In the process of urbanization, Manaus acquired most of the characteristics and problems associated with urban-industrial growth throughout much of Brazil and Latin America. In almost every area affecting the quality of life, the growth in population dramatically outpaced the provision of human needs. As wages remained low and the cost of living and property values soared, and as public housing and services of every type became more and more inadequate, large segments of the working class were forced to live at poverty's edge. Thus, favelization (the creation of squatments) became widespread.

Joinville. The cultural and economic history of Joinville assumes a somewhat different character from that of Manaus. Located in the northeast of Santa Catarina, on the Bay of Babitonga, the *município* was founded 1850 when lands in the area were donated to the Princesa Dona Francisca upon her marriage to the Príncipe of Joinville. The colony of Joinville was subsequently settled by mostly German migrants—the latter arriving in the region in such large

---

[4]It may also be noted that during this period the number of economically active women increased from 6700 to 64,000, a relatively increase of 855%. By 1980, women comprised nearly one-third of the economically active labor force.

number that, by the 1930s, the three southern states of Brazil contained approximately 2500 schools in which all instruction was carried out in German.[5]

For more than a century following its colonization, the economy of Joinville was tied to the extraction of timber, the cultivation of tea for export, and the production of various food crops mainly for local and regional markets. In 1926, the city listed less than 100 industries and all but a few of these were engaged in the processing of agricultural products, mainly tea, tobacco, wood, sugar, and leather. A few relatively small firms were engaged in the manufacturing of textiles and various articles of clothing. During this period, the *município* contained 46,000 inhabitants. Of these, 36,000 lived outside the city and were mostly self-employed on family farms.

Unlike Manaus, the industrialization of Joinville resulted not from programs involving the massive intervention of the federal government, but rather from local capital investment. Moreover, industrial development centered mainly on the establishment of heavy, mechanical industries, rather than industries of the assemblage type. The process began most noticeably in 1938 when a group of local investors created Fundição Tupy S/A. Initially, Tupy produced iron castings and hydraulic connections. It then diversified its production to include a wide variety of heavy industrial products. Subsequently, Tupy evolved into a group of 18 companies, of which ten were located in Joinville. Today, it is the city's largest employer. Following Tupy, in 1941, Hansen Industrial was formed. Engaged mainly in the production of plastic piping, Hansen continued to expand its operations in Joinville while becoming a conglomerate of 25 firms spread over 15 Brazilian states and three foreign countries. A third firm, Consul, was organized in 1950 for the production of refrigeration units. Vertically integrating its production, shipping, and marketing operations in Joinville, Consul now controls

---

[5]In 1937, at the same time as the institution of the Estado Novo, President Vargas (fearing that these schools and the German population of the region were falling under the control of "Nazistas do Brasil") initiated a "Campaign of Nationalization" which, among other things, required that instruction in Brazilian schools be conducted in Portuguese.

approximately 50% of the Brazilian market for household refrigerators and related appliances. A fourth company, Embraco, was organized in 1974 for the production of compressors. While first servicing only Consul's need for compressors, Embraco now exports approximately half of its total production to more than 30 countries. Together, these firms are known as the "big four" and they form the hegemonic core of Joinville's new industrial economy.[6]

Through the local *Associação Comercial e Industrial*, the directors of these four firms have virtually controlled the economic and political life of Joinville. Over the years, the *Associação* has worked assiduously to stimulate the local development of cognate industries and to free "the big four" from any dependency they might have on the São Paulo market for the purchase of capital goods and unit components for the products they manufacture. The *Associação* has had as one of it objectives to make of Joinville the industrial center of Santa Catarina. Thus, during the 1970s, the *Associação* provided the political momentum for the development of an industrial park in Joinville and then, with its research division and financial connections, it proceeded to attract 282 new industrial firms to the city. With the addition of 141 new firms, the heavy industrial sector represented the major source of growth. Still, 60 new firms were added in sectors involving the production of plastics, textiles, and clothing. Associated with this growth, the number of commercial establishments in the city increased from 1036 (employing 4000 workers) to 1551 (employing almost 7000 workers).

---

[6] All four of these industries are capital intensive and unlike most of those that were implanted in Manaus, none of them are fundamentally assemblage in type. In addition, all four of these enterprises were initially capitalized by entrepreneurs, mostly engineers and bankers of German descent, living in Joinville. Even today, all four of them remain largely under the control of directors who live in Joinville and who form the majority of their governing boards. It should be noted, however, that Consul owns 51% of Embraco. To raise capital for further expansion, in 1977 Consul sold 30% of its shares and 8% of Embraco's shares to Whirlpool, an American firm based in Michigan. However, controlling shares in these two firms continue to be held by investors in Joinville.

With all of this development, between 1970 and 1980 the economically active population in the city grew from 40,000 to 94,000 workers, a relative increase of 135% as compared to the 104% increase recorded in Manaus during the same period. However, judging from the available data, the proportion of self-employed workers remained relatively constant at approximately 15% of the total. Excluding taxi operators and a suprisingly small number of street vendors, most of the self-employed appear to be shopkeepers or the proprietors of small-scale service and industrial enterprises dependent almost exclusively on family labor.

Although industrialization in Joinville has proceeded at somewhat slower and more integrated pace than it did in Manaus, it nevertheless has been accompanied by a substantial growth in the city's population. In 1940, shortly after Tupy was established, the city had a population of 34,000. By 1964, this number more than tripled, reaching a level of 108,000. In 1986, based on data collected by the city's planning division, the population exceeded 325,000, a relative increase of 38% over 1980. Of this number, 48% is comprised of individuals who migrated to Joinville principally for reasons of work and only 38% of these migrants have lived in the community ten years or longer. Slightly more than half of these migrants have proceeded from areas classified as rural. The major source of this migratory flow has been the littoral of São Francisco do Sul and Vale do Itajai in Santa Catarina but, in recent years, increasing numbers of migrants have come from the states of Paraná and Rio Grande do Sul. Despite the magnitude of this migratory flow, industrialists and union leaders alike acknowledge that there exists such a shortage of labor in Joinville and its surrounding area that further industrial expansion may require the organized recruitment of "less desirable" workers from outside the region.[7]

As in the case of Manaus, the magnitude and rapidity of the migratory flow to Joinville has exceeded the city's capacity to

---

[7]At the time of research, Consul was in the process of completing the construction of a new division that would necessitate the recruitment of 1,000 workers. Comments relating to "less desirable" workers generally include a reference not only to the level of skill but also to workers whose ethnic origins are not German.

provide adequate housing and public services. Thus, industrialization has meant favelization. In the words of a local historian (Ternes 1986: 246):

In truth, the process of industrialization disfigured the city, polluted the rivers, compromised its green areas, while the immigrant populations were establishing themselves in a disorderly manner, occupying areas not recommended for human habitation.[8]

The most notorious of the areas unfit for human habitation is a large sea mangue or marsh owned by Tupy and now occupied by more than 7000 squatters.

Juiz de Fora. Juiz de Fora provides still another microcontext in which the conditions relating to wage-work and self-employment would appear to differ. Located approximately 275 kilometers from Rio, Juiz de Fora is the most important socioeconomic magnet of the Zona da Mata in southern Minas Gerais. Founded in 1850, the city's early population included a substantial number of German, Italian, and Portuguese immigrants who came to construct the railroad over which coffee and other agricultural products could be more easily transported from the Zona da Mata to the port of Rio. Engineers among these immigrants combined with *fazendeiros* to form a local oligarchy similar to that which existed in Joinville. In 1889, they capitalized the construction of the first hydroelectric power plant to be built in Latin America. A textile industry soon followed. By the turn of the century, with 37 cotton mills, Juiz de Fora had acquired a reputation, as the "Manchester of Brazil," a reputation of which the city still boasts.[9]

In her study of one of the city's textile mills, Maria Andréa Rios Loyola (1972) relates that the industrialization of Juiz de Fora was affected both positively and negatively by its centralized location

---

[8]My translation from the Portuguese.
[9]For details relating to the history of Juiz de Fora, see Paulino de Oliveira (1966), Maria Andréa Rios Loyola (1972), and Silvia Maria Belfort Vilela de Andrade (1984).

in the highway and railroad networks that connect the Zona da Mata to the large urban markets in Belo Horizonte, Rio, and São Paulo. Coffee provided much of the capital with which local entrepreneurs established the textile and garment sector as the main branch of industrial activity in relationship to these markets. With the collapse of coffee, the agricultural economy shifted to livestock and the production of dairy products, and Juiz de Fora became and remains today the largest milk and cheese producing municipality in the region. In recent years, because of competition from Rio and São Paulo, the local oligarchy has turned its investment interests away from textiles to the capitalization of new industries, mainly in the mechanical, paper, and chemical sectors.[10] As a consequence, the textile and food processing sectors no longer dominate the city's economy in terms of total production. Still, these traditional industries continue to absorb the majority of the city's labor force.[11] However, it is the newer industries that have attracted the most recent wave of migrants, mainly from the Zona da Mata but also from Rio.

In 1970, Juiz de Fora reported a population of 239,000 inhabitants, of which 76,000 (32%) were economically active. Although 35% of the 1970 population could be counted as migrants (82% proceeding from the Zona da Mata), more than 90% of these migrants had already lived in the city ten years or longer. Also in 1970, the city registered a total of 696 industrial and 1717 commercial establishments. Buried in these figures, however, is a deeply rooted tradition of cottage industry and family-based commercial establishments. As evidence of this, in 1970 only 6% of the city's 696 industrial establishments employed in excess of 100 workers and no less than 61% were family-operated enterprises

---

[10]The most significant of the new mechanical industries is Siderúrgica Mendes Júnior, a steel mill which produces six million tons of non-flat steel products annually. Largely because of the transportation requirements of this plant, the Federal Brazilian Railway elected to move its regional headquarters from Rio and thus base a substantial number of its workers in Juiz de Fora.

[11]Juiz de Fora still has many industrial establishments that were founded prior to 1920.

employing five workers or less.[12] The vast majority of these small-scale industries continue to be engaged in the production of various articles of clothing either on consignment or for retail sale in family shops.

Between 1970 and 1980 an industrial park was established in Juiz de Fora. During the decade, 217 industrial and 886 commercial establishments were added to the city's economy. As near as can be determined, these developments did not greatly transform the cultural character of the community. All of the new industrial firms were locally capitalized and a great many of their directors and their majority shareholders resided in the community and continued to form its economic oligarchy. Moreover, the textile and food-processing industries remained the major source of employment. Regarding the textile sector, the city's planning commission estimated that in 1986 there existed perhaps 1500 registered and unregistered household enterprises engaged primarily in the manufacture and sale of clothing. Thus, while the city's economically active population increased from 76,000 to 115,000 between 1970 and 1980, it was the belief of public officials that the number of self-employed workers had remained more or less at the level of approximately 25% of the total and that this figure had not increased as a result of a surplus flow of migrants looking for work. Indeed, they suggested that most migrants coming to the city were workers who secured employment in the mechanical, chemical, paper, and railroad industries prior to leaving their previous places of residence.

As compared to the 84% increase in population recorded in Joinville and the 104% increase in Manaus, during the decade of the 1970s, the population in Juiz de Fora increased by only 29%. The establishment of new industries during the period 1970-80 generated a flow of workers from the Zona da Mata, but the migratory wave was not large. While the proportion of migrants who had lived in the city ten years or longer declined from 90% to 60% during the

---

[12]Informed sources estimate that 15-20% of the small scale enterprises operating in the city are not registered; thus, it is difficult to know how much these figures underestimate the true number of family-based cottage enterprises.

decade, the proportion of total population born outside the city increased only from 35% to 41%.

Thus, urban industrialization in Juiz de Fora has been less rapid and considerably more manageable in its social impact than it has been in Manaus or Joinville. This is evidenced by the success with which city government in Juiz de Fora has confronted urban industrial growth with a well organized program of urban development. Almost as rapidly as squatter settlements appear, self-help groups are organized and the city provides them with land titles and with the financial assistance and materials they need to construct decent houses. These new *bairros* are then targeted for infrastructural development, including the pavement of streets, the construction of schools, clinics, recreation facilities, and the like. As a consequence of this program, compared to Manaus and Joinville, there are surprisingly few *favelas* in Juiz de Fora and those that remained were rapidly being reconstructed at the time of research.

Self-Employment: Macrotheories and Urban Contexts.

The process of urban-industrial change in these three cities has been contextualized at least in part by local social, political, and economic forces. Accordingly, in each city the developmental process has assumed a somewhat different pattern by virtue of the decisions taken by public agencies, entrepreneurs, or both to establish different types of industrial firms and commercial establishments in relationship to product and factor markets. Thus, independent of the general consensus that exists among political and economic elites regarding the capitalist mode of production, the process of urban-industrial change has assumed a sufficiently distinct character in each of these cities as to render problematic efforts to assimilate the explanation of such microcontextual phenomena as wage-earning and self-employment to macrotheories of political economy.

Consider, for example, the thesis that modern enterprises enter into a backward economy and, in the process of their expanding influence, surplus workers are marginalized and forced to make their way by self-employment in the so-called informal sector. The thesis assumes, *inter alia*, that modern enterprises are more demanding of skill than traditional enterprises, more selective in recruitment on the basis of skills and, thus, more renumerative in the wage employment they offer. It also tends to assume that rural areas are more traditional or backward than urban areas and migrants from rural areas are disproportionately disadvantaged with respect to wage employment and, consequently, more likely to be counted among the self-employed.

Among the 211 economically active workers interviewed in Manaus, 77% could be counted as migrants. However, virtually no difference existed in the distribution of migrants and non-migrants among wage workers and the proportion of migrants among self-employed workers was only slightly higher than that of wage workers. Moreover, migrants who were self-employed were far more likely to have lived in the city ten years or longer than wage workers. Personnel managers among some of the new assemblage industries did express a strong preference for recruiting non-migrants, particularly younger men and women of urban rather than rural origins and persons who generally possessed a higher level of education. In rationalizing this preference, they reasoned that younger men and women of higher educational achievement had fewer family responsibilities and were less inclined than older workers to want to make a career of their factory employment; as a consequence, personnel managers believed that these young and better educated urban workers could be more easily dismissed when production levels needed to be lowered in response to market assessments. Because of these recruitment preferences, it is the case in Manaus that migrants who work for wages are more likely to be found in the traditional rather than the new industrial sectors. It should be noted, however, that employment in the traditional industries in Manaus is generally more secure. In addition, the wages earned by workers in these traditional industries are as high, and in many cases higher, than those paid by the new industrial firms.

Thus, 81% of all the industrial workers interviewed in Manaus reported earning two minimum salaries per month or less. By way of comparison, 51% of the lower echelon white collar workers, and 49% of the self-employed workers, reported earning three minimum salaries per month or more. In sum, based on our data, self-employed workers in Manaus are not persons who have been significantly marginalized relative to wage workers by virtue of their social and cultural origins, their migratory status, their lack of skills or, in the final analysis, their income-earning potential.

In Juiz de Fora where the locally capitalized textile, mechanical, chemical, and paper industries are not of the assemblage type, and where, by tradition, there exists a relatively high level of self-employment based in cottage industries and small-scale retail enterprises, the data differ but they generally support the same conclusion. In Juiz de Fora, only 34% of the 135 workers interviewed were migrants. Of these migrants, 72% worked for wages and almost two-thirds of them were employed in the new mechanical industries. Moreover, 70% of the migrants who were self-employed, as compared to only 30% of those working for wages, had lived in the community ten years or longer. Regarding recruitment, the firms studied in Juiz de Fora placed a high value on the personal character and previous work habits of applicants almost to the exclusion of their educational and technical qualifications and they expressed no interest in whether or not job applicants were migrants from rural or urban areas.

As for wages and incomes, the situation in Juiz de Fora is very different from that of Manaus. In Manaus, 82% of the new industrial workers earned two minimum wages/month or less. In Juiz de Fora, 92% of the new industrial workers interviewed reported earning three minimum wages per month or more, a level of income achieved by only 65% of the self-employed workers, 48% of the lower echelon white collar workers, and 41% of the wage workers drawn from the textile industry. In other words, in Juiz de Fora the new mechanical, chemical, and paper industries have a significantly higher wage structure than do the assemblage industries in Manaus. Still, wage employment opportunities in these new industries have not diminished the proportion of self-employed workers in the urban economy. Accordingly, the marginality thesis simply cannot account for the large number of self-employed workers operating in the urban economy of Juiz de Fora.

In Joinville, 75% of the workers interviewed were migrants and no difference existed among wage and self-employed workers according to whether or not they were migrants or non-migrants. As a group, self-employed workers showed a much lower level of educational achievement than all categories of wage workers. However, partly because of the shortage of labor, in Joinville the largest of the new industrial firms (i.e., Consul, Tupy, and Hansen) have professionally organized training programs designed to develop and maintain a permanent cadre of highly skilled workers. These programs are open to applicants more or less independent of their level of educational achievement. As a consequence, in Joinville, migrants of low educational status are not marginalized and forced to work for themselves in order to earn a living.

The low level of self-employment in Joinville (approximately 15% in comparison to 21% and 25% for Manaus and Juiz de Fora respectively) invites the question of whether or not self-employment in these microcontexts can be explained as a function of capitalist enterprises lowering labor costs by seeking to maintain a reserve of surplus labor. Certainly in Joinville there existed a critical shortage of labor and the wages paid by new industrial firms were relatively high by comparison to Manaus (but not as high as those paid by the new industrial firms in Juiz de Fora). Still, a substantially higher percentage of the self-employed workers in Joinville (80% as compared to 55% of the new industrial workers and 42% of the traditional industrial workers) reported earning three minimum wages per month or more. Thus, given the shortage of labor and the earning potential of self-employment, if the reserve of surplus labor thesis is correct, one would think that either industrial wages would be higher in Joinville or that the number of self-employed workers among the economically active would be larger.

Manaus is another matter. As previously noted, despite the massive increase of population in Manaus, the proportion of self-employed workers has declined. This may be related to a low level of unemployment and the availability of wage opportunities, but these explanations ignore the fact that the wages paid in both the new and traditional industrial sectors (and in much of the commercial sector) are uniformly low. Approximately 50% of the self-

112

employed workers interviewed, including street vendors, reported earnings in excess of those reported by 80% of the industrial workers. In truth, industrial firms in Manaus do not need a reserve surplus of workers to lower labor costs. By tacit agreement among themselves and with the support of government, most of these firms have taken the federal government's minimum wage floor and used it as the ceiling above which they concede little or nothing to the contract demands of the *sindicatos*. With few exceptions, industrial firms and commercial establishments in Manaus pay but a small percentage of their employees more than the minimum wage.

The reserve army of surplus labor thesis is even more problematic in the case of Juiz de Fora. Relative to Manaus and Joinville, the number of migrants flowing into Juiz de Fora is not large and a substantial proportion of these migrants secure employment, mainly in the new industrial sector, even before they migrate. Moreover, the wages paid by the new industrial firms in Juiz de Fora are well above those required by the minimum wage law. Of the new industrial workers interviewed, 92% reported earning three minimum wages per month or more; no less than 35% reported earning in excess of six minimum wages. Despite these attractive wages and the employment opportunities that now exist in these new industries, the number of self-employed workers engaged in cottage industries and family-based retail enterprises continues to remain high. If there exists a surplus of labor in Juiz de Fora to explain this, then why is it that the new industries pay wages higher than what is required by law and considerably higher than the wages earned by virtually all categories of textile workers? Further, if there exists a surplus reserve of labor, why is it that as many as three out of every ten of the new industrial workers interviewed were migrants, mainly from the Zona da Mata, who had lived in the city less than five years? In sum, we could find little evidence in Juiz de Fora that wage-work and self-employment were somehow significantly related to efforts by industrial firms to lower labor costs by maintaining a reserve of surplus labor.

As applied to the analysis of self-employment, structural theories would give focus to the complex linkages and dependent relationships between petty commodity production and monopoly capital (see, e.g., Faria 1976; Moser 1978; Tokman 1978). The general thesis of this approach is that large-scale capitalist enterprises relegate to small-scale enterprises subsidiary functions and operations they consider risky or too costly to provide for themselves. This thesis is certainly relevant to the position assumed by a great many cottage industries in the urban economy of Juiz de Fora. However, as an explanation of self-employment in Juiz de Fora or elsewhere, it is both erroneous and tautological. It is tautological because it suggests that individuals who subcontract work are self-employed because they subcontract work. It is erroneous because the majority of the self-employed workers interviewed in all three cities were engaged in the production, sale, or both, of goods and services for which they did not have orders or contractual arrangements with large-scale firms. To the contrary, in Manaus it was a common complaint of street vendors that they were continuously harassed by public authorities on the behalf of commercial establishments with which they competed.

Workers as actors.

Whether monistic or dualistic in conception, and whether evolutionary, structural, or functional in mode of analysis, the macrotheories from which explanations of the so-called "informal sector" have been deduced generally treat firms and enterprises as economic actors whose decisions are more or less based on the economic calculus of the market. By a strange twist of logic, however, workers are generally denied the status of economic actors. As commoditized labor, workers form a class which has the potential of collective action but, as individuals, they are dealt with as if they did not make decisions for themselves. What all of this tends to ignore is that, despite their limited quotient of power, workers are economic actors. At the very least, they generally decide for themselves whether or not they will make of their labor power a marketable commodity or use it themselves in the production of marketable goods and services. The question is: By what rationality or rationalities do workers take this decision? Given the limitations of space, we shall confine the discussion of this question to a consideration of (1) the previous work experience of the workers interviewed, (2) the reasons self-employed workers give for their self-employment, and (3) the circumstances under which wage and self-employed workers would change the work they are doing in favor of something else.

By comparison, wage-workers and the self-employed seem to respond differently to their earlier work experiences. In Joinville, 57% of the wage workers interviewed had never changed employers and only 11% had changed employers more than once. In Juiz de Fora, 50% had never changed employers, and only 5% had changed more than once. This would seem to suggest that wage employment in these communities has been relatively stable and workers are not shunted, nor do they shunt themselves, from one employer to another. This is not the case in Manaus where 70% percent of the wage workers interviewed had changed employers at least twice and 27% of them had changed employers no less than four times. This certainly underscores a feature of an urban economy dominated by industries of the assemblage type. Still, excluding the few individuals who had once worked in agriculture or who might have sold goods in the streets when they were young, 93% of the wage workers in Manaus, 97% in Juiz de Fora, and 95% of the wage workers in Joinville had never been gainfully employed except for wages. This would seem to suggest that unless their early experience with employers somehow had been difficult and negative, wage workers in general tend to become locked into wage employment as a way of earning a living.

The opposite tends to be the case with self-employed workers. Of the self-employed workers interviewed, 93% considered themselves capable of securing wage employment. Moreover, 75% of these workers in Manaus, 65% in Juiz de Fora, and 50% in Joinville, had at one time or another worked for wages. Of this entire sample, only 13% had turned to self-employment because they had lost their previous job and could not find what they considered to be acceptable wage employment. In other words, the overwhelming majority of these workers had quit whatever work they were doing for wages in favor of working for themselves.

Each self-employed worker interviewed was asked to specify the various reasons why they had decided to become self-employed.

Only 43% of them took the decision, in part, because they thought they could earn more money.[13] A slightly larger number, 47%, elected self-employment because they "disliked working in a factory or for a *patrão*." Related to this, 60% indicated they decided in favor of self-employment because they did not like taking orders from an employer or a *patrão*. As self-employed workers, 67% were economically engaged with other members of the family and most of this group indicated that, in part, they were persuaded to quit their jobs in order to work at home or elsewhere with relatives. In addition to this, a little over 60% of them took the decision, again in part because they considered the work they were doing for themselves to be more interesting, more challenging, and it afforded them a greater opportunity for growth. Whatever, the most commonly agreed upon reason given for their preference, cited by 79% of those interviewed, was that self-employment provided them the independence with which they could decide for themselves how, when, and to what purpose they would perform their work.

In light of these considerations, it is interesting to compare wage and self-employed workers according to the circumstances that would motivate them to change their employment (i.e., leave their present employer or give up self-employment for wage work). Of the wage workers interviewed, 78% would change their present employer for higher wages; 70% of the self-employed workers would not take on wage employment for a higher income. Fifty-three percent of the wage workers would change jobs to work for a better employer; 73% of the self-employed workers would not give up their self-employment in order to work for a "good company." Of the wage workers, 69% would change employers for better working conditions; 73% of the self-employed workers would not. Of the wage workers, 52% would change employers if they could find a more "intellectual" type of work; 90% of the self-employed workers would not.[14] In sum, as compared to wage workers, self-

---

[13]Workers were not compelled in the interview situation to rank the reasons for their decision according to priority but rather they were asked simply to indicate what factors they had considered in making the decision.

[14]It perhaps should be noted here that these and the above value orientations of self-employed workers did not vary significantly from one urban context to another. This is not always the case with wage workers. Assembly workers in

employed workers held extremely positive attitudes with respect to the character and organization of their work and most of them would not be inclined to change it for more income or an opportunity to work for a good company or *patrão*.

Conclusions.

These data suggest that, somewhat independent of the macrodevelopments affecting the labor markets of these three urban economies, wage earners and self-employed workers disclose very different rationalities in reference to the labor process. Whether they worked in the white collar sectors of these urban economies, for the assemblage industries in Manaus, or the mechanical or textile industries in Juiz de Fora or Joinville, most of the wage workers interviewed acquiesced to a system of values in terms of which they viewed their economic well being as inextricably linked to the commoditization of their labor for sale in the market. Accordingly, whatever dissatisfaction they might have with wages they were paid, with the conditions of their employment, or with those for whom they worked, for most, their only conceivable option was to withdrawn their labor and return it to the market. Thus, in conformity with the logic of economic rationality, most of these workers were more or less prepared "to go to market" whenever they thought they could incrementally improve the material conditions of their social and cultural lives.

By way of contrast, the self-employed workers interviewed held extremely positive attitudes concerning the character and organization of their work. Most of them considered their work interesting and challenging. They perceived that it afforded them the opportunity for advancement, the opportunity to reward their own initiative. Laboring alone or with family and kin, they were their own bosses. They did not have to take orders, submit to authority, or worry about relationships with supervisors or *patrões*. They did

---

Manaus, followed by textile mill workers in Juiz de Fora, were much more inclined to change employers than were workers employed by the mechanical industries in Juiz de Fora and Joinville, or sawmill workers in Manaus. Compared to textile workers in Juiz de Fora, sawmill workers in Manaus tended to view their *"patrões "* in more positive light.

not have to worry about lay-offs or dismissals. They considered that their work provided them with a sense of self-reliance, freedom of movement, and the independence with which they were able to perform their work according to their own sense of priorities. Accordingly, even if it meant somewhat less income for themselves and their families, most of the self-employed workers interviewed strongly preferred to commoditize *not themselves and their labor but the products of their labor.* The decision they made in this regard tends to follow upon decisions they had already made as to how they wanted to conduct their individual lives with family and friends. Thus, their decision with respect to self-employment as a mode of economic action was embedded in a system of social relationships that did not conform entirely to the symbolic-cultural logic of economic rationality.

All of this is not to suggest that the various macrotheories that conform to the logic of economic rationality are not without some value for understanding the dynamic processes that affect working class populations in these Brazilian cities. Clearly, the opportunities of wage earning and self-employment do not exist completely independent of the forces that have transformed the economies of these cities and the composition of their populations. However, self-employment appears to involve considerations that engage values which are not entirely structured by these macroinstitutional forces. Further, the character of these values is not clearly revealed by subsuming the description of workers or the type of work they do under such *a priori* categories as the "informal sector" or "petty commodity production." Finally, it is also the case that self-employment in these cities may be found in all sectors of the economy and in relationship to the organization of firms or enterprises of varying scale and capitalization.[15]

---

[15]Although she continues to employ the dualistic conception of the economy, in a recent article Lorissa Adler Lomnitz (1988) describes the extent to which "informal activities" are socially embedded even in the formal sector of State controlled, centrally planned economies like that of the Soviet Union.

References.

Andrade, Silvia Maria Belford Vilela de.
1984   Classe Operária em Juiz de Fora: Uma História de Lutas (1912-1924). Campinas, Brasil: Dissertação apresentado como exigência parcial para obtenção do grau de Mestre em História à Comissão Julgadora da Universidade Estadual de Campinas.

Boeke, J.H.
1953   Economics and Economic Policy of Dual Societies as Exemplified by Indonesia. New York: International Secretariat of Pacific Relations.

Despres, Leo A.
1988   Dependent Development and the Marginality Thesis: A Case Study from Manaus. In John W. Bennett and John R. Bowen, eds., Proceedings, Society for Economic Anthropology. New York: University Press of The Americas, pp.293-310.
1987   Urban-industrial Development and the Marginality of Workers in Manaus: Some Theoretical Implications. In Werner von der Ohe, ed., Kulturanthropologie. Berlin: Duncker and Humbolt, pp. 67-88.

1988   Dependent Development and the Marginality Thesis: A Case Study from Manaus. In John W. Bennett and John R. Bowen, eds., Production and Autonomy— Anthropological Studies and Critiques of Development. Lanham MD: University Press of America, pp. 293-310.

Faria, Vilmar
1976   Occupational Marginality, Employment and Poverty in Urban Brazil. Unpublished Ph.D. Dissertation. Harvard University.

Frank, A.G.
1970   Latin America: Underdevelopment or Revolution.
        New York: Monthly Review Press.

Gerry, Chris
1978   Petty Production and Capitalist Production in Dakar:
        The crisis of the Self-Employed. World Development
        6 (9/10): 1147-1160.

Geertz, C.
1963   Peddlers and Princes. Chicago: University of Chicago
        Press.

Hart, Keith
1973   Informal Income Opportunities and Urban
        Employment in Ghana. The Journal of Modern
        African Studies 11: 61-89.

Lomnitz, Larissa Adler
1988   Informal Exchange Networks in Formal Systems: A
        Theoretical Model. American Anthropologist 90: 42-
        55.

Loyola, Maria Andréa Rios
1972   Trabalho e Modernização na Indústria Têxtil. Rio de
        Janeiro: Dissertação de mestrado apresentada ao
        Programa de Pós-Graduação em Antropologia Social
        do Museu Nacional da Universidade Federal do Rio de
        Janeiro.

McGee, T.G.
1973   Peasants in the Cities: a Paradox, a Paradox, a most
        Ingenious Paradox. Human Organization 2: 135-142.

Mingione, Enzo
1984   The Informal Sector and the Development of Third
        World Cities. Regional Development Dialogue 5: 63-
        76.

Moser, Caroline O.N.
1978   Informal Sector or Petty Commodity Production: Dualism or Dependence in Urban Development? World Development 6: 1041-1064.
1984   The Informal Sector Reworked: Viability and Vulnerability in Urban Development. Regional Development Dialogue 5: 135-178.

Nattrass, Nicoli Jean
1987   Street Trading in Transkei: A Struggle Against Poverty, Persecution, and Prosecution. World Development 15: 861-875.

Nun, J.
1969   Superpoblación relativa, ejército industrial de reserva y masa marginal. Revista Latinoamericana de Sociología 2: 128-235.

Oliveira, Paulino de.
1966   História de Juiz de Fora. Juiz de Fora, Brasil.

Peattie, L.
1984   Comment. Regional Development Dialogue 5: 179-180.
1987   An Idea in Good Currency and How it Grew: The Informal Sector. World Development 15: 851-860.

Portes, Alejandro and John Walton.
1981   Labor, Class, and the International System. New York: Academic Press.

Quijano, Aníbal
1974   The Marginal Pole of the Economy and the Marginalized Labor Force. Economy and Society 3: 393-428.

Richardson, Harry W.
1984 The Role of the Informal Sector in Developing Countries: An Overview. Regional Development Dialogue 5: 3-54.

Roberts, Bryan
1978 Cities of Peasants: The Political Economy of Urbanization in the Third World. London: Sage Publications

Souza, Paulo R. and V. E. Tokman
1976 The Informal Urban Sector in Latin America. International Labor Review 114: 355-365.

Ternes, Apolinário.
1986 História Econômica de Joinville. Joinville, Brasil: Meyer.

Tokman, V.
1978 An Exploration into the Nature of the Formal-Informal Sector Relationships. World Development 6(9/10): 1065-1075.

POPULAR RELIGION, PATRONAGE, AND RESOURCE DISTRIBUTION IN BRAZIL: A MODEL OF AN HYPOTHESIS FOR THE SURIVIVAL OF THE ECONOMICALLY MARGINAL.

Sidney M. Greenfield
Department of Anthropology
The University of Wisconsin-Milwaukee

Russell R. Prust
Compact for Educational Opportunity
Milwaukee, Wisconsin

The initial survival value of a favorable innovation is conservative, in that it renders possible the maintenance of a traditional way of life ithe face of changed circumstances (Hockett and Ascher 1964:137).

Introduction.

In the four decades since the end of World War II the economy of Brazil, the fifth largest country in the world, has been transformed from an underdeveloped provider of raw materials and foodstuffs for the markets of Europe and North America into an industrializing producer of automobiles, trucks, airplanes, tanks, weapons, and other manufactured goods for export as well as for a growing domestic market. From 1948 through 1976, for example, the economy grew at a rate of 7% per year, making it at present the eighth largest in the free world (Salazar-Carnillo and Fendt 1985).

During approximately the same period Brazil's population quadrupled, increasing from slightly under 41 million in 1940 to its recently estimated level of more than 140 million. The country also urbanized (Merrick and Graham 1979): In 1940, two-thirds of the population was rural; by 1980 the rural/urban percentages had reversed themselves with two-thirds or more of Brazil's people living in urban areas. At present, there are 10 cities with more than a million inhabitants and Recife, where the research on which this paper is based was conducted, is one of several cities with an excess of two million inhabitants (Anuário Estatística do Brasil 1985).

However, as is the case in so many other developing nations, Brazil's rapidly expanding economy has become capital- rather than labor-intensive. Consequently, jobs have not been created in numbers anywhere near the increase in the population, especially in the urban centers. Unemployment rates are high and underemployment is a factor of life, particularly among the more recent rural migrants and the less educated segments of the urban born. It has been estimated that as many as 60% or more of the population is marginal to the formal economy; i.e., they are not integrated into the society by means of incomes earned at jobs that allow them to purchase in the market goods and services produced by the new industries. For many scholars, the term "informal sector" has become a catch-all to refer to the varied and diverse ways this marginalized population obtains the material resources it needs to survive.

Brazil's vertically stratified society often has been characterized in terms of its extremes. With respect to the distribution of its rapidly expanding national wealth, the rich, who always have been very rich, have become even more so, while the poor, especially the urban poor, often have so little that one wonders how they manage to survive. To complicate matters, the cities have been unable to provide the most basic services for the growing number of poor; few welfare and assistance programs have been established by governmental agencies at any level. Thus, countless millions live at the brink of poverty and destitution, often by squatting in *favelas* where they are without water, sewage, electricity, public transportation, and other basic facilities. They live in dwellings often assembled from materials found in other people's trash, on land whose legal title rests with others or whose ownership often is in dispute.

This paper is about Brazil's unemployed and underemployed urban masses. Specifically, we are interested in how those marginal to and, for the most part, outside of the formal economy of the nation obtain the minimum material resources needed to enable them to survive. In this respect, the paper is about the informal sector; but, as we shall see, it is really about a way in which people in the formal and the informal sectors are brought together in the distribution of a part of the national wealth (cf. Prust 1985). We shall focus on one dimension of what is a complicated situation. What is important about the model we propose as an hypothesis to be tested by future studies, however, is that it focuses on a domain of culture—religion—not usually examined in any detail by students of economic behavior and resource distribution. The life events to be presented in the case materials below had as their common element the relationship that each of the individuals was to develop with Sr. Luiz, a *pai-de-santo* and head of an *Umbanda* center. In order to demonstrate one way the poor and the marginal in the informal sector in Brazil's cities survive, and how the formal and informal sectors are brought together in the redistribution of wealth, we shall look at *Umbanda* as an example of a new, urban religion, at Sr. Luiz's center in Recife and, in particular, at a sample of his clients.

The case materials.

Case #1. Pedro Moreira lives in a small shack in a *favela*, or slum, in the city of Recife in northeast Brazil. Although he was born in the interior of the state, he has spent the last dozen years in Recife. During his childhood he remembers his parents moving from one *fazenda* (plantation) to the next, unsuccesfully trying to improve their circumstances. He occasionally speaks of the squalor of their lives, and their insecurity.

When Sr. Moreira was 13, he decided to follow his uncle who had moved to Recife. The boy hoped that he would be able to find there conditions that would enable him to live a more secure and satisfying life than he had experienced thus far. Unfortunately, this was not to be. Although young, strong, and energetic when he arrived, Pedro was unable to find work. At first, he lived with his uncle who had obtained employment as a gardener for the manager of a medium sized food market. Although the pay was not much, the store manager helped Pedro's uncle and his family with food, old clothing, and other things they needed. Pedro found odd jobs from which he earned a small amount of money, part of which he gave to his uncle while he continued to live with him.

When he was 18 Pedro met Luiza, the daughter of a friend of his uncle, whose parents also had moved to Recife from the interior of the state. When Luiza became pregnant with his child a short time later, Pedro tried even harder to find a job and a house into which they could move together. Unable to obtain steady work, however, he could not rent let alone buy a home. So, when he heard from friends that an *invasão* (invasion) of an unsettled area at the outskirts of the city was being planned, with help from his uncle and Luiza's parents he assembled some poles, thatch, cardboard, and other materials from which he made a small shack placed on a plot in the new squatter settlement. On three occasions over the next five years, Pedro, Luiza, and their children moved to new shacks in new squatter settlements. Pedro still has not been able to find steady employment. He works at odd jobs, in what has come to be called the informal sector. Luiza takes in washing to help support the family.

In February of 1980, their oldest child took seriously ill. The herbal remedies provided by a neighbor did nothing to bring down her high fever. The prayers of the local *rezador* (faith healer) also did not help. Pedro and Luiza could not afford to take the child to a doctor. They silently feared that their little one would die, as do thousands of poor children daily in Brazil's many slums. A friend of Pedro's then suggested that he take the child to Sr. Luiz, a well known *pai-de-santo*, a healer, and the head of an *Umbanda* center located several miles from where Pedro and Luiza lived.

Case #2. Armando Soares also had been born in the interior of the state of Pernambuco. As a child he lived and worked on the small plot of land owned by his parents. Unlike Pedro Moreira, who had been unable to complete even the first year of primary school, Armando had finished six years of schooling. At the age of 20, he moved to Recife where he joined the merchant marine. He served until 1978, when he retired. Then he ran into problems. Try as he might, he found himself unable to obtain the pension to which he was legally entitled. Every time he went to the office in Recife that administered such benefits, he was given numerous forms to fill out, sent from one office to the next, and then told to return at a later date. As time passed, Armando found that he was using up his small savings. Without his pension, he feared that soon he would become destitute. A friend suggested that he go to Sr. Luiz, the *pai-de-santo*, and ask for his help.

Case #3. Amalia Ferreira is a slight, attractive woman in her late twenties with long dark hair. She, her husband—an unemployed tailor—and their three children live in the same *favela* where Amalia and her parents lived when she was a child. For several years, she had been suffering from debilitating headaches and back pain so severe that she no longer was able to work as a part time maid. She also was finding it more and more difficult to care for her children. Her husband, who had been raised in a *favela* in the neighborhood of Sr. Luiz's *Umbanda* center, suggested that she go to the religious leader and ask for his help.

Case #4. Edson Miranda had been the assistant to an influential and outspoken member of the legislature of the state of Pernambuco. He also ran a successful real estate agency in the state capital. In the 1970s, the deputy for whom he worked was *cassado* (stripped) of his political rights by the conservative military regime in Brasilia. When the legislator left office, Edson was out of a job. His real estate business then began to suffer, partly because of a building slump and partly because Edson was considered by many potential clients to be "subversive" as the result of his close association with his former employer. In 1978, Edson co-signed a promissory note for a friend. When the friend defaulted, the bank turned to Edson to make payment. Unable to do so, Edson asked his brother, who was doing well financially at the time, and other members of his and his wife's families to help. When they all turned him down, he too sought the help of Sr. Luiz, the *pai-de-santo*.

Umbanda and its clients.

Umbanda is one of several religious traditions to have taken roots and flourished in Brazil in recent years (Brown 1986; Camargo 1973; Willems 1967). While Brazil's growing population has been urbanizing and industrializing, new or syncretized religions have appeared in this largest Roman Catholic country in the world. Most of the new religions, as is the case with *Umbanda*, are urban in origin and the majority of their followers are city dwellers.

Umbanda first appeared in Brazil in the vicinity of Rio de Janeiro in the 1920s. As a syncretic religion, it combined Spiritism brought from France in the 19th century with a range of Afro-Brazilian practices referred to locally as *Macumba* (Brown 1986, chapters 2 and 3; Ortiz 1978). The Afro-Brazilian traditions already represented a syncretism of the beliefs and practices of the slaves with the Roman Catholic beliefs and practices of their Iberian masters (Bastide 1978). Most of the West African cultural heritages of the slaves shared a belief in a supreme Creator and a pantheon of more specialized deities who assisted and communicated with their human worshippers. Although the Iberians tried to stamp out what they called the "fetishistic" and "pagan" beliefs of the Africans by converting them to Roman Catholicism, the slaves recognized early the parallels between their own beliefs and the cult of the saints of the masters. To make it appear to the masters that they had accepted Christianity and, to hide their continuing worship of their African supernaturals, equivalencies were established between specific *Orixás*, (the Yoruba term generally used in Brazil to refer to the African deities, and specific Roman Catholic saints). The name of a saint came to represent both its African and Roman Catholic forms (Bastide 1978; Herskovits 1937).

To this already syncretized pantheon of supernaturals, *Umbanda* added the Spiritist belief in a universe of deceased spirits. It then added several new categories of deities who became the more immediate contacts between the supernatural world and the world of the living (Gabriel 1980; Ortiz 1978; Pressel 1974). The new *Umbanda* cosmology is organized in sevens. Seven lines, each headed by a powerful syncretized entity, are seen as part of a vast army of supernatural beings that resembles a bureaucracy and, at the top of the hierarchically-ordered system, is the distant Creator. Each of the seven lines, is, in turn, subdivided, into seven sub-lines, which in turn are subdivided into seven legions. Each legion is subdivided into seven sub-legions, in turn subdivided into phalanxes and sub-phalanxes. At each level, each unit has its own leader.

At the upper reaches of the hierarchy are the saints, *Orixás*, or both. At the lower echelons are the entities unique to *Umbanda*—not deities proper but, rather, disincarnate spirits—the *Pretos Velhos*, the *Caboclos*, the *Exus*, and the *Crianças*. In Spiritism, however, the disincarnate spirits once were real historical personages; the *Pretos Velhos, Caboclos, Exus,* and *Crianças* are stereotyped categories drawn from earlier periods in Brazilian history. The *Pretos Velhos* are the wise old slaves who loyally served their masters; the *Caboclos* are the brave and noble Indians who resisted captivity; the *Exus*, originally the messengers of the *Oriaxás*, are a varieity of types ranging from bums and prostitutes to other picturesque characters familiar in Brazilian history; and the *Crianças* are children who represent the biologically and culturally unified Brazilian people of the future.

Like its African and Spiritist predecessors, *Umbanda* is a religion based on mediumship and spirit possession. The supernaturals are believed to come down to the earth and make their presence known and felt through the bodies of their worshippers and caretakers who are mediums. Also like its predecessors, *Umbanda* has taken as its central value *caridade*, the doing of charity. The supernaturals are believed to come down to the earth through the bodies of their mediums to help the needy. Though *Umbanda* mediums are able to receive entities from across the range of the vertically ordered pantheon, those entities who perform the works of charity that are the basis of *Umbanda's* public appeal are the stereotyped, disincarnate personages drawn from Brazilian history— the *Pretos Velhos*, the *Caboclos*, the *Exus*, and the *Crianças* at the lower end of the spiritual hierarchy. Applying the bureaucratic, military imagery used so often by *Umbandistas*, it is as if the old deities from Africa—along with their counterparts, the Roman Catholic saints—have been moved upstairs to desks, along with the Creator, leaving charitable tasks in the field to the *Pretos Velhos*, the *Caboclos*, the *Exus*, and the *Crianças*.

Umbanda is organized in local centers usually called *terreiros*. The bureaucratic model is applied to both the religious and secular organization. Each center is directed by a leader who is the medium who receives the most powerful spirit entity to come to the center. The religious leader is the authority over a cadre of assistant mediums and mediums-in-training, called *filhos/filhas-de-santo*, who assist in the performance of the rituals. On the secular side, each center has a president, vice-president, secretary, treasurer, and other officers who manage the affairs of the center like those of any other organization. There is, of course, a membership that includes believers who are not mediums. Public rituals are attended by the corps of mediums and the members but are open to anyone.

At public rituals the mediums invoke and receive serially (are possessed by) the particular spirits with whom they have developed a special relationship and for whom they serve as mediums. The high point of the evening are the *consultas* (consultations). The most powerful spirit to come to the center, its *padroeiro* (patron), invariably is received by the religious leader and speaks, one at a time and in order, with anyone present wishing to do so. The mediums, other members of the center, and non-members who have come specifically to consult with the spirit, perhaps for advice or for help with a variety of problems, line up according to the number given them when they entered, and await their turn.

As noted above, the symbolic imagery of the *Umbanda* cosmos is one of a hierarchically-ordered pantheon of other-worldly entities who, in the broad sense, are committed to giving charitable help to those in need on earth.below them. The *Pretos Velhos*, the *Caboclos*, the *Exus*, and the *Crianças*, come down and, through spirit mediums, bring power and spiritual resources to those who need them to modify and improve their worldly situation. It is believed quite generally in Brazil that one's worldly situation or fate can be modified significantly only through the intercession of the supernaturals. As Brown (1986: 189) has summarized it, "spiritual powers...move downward in exchange for loyal and faithful homage and service, which moves upwards." She explicitly states that the symbolic imagery that pervades *Umbanda* is that of patron/client exchange, the system of social relations that dominated traditional

130

Brazilian society and culture prior to its urbanization and industrialization (see Forman and Riegelhaut 1979; Greenfield 1968, 1972, 1977, 1979; Hutchinson 1966; Roniger 1987). The symbolic patron/client ties are between the spirit entities from above, the *Pretos Velhos*, the *Caboclos*, the *Exus*, and the *Crianças*, and their human clients seeking help below.

At least in theory, the resources exchanged are spiritual and symbolic—power and homage. However, as in the cases described above, many of the problems for which individuals seek help from the spirits also have a material dimension. Consequently, material resources are added to the symbolic exchanges between the spirit entities and their clients. Before examining them, however, the role of the medium requires further comment.

Spirit mediums such as Sr. Luiz are not part of the patron/client exchanges and subsequent relationships between the spirits and their human clients. Strictly speaking, they are intermediaries who bridge the two theoretically distinct orders of reality, thereby making it possible for the patrons and their clients to interact—for the resources of each to be exchanged. We might refer to the spirit mediums as "brokers" (cf. Allum 1973) who facilitate transactions between otherwise separate planes of reality. In practice, however, the brokerage role often is lost in confusion; most clients do not separate the spirit mediums from the spirit guides the latter incorporate. As a result, powerful mediums like Sr. Luiz are often considered to be, and are treated by the clients of their spirit guides, as the patrons of those who become center clients. Since, usually, material resources are part of a client's problem, they become part of the transaction and the medium becomes a broker through whom extensive material resources flow as part of a network of patron/client exchanges. As the broker of material resources, the medium, his (or her) religious center, or both (Lerch 1978), assist segments of the unemployed and underemployed urban poor in the informal sector in the latter's quest to survive. To see how this functions, let us now return to those individuals and their stories that we introduced earlier.

131

Umbanda at work.

Pedro and Luiza Moreira, Armando Soares, Amalia Ferreira, and Edson Miranda are among the tens of thousands who have come to Sr. Luiz for his help over the past several decades. Each, at different times, made the first visit to the spiritual leader of the *Centro Espirita João de Deus* on the evening of a public session. Clients and the public generally usually arrive shortly after sundown and are seated in a large room in an area across from an open space that soon will be occupied by Sr. Luiz, the medium corps, and other members of the Center. When arrivals indicate to the attendant who does the seating that a consultation is desired with Sr. Luiz's spirit guide, they are given a number.

A typical evening began with the cleansing by incense of the numerous statues of the deities on an altar in the front of the open space. Then, standing in the open space, the white-clad medium corps were cleansed, as were, finally, the visitors seated across from them. Then drums, located across the open space from the altar, began to beat rhythmically. Those in the open space, and some of those seated began to sing *pontos*, (songs) that were invocations to the various deities. The white-robed mediums then began to dance, gyrating slowly in a circle. After several songs and a period of dancing, the body of one of the participants convulsed; the first of what were to be a series of deities had arrived to occupy the bodies of their devotees. As the evening progressed, one white-clad devotee after another entered into trance in response to almost non-stop singing, drumming, and dancing. Then, after several hours, many of the seated observers stood up and, according to the number they had received, left to line up at the side of the building. João de Deus, Sr. Luiz's *Preto Velho*, had arrived and was attending to clients.

We shall begin our summary of what happened to each of the individuals introduced above with the story of *Armando Soares*. As his turn approached, Armando was directed by a male assistant to sit in a chair next to the almost unrecognizable figure of Sr. Luiz. The tall, large body of the medium appeared to be smaller and considerably older than it had seem a few hours earlier, and walked

132

bent over, with a stoop. The figure held a pipe in its mouth and a glass of *cachaça* (Brazilian rum) in its hand.

When the medium turned to him, Armando tried to explain the problem he was having obtaining his retirement benefits. The figure, however, paid no attention. Instead it wrote something on a piece of paper, handed it to Armando and, in a gruff, raspy voice (significantly different from that of Sr. Luiz), instructed him on what to do. If that did not work, the figure added, Armando should come back and see him again. A white-robed male medium then took Armando by the arm and directed him to a table in another part of the building where several similarly dressed men were seated. One took the piece of paper, entered Armando's name, address, diagnosis, and prescribed treatment into a ledger book, and explained the treatment. The assisting medium then directed Armando to another room where the latter was given incense for burning and a combination of herbs and roots with which to prepare prescribed ritual baths. The old man who dispensed the materials also instructed Armando in the dietary restrictions he was to observe during the two-week period he was to take the treatment.

After completing the regimen, Armando returned to the pension office. He was told that his file had been lost and that he would have to fill out new forms and repeat yet again the procedure he had gone through several times before. Totally frustrated now, he returned to the Center and requested another consultation with Sr. Luiz and his spirit guide. Late that night, after the public ritual had been completed and when all but a few of the visitors and most of the mediums had left the Center, Armando was conducted into a small room in which Sr. Luiz, incorporating João de Deus, attended selected individuals. Armando poured out his anger and frustration, explaining again what had happened with his efforts to obtain his benefits. João de Deus, through Sr. Luiz, explained slowly, in an accent so thick that it was difficult at times for Armando to understand what was being said to him, that he had been the victim of black magic used against him by his former supervisor who had been jealous of him. The spell, however, had been broken by the ritual treatment. But to protect himself from any further harm through black magic, Armando would have to continue taking the

133

ritual baths prescribed, and follow the dietary proscriptions. He also would have to be prepared to take a trip to Rio de Janeiro.

Armando decided to do as he was instructed. In addition, he went to the Center several evenings a week where he talked with the younger mediums and others about spiritism generally and about *Umbanda* in particular. He learned some of the songs of the dieties and some of the rituals. He heard stories about the many wonderful charitable deeds performed by Sr. Luiz's spirit guide, the *Preto Velho*/João de Deus. After a few weeks, Sr. Luiz called Armando into his private consultation room one evening and handed him a piece of paper that had written on it the name and address of a military officer in Rio de Janeiro. Armando was instructed to go to the man.

Armando, who had very little money left, borrowed the fare from his friends. A week later he boarded a bus that would take him the almost 2000 kilometers to Rio de Janeiro. When he arrived several days later, he went directly to the address on the paper. He showed his documents and explained the situation to the army officer who received him. Under the *coronel's* (colonel) supervision, Armando once more completed the papers he had submitted several times to the officials in the pension office in Recife and left. The following day he returned as instructed and was given his documents, all appropriately signed and stamped. He was told to return to Recife and to present them to a specific individual in the pension office. He did so, and at the end of the month, just six weeks after he first visited Sr. Luiz, he received his first benefit payment. He now receives his pension regularly.

Armando continued to visit the Center, learning more about spiritism and consulting with Sr. Luiz whenever he was confronted with other problems, or had major decisions to make. After several consultations, João de Deus (through Sr. Luiz) told him that he had mediumistic abilities and should develop himself spiritually in order to assure his future health and well-being. He moved into a house near the Center and is now a member of the corps of mediums in training.

Amalia Ferreira also attended the Center the first time on the evening of a public ritual. When her turn came to consult with the spirit, she took the piece of paper handed her while she nervously tried to explain her problem. As with Soares, she was told to return if things did not improve. A young medium also interpreted for her the details of the prescription and the dietary restrictions, and the old man provided her with the herbs and incense she would need. For two weeks she took the baths and ate only what she was told. Not only did her physical condition not improve but, during the same period, her husband, the tailor, lost his job. In desperation she returned to Sr. Luiz who explained to her that black magic had been used against her. The ritual baths she had taken, plus what Sr. Luiz had done without her knowledge, had broken the spell. She then was given a note with instructions to go the clinic of Dr. João Leite. She also was given a small amount of money by one of the assistant mediums to help the family until things improved.

When she arrived at the crowded medical clinic the next afternoon, she nervously presented the note to the nurse, not knowing what to expect. She was instructed to wait along with the many other patients who crowded the small waiting room. After several hours (during which she had to resist the urge to leave and return home), she breathed a sigh of relief when she was ushered into a consulting room where the doctor stood waiting for her. Dr. João then treated her for her back and other problems. The treatment continued for the next three months. Amalia was not charged, nor was she asked to pay for the medicines dispensed by the nurse at the clinic. As the weeks passed, she gradually improved until eventually she was able to return to work. She also returned to the Center where she attends rituals, is instructed in spiritism, and tries to do whatever she can to show her gratitude for what had been done for her.

The Moreira family. When Pedro and Luiza Moreira came to Sr. Luiz about their sick child, in addition to the ritual and dietary treatment prescribed for all three, they also were instructed to take the child to Dr. João Leite. Fortunately, since not much time had elapsed between the onset of the illness and the beginning of treatment, the doctor was able to help the child. As the child recovered physically, the parents also recovered spiritually and materially. Pedro and Luiza have learned about *Umbanda*. Luiza was told that she had mediumship abilities. She is now a member of the corps of mediums in training; Pedro has a job.

Fernando Rodrigues is a dentist who, following help received from Sr. Luiz, now contributes his professional services as part of the Center's health care program. He mentioned in passing one day that he needed a gardener, someone he could trust. Sr. Luiz remembered that Pedro's uncle was a gardener and that Pedro, who had grown up working on a plantation, had worked with his uncle. One evening, the spiritual leader told Pedro to go to Fernando's home where, because of Sr. Luiz's recommendation, Pedro was hired. Although he is not paid much, it is steady work and, when his wages are combined with the extras given him occasionally by Fernando, plus what Luiza earns doing washing, added to what both of them receive periodically from the Center, it is sufficient to have allowed Pedro to enlarge his home in the *favela*, put food on the table, and clothe his childen. Perhaps more importantly, Pedro and Luiza know that they have someone to whom they can turn if they need help in the future.

Edson Miranda, former assistant to the deputy and realtor whose business had declined, first came to the Center at perhaps the lowest point in his life. When his turn came to consult with Sr. Luiz's spirit guide, he also was given a prescription for ritual treatment and instructions to restrict his diet. In addition, he was advised by the spirit to *aquentar firme* (endure; stick it out). For the next seven months Sr. Luiz paid Edson's grocery bills and supplied him with gasoline for his car. Then Edson received a visit from João Freitas, a representative of Aluisio Duarte, the mayor of the interior municipality of São Leonardo. The mayor, a politician who himself had benefited from the advice of Sr. Luiz and his spirit guide, and who still consulted Sr. Luiz about personal and professional matters, was running for the office of state deputy. When he had asked for the religious leader's approval and assistance, he was told to seek out Edson Miranda. Edson eagerly joined the campaign.

During the campaign, candidate Duarte regularly visited Sr. Luiz. When he did, the *pai-de-santo* invited other clients of his— lawyers, doctors, architects, businessmen and other influential citizens from around the state—to meet the candidate. Leaflets were prepared carrying Sr. Luiz' endorsement and boxes of these were given to those who came to the meetings with instructions to distribute them in their neighborhoods. The leaflets also were given by mediums to visitors to the Center who were told, as were the mediums and other members of the Center, that it was their *dever sagrado* (sacred duty) to vote for candidates endorsed by Sr. Luiz.

When Aluisio was elected, thanks not only to Sr. Luiz' efforts but also to Edson's extensive knowledge and political expertise, he offered the still desperate Edson a job as his assistant. Clients, many of them sent by Sr. Luiz, began to come again to Edson's real estate office. In time Edson was back on his feet financially and was able to repay the loan Sr. Luiz had arranged for him with a banker. He also was in a position to help those who were sent to him by Sr. Luiz because they needed assistance with the state legislature and its many bureaucracies.

Networks: Doctor, lawyer, military chief.

Dr. João Leite is one of a number of medical doctors in Recife and elsewhere in Brazil who gives his time and services freely as part of what may be considered a health care program dispensed as charity by *Umbanda* and other Spiritist centers. Several years ago, Dr. Leite himself had come to Sr. Luiz for help. His young bride of several months had inherited a small piece of land located not far from Sr. Luiz's Center. The physician wished to build a clinic on the land but another relative was contesting the will. Having only recently completed his medical training, the young doctor did not have money at the time to hire a lawyer. On the advice of one of his wife's relatives who lived near the Center, he went to Sr. Luiz. The doctor was given materials and instructions for ritual treatment and dietary restrictions. On his second visit he was given the name and address of Renato Pontes, a young lawyer who also had come to Sr. Luiz for help some time before, and told to see him.

137

Renato had come to the *pai-de-santo* when he was having difficulty starting his career. The only son of poor parents, Renato had worked his way through law school and had borrowed heavily to pay his fees. When he graduated he was unable to obtain clients because, unlike his more affluent classmates, he did not have any wealthy and influential kinsmen and friends to help him. After taking the prescribed ritual baths and observing the dietary restrictions, Renato returned occasionally to the Center where he would sit and chat with Sr. Luiz on quiet afternoons. Sr. Luiz began to send people who came to him with legal problems to Renato. Most, of course, were unable to pay the young lawyer a fee. But after he won a few cases, Sr. Luiz began recommending him to more affluent friends who did pay fees. In time, Renato's office was bustling and he was able to provide modestly for his family.

Several clients, like Dr. João, needed help with government bureaucracies. After sending them to Renato, Sr. Luiz also would contact other clients, like the colonel in Rio—who then would assist Renato in maneuvering through the bureaucracy. Renato, in effect, did the leg work and legalistic maneuvering as part of a group being coordinated by Sr. Luiz. Soon, Renato had a reputation as a specialist in this area. Other clients sought him out, and his financial situation improved. He bought a comfortable home and a new car. Renato continued to visit the Center, both to seek the advice of Sr. Luiz and his spirit guide on personal and professional matters, and to socialize with the man who had helped him so much. He was asked to serve as the Juridical Counsel on the Center's Board of Directors. As his career and fortune improved, Renato both made money for and gave money to his patron. On one occasion, for example, he was asked to complete a real estate transaction involving one of Sr. Luiz's client-friends. Renato gave part of the fee he received to Sr. Luiz. On another occasion, he and three other members of the board "lent" Sr. Luiz the money to buy a new car. Whenever repayment was mentioned, Renato insisted in public (in a way that forced the others to do so also) that he owed Sr. Luiz so much that he would not accept repayment.

When Renato succeeded in getting Dr. João title to his wife's land so that he could build his clinic, the doctor (who had not paid a fee) was indebted both to the lawyer and to the religious leader. Therefore, when Sr. Luiz sent poor patients, such as Amalia Ferreira, to him, the doctor would treat them without charge and help them with free medicines and the like. Dr. João joined with other doctors, dentists, and nurses who had benefited from Sr. Luiz's help, to staff the clinic set up at the Center to provide health care for the poor.

Sacred/secular transactions: João de Deus/Sr. Luiz.

In theory, Sr. Luiz, as the medium for João de Deus, is an intermediary who facilitates and brokers transactions and exchanges of the patron/client type between the *Preto Velho* and living humans. Needy clients, however, equate Sr. Luiz and others like him with the spirit, perceiving him as the patron to whom they are indebted for the benefits they receive. Ideally, the spiritual power, by means of which the worldly situation for the living is modified, moves down in exchange for loyalty that moves up. Invariably, however, there is a material component to the requests made of the spirit by the human clients. In practice, material resources become involved in the transactions. Sr. Luiz, as medium for João de Deus, is at the center of these transactions. Consequently, all resources, spiritual and material, move through him. As we have seen, Sr. Luiz's clients come from all races, classes, occupations, and sectors of Brazilian society. In terms of their material wealth, they range from the uppermost sectors of the vertically stratified society to the lowest. Included are professionals, businessmen, politicians, members of the middle and lower sectors, and the unemployed and underemployed who make their living in the informal sector. Materially, some of Sr. Luiz's clients are above him in terms of wealth; many more are below him. Sr. Luiz does not charge any of them, nor does he accept fees for his services. However, businessmen, professionals, and other affluent clients give him gifts of goods (including: automobiles), services, or money—a portion of the profits they earn from the deals he and his spirit guide help them to make. Sr. Luiz uses these commodities at times to satisfy his personal needs (e.g., in the support of his family) as well as to maintain and improve the Center and its ability to care for and serve the deities. He also uses

139

what he receives to help solve the problems brought to him by the many who need material assistance.

Sr. Luiz is both patron and client to many individuals from the stratified segments and sectors of Brazilian society. More significantly for our purposes, he is the hub in a network of patron/client exchanges through which material resources flow. As broker for these resources, he is able to make them available to those who need them. While serving as the leader of a religious group that values charity, he is able to translate the symbolic and ritual deeds of the spirits into material benefits. He is able to apply the goods and services given to him, along with others he can claim, such as the services of doctors, dentists, lawyers, politicians, and bureaucrats, to solve the problems of those who come to him in need of these services. As a result, material goods and services flow through and are redistributed by the network of relations of spiritual patronage and clientage of which he is at the center. In this way, resources from the formal economy become available to individuals in the informal sector and vice verse.

Obviously, Sr. Luiz is not the only head of an *Umbanda* center to perform this brokerage function in the redistribution of wealth in Brazil. Diana Brown, in her study of *Umbanda* in Rio de Janeiro, writes

Umbanda *centros* extend the concept of *caridade* beyond the spiritual aid provided in the consultas to include material forms of aid, such as access to doctors (both homeopathic and allopathic) or dentists, free or cut-rate medicines, burial funds, and food and clothing. These are often made available free or at a minimal cost to members and, occasionally, to the local community as well....In addition to such regularly available forms of aid, in certain cases employment, loans, and other forms of help may be arranged on a personal basis...(Brown 1986:100).

140

Conclusion.

We began this paper with Romer's Rule, an epigraph on the survival value of conservative innovations that render possible the maintenance of a traditional way of life in the face of changed circumstances. Although referring to the adaptation of organisms in the context of biological evolution, the rule seems to shed light on the development of *Umbanda* and other primarily urban religions in Brazil. *Umbanda*, as we have seen, was an innovative religious form that appeared as Brazilian society was in the throes of urbanization and industrialization. Its organization, however, was conservative in that it emphasized patron/client exchanges and relationships, the patterns that characterized traditional Brazilian social structure. These relationships, among other things, have enabled large numbers of the poor—the unemployed, and the underemployed who find themselves outside of and marginal to the formal Brazilian economy—to survive. It has provided them with new patrons who, in a new context and in terms of a new set of symbols and beliefs, have been able to articulate networks through which resources flow at times from successful individuals in the formal economy to those in the informal sector who lack those resources—from the elite to those like Pedro, Luiza, Amalia, and others. Although their old rural patrons are not to be found in the cities, by organizing in terms of networks of patron/client exchanges, *Umbanda* and other new religions are providing the means for those in need to utilize traditional patterns of social relations in the face of changed circumstances.

We suggest that the data presented here bring into question two of the major theories that have been applied in social science studies of Brazilian and Latin American societies. Modernization theory predicted that urbanization and industrialization would bring radical changes in the forms of social organization. *Umbanda*, and the other religions to appear in Brazil, however, are conservative in that they are organized as patron/client exchange systems. They have made possible the maintenance of the traditional social structure—which, in turn, has made possible the articulation of the formal and the informal sectors. Meanwhile, Marxism predicted the revolutionary upheaval by the disenfranchised and destitute. This too has not happened. Instead, traditional Brazilian social structure has been utilized by new religions and other organizations to enable the society to adapt in spite of the radical changes.

References.

Allum, P. A.
1973 Politics and Society in Postwar Naples. Cambridge: Cambridge University Press.

Anuário Estatística do Brasil
1985 Rio de Janeiro. Fundação Instituto Brasileiro de Geografía e Estatística.

Bastide, Roger
1978 The African Religions of Brazil. Translated by Helen Sebba. Baltimore: The Johns Hopkins University Press.

Brown, Diana DeG.
1986 Umbanda: Religion and Politics in Urban Brazil. Ann Arbor: UMI Research Press.

Camargo, Candido Procopio Ferreira de
1973 Católicos, Protestantes e Espíritas. Petrópolis. Editôra Vozes.

Forman, Shepard and Joyce F. Riegelhaupt
1979 The Political Economy of Patron-Clientship: Brazil and Portugal Compared. In M. L. Margolis and W. E. Carter, eds., Brazil: Anthropological Perspectives. New York: Columbia University Press, pp. 379-400.

Gabriel, Chester E.
1980 Communications of the Spirits: Umbanda, Regional Cults in Manaus and the Dynamics of Mediumistic Trance. Ph.D. dissertation. Department of Anthropology, McGill University

Greenfield, Sidney M.
1968 Patronage Networks, Factions, Political Parties, and National Integration in Contemporary Brazilian Society. Discussion Paper No. 12, Center for Latin America, The University of Wisconsin-Milwaukee.

1972 Charwomen, Cesspools and Road Building: An Examination of Patronage, Clientage and Political Power in Southestern Minas Gerais. In Arnold Strickon and Sidney M. Greenfield, eds., Structure and Process in Latin America. Albuquerque: University of New Mexico Press, pp. 71-100.

1977 Patronage, Politics and the Articulation of Local Community and National Society in Pre-1968 Brazil. Journal of Inter-American Studies and World Affairs 19: 139-172.

1979 Domestic Crises, Schools and Patron-Clientage in Southeastern Minas Gerais. In M.L. Margolis and W.E. Carter, eds., Brazil: Anthropologial Perspectives. New York: Columbia University Press, pp. 362-378.

Herskovits, Melville J.
1937 African Gods and Catholic Saints in New World Negro Belief. American Anthropologist 39: 635-643.

Hockett, Charles F. and Robert Ascher
1964 The Human Revolution. Current Anthropology 5: 135-147.

Hutchinson, Bertram
1966 The Patron-Dependent Relationship in Brazil: A Preliminary Examination. Sociologia Ruralis 6: 3-30.

Lerch, Patricia
1978 Warriors of Justice: A Study of Women's Roles in Umbanda in Porto Alegre, Brazil. Ph. D. dissertation. The Ohio State University.

Merrick, Thomas W. and Douglas H.Graham
1979 Population and Economic Development in Brazil, 1800 to the Present. Baltimore: The Johns Hopkins University Press.

Ortiz, Renato
1978 A Morte Branca do Feiticeiro Negro. Petrópolis. Editôra Vozes.

Pressel, Esther J.
1974 Umbanda Trance and Possession in São Paulo, Brazil. In F. Goodman, J. Henney and E. Pressel, eds., Trance, Healing and Hallucination. New York: John Wiley and Sons, pp. 113-225.

Prust, Russell R.
1985 Brazilian Umbanda: An Urban Resource Distributional System. Ph. D. dissertation. The University of Wisconsin-Milwaukee.

Roniger, Luis
1981 Clientelism and Patron-Client Relations: A Bibliography. In S.N. Eisenstadt and R. Lemarchand, eds., Political Clientelism, Patronage and Development. London: Sage Publications.
1987 Caciquismo and Coronelismo: Contextual Dimensions of Patron Brokerage in Mexico and Brazil. Latin American Research Review 22: 71-100.

Salazar-Carnillo, Jorge and Roberto Fendt, Jr., eds.
1985 The Brazilian Economy in the Eighties. London: Pergamon Press.

Willems, Emilio
1967 Followers of the New Faith: Culture Change and the Rise of Protestantism in Brazil and Chile. Nashville: Vanderbilt University Press, pp. 205-232.

CRISIS AND SECTOR IN OAXACA, MEXICO: A COMPARISON OF HOUSEHOLDS 1977-1987.

Arthur D. Murphy, Martha W. Rees
Anthropology and Environmental Studies
Baylor University

Karen French
Department of Anthropology
Emory University

Earl W. Morris
Department of Design
University of Minnesota

Mary Winter
Family Environment
Iowa State University

Henry Selby
Department of Anthropology
University of Texas

Introduction.

In 1977, the Mexican Housing and Urban Development Agency (INDECO) conducted a study of households in the city of Oaxaca, Mexico (Murphy 1979, 1982). At the time, Mexico was in the midst of an economic boom. The discovery of vast oil reserves along Mexico's coast had led to a period of economic optimism unlike any experienced in modern Mexican history. The optimism, however, was short lived. By 1983, Mexico was in deep economic crisis, the result of change in the world structure. The peso, which President López Portillo had promised to "defend like a dog," was suffering constant devaluations, inflation was on the rise, and the price of oil on the world market was tumbling. Mexico's economy slowed and even experienced several years of negative growth.

The effects of *la crisis*, as it became known in Mexico, were similar in Oaxaca to those on the national level. As the state capital, Oaxaca was directly affected by the government's need to cut back on spending. The central government's initial commitment not to lay off any workers, however, moderated some of the more drastic effects felt in cities more dependent upon industrial employment. Further, other than governmental activity, Oaxaca's major source of income is tourism and, with the fall in the value of the peso on the international market, Oaxaca gained from the increased tourism. The effects of inflation were dramatic, however, especially when coupled with the fact that official wage increases in the city as well as the nation stayed about 30% below the inflation rate.

In this context, a follow-up survey was conducted in Oaxaca in 1987 to assess the impact of the crisis on the city's households.[1] A major question for the 1987 study was how households had adjusted to meet the demands of the new economic reality.

The sample for the 1987 study is a two-stage cluster sample of the city of Oaxaca. The first stage consisted of a random sample of the blocks within each of the 54 fiscal sectors of the city. The second stage was a systematic sample of the approximately 3600 households living on the blocks selected. Approximately 800 of the occupied dwellings were selected for interviewing. After eliminating ineligible households (those with no female who had ever been married or had a child and those with a male head without a spouse), as well as those where we could not interview because of refusals, sickness, and absence, 609 households remained. In each of those households, an interview with the female household head was completed. In addition, interviews with 404 of the husbands of the

---

[1]The research project was titled "A Decade of Change in Oaxaca, Mexico," and was co-directed by Arthur D. Murphy, Earl Morris and Mary Winter. The project was funded by the National Science Foundation. Additional funding was received from the World Food Institute, the Graduate College, the Department of Family Environment, and the College of Home Economics at Iowa State University, and the University Research Committee, Baylor University.

married females in the sample were obtained. The interviews were conducted by a team of trained Mexican interviewers. Women's interviews lasted approximately one hour and the husbands' interviews about 45 minutes.

The informal sector.

The term "informal sector" has been used to describe income generating activities that are characterized by ease of entry, reliance on indigenous resources, family ownership and labor, small-scale operation, labor-intensive technology, and unregulated markets (Bromley 1978; Winter et al. 1987). For the most part, the informal sector is officially ignored by governments; its activities are not included in measures of national economic activity (e.g., GNP) nor are they generally taxed, although members of the informal sector are often subject to indirect taxation through sales taxes as well as the bribes they must pay in order to continue working. Historically, in particular, activity in the informal sector has not been included in national employment statistics, although recently the inclusion of the "underemployed" in national figures is an attempt to bring this group to national attention as well as reduce the frightening absolute unemployment figures in many developing nations.

In this paper we will compare Oaxacan households in the informal and formal sectors of the economy in 1977 and 1987 in order to see how the city's economic structure, households, and employment market have changed with the crisis and how households have adjusted to the new condition.

While researchers have focused on the role of the informal sector in the economies of both nations and households, there is no consistent definition of what constitutes the informal sector (Hart 1973; Roberts 1978; Geertz 1963; Davies 1979; ILO 1972). In this paper we take our direction from Eckstein's argument that, in Latin America, "access to social security—including medical insurance, compensation for work-related disabilities, old-age pensions and job security—as well as income and prestige" is the primary characteristic distinguishing workers in the informal or traditional sector from those in the modern sector (Eckstein 1967: 109).

As with many definitions of the informal sector, one can argue with categorizing households on the basis of the benefits received by one worker in the household. This definition, however, has two important advantages for our study. The first is methodological: It is clear and for the most part unambiguous. If a member of the household has a job registered with a government agency then that individual receives some type of benefit.[2] The most important of these is *base* (a permanent contract). Less significant but still important benefits may include health insurance, unemployment compensation, life insurance, paid vacations and the like. This measure is, in some way, an indicator of government tracking of business activities since in Mexico there is no reliable statistical base on small businesses.

The second reason for using this definition is more theoretical. An important issue is raised when dividing the labor market into "sectors": just how does such a classification relate to the concept of class? Is the informal sector just another term for a particular social class? If so, what is the nature of that class and how does it articulate with other classes in the society? We would argue that by using access to fringe benefits as a marker we are recognizing two important groups of workers within a modern capitalist State—on the one hand, those in whom the system, through the State, is willing to invest resources in order to provide them with a modicum of security and, on the other hand, those who are left entirely to their own devices. In more Marxist terms, we would suggest that workers in what we call the formal sector are those for whom the State is willing to provide a greater portion of the reproductive costs than for workers in the informal sector. In this sense, the informal sector has a different relation to production and reproduction than the formal sector. Roberts (1988: 8) points out that a distinction between protected and unprotected workers grew up in Latin America as key workers in strategic industries received coverage and others were left out.

---

[2]In Mexico, every employer of over 100 individuals is required to register with the national social security system.

With these questions in mind, we have divided our households into two groups on the basis of whether one of the major wage earners in the household has access to fringe benefits. In Mexico, it is important to look at all the major bread winners when making such a classification; wage laws in Mexico give all members of a family benefits if one member of the family is employed in the formal sector. Thus it does not matter if the husband, wife, or son work in the formal sector, all members of the household can get medical assistance at the Social Security Hospital or purchase goods from the subsidized store.

Table 1 demonstrates a major shift in the nature of the labor market in Oaxaca over the past decade. In 1977, a majority of the households had a worker in the formal sector giving the unit some degree of protection against short term economic crisis. By 1987, the situation had reversed, with over 60% of the households having with no State supported benefits.

Table 1
INFORMAL SECTOR RELIANCE:
PERCENT OF HOUSEHOLDS AND HOUSEHOLD HEADS.

	1977	1987
Informal Sector households	38.9	62.7
Male household heads in the informal sector	43.5	66.2
Female household heads in the informal sector	63.0	73.0

The lower portion of Table 1 demonstrates that the shift towards informal sector work is mirrored in the types of jobs held by the heads of households. The percentage of male household heads working in the informal sector has risen by over 65% in the past ten years. What is clear is that, with the economic crisis, individuals are losing jobs in the formal sector and those entering the work force are working on temporary contracts offering no security. The common practice is for workers to be fired just before they would earn a permanent *base* with full benefits and rehired as "new" employees to whom no commitment is owed. The important distinction between the 1977 and the 1987 data is that, in 1977, the category "Male household heads" contained the most members in the formal sector. As the portion of Table 1 dealing with female heads of households indicates, the removal of workers from the formal sector is across the board. Females, of whom only 37% were in the formal sector in 1977, have been reduced to 27% in 1987. For the most part, this represents a restructuring of the service economy in Oaxaca in such a way that job security for women working the tourist industry is eliminated.

Comparison of formal and informal sector households.

When comparing the formal and informal sectors of Oaxaca, Kim (1982) examined the income from employment in each sector, the worker/non-worker dependency ratios, the style of living each strategy affords, and the proportion of migrants in each sector. In the remainder of this paper we will compare the formal and informal sectors of Oaxaca in 1987 on each of these variables and then compare those results with Kim's analysis of the 1977 data.

Income. As expected, in 1977 Kim found that informal sector households tended to have lower incomes than formal sector households. Neither median income nor the differential between formal and informal sector employment has changed. Mean income fell by more than half in both sectors, indicating a reduction in salaries at the upper end.

One of the basic suppositions in comparisons between the formal and informal sector is that formal sector employment pays more. These data support this supposition: In 1977, the informal sector mean income is 70% that of the formal; in 1987 it is 74%. There is basically no change in median income between sectors or over time.

Table 2
HOUSEHOLD INCOMES*

	1977		1987	
	Mean	Median	Mean	Median
Informal	284.3	102.5	138.1	105.0
Formal	406.6	156.6	186.5	153.0

*In constant 1987 pesos (thousands)

One of the basic questions is the effect of the crisis on income. All mean incomes fell. These data show that mean income of (formal sector) salaried workers has decreased slightly more (56%) than that of informal sector workers (51%) between 1977 and 1987. This indicates that formal sector incomes are the hardest hit by the crisis and that consequently, the gap between the two sectors is decreasing.

Worker Dependency Ratio. The worker dependency ratio is a measure of the number of individuals supported by each worker in the household (household size/number of workers). In 1977, the ratios of each sector were the opposite of what was expected. Households in the formal sector had a significantly larger dependency ratio. Kim accounted for this by suggesting that formal sector jobs were able to support more people because of their higher wages and fringe benefits. Informal jobs were easier to obtain because they required a smaller investment in formal education. Thus, the families who had lower wages and no benefits were able to put more members to work. These patterns seem to hold for the 1987 data (Table 3).

Table 3
WORKER DEPENDENCY RATIO

	1977	1987
Informal sector	3.0	3.4
Formal sector	3.3	3.5

We contend that as a result of the crisis, wages and benefits in the formal sector have decreased, closing the gap between the two strategies; the more balanced ratios would appear to reflect this trend. The overall increase in the number of people each worker supports is a result of the shrinking job market. As formal sector opportunities disappear, many formal sector households are forced into implementing a more informal strategy. This, in turn, makes entrance into the informal sector more competitive, keeping younger less experienced workers out of the job market all together.

Table 4
DWELLING TYPE AND TENURE (PERCENT)

| | 1977 | | 1987 | |
	Informal Sector	Formal Sector	Informal Sector	Formal Sector
TYPE				
Shack	28.9	15.8	13.6	6.3
Room	14.0	11.9.	9.1	13.6
Apartment	1.7	2.8	1.4	4.4
House	55.4	69.4	76.1	85.7
TENURE				
Own	75.4	77.5	70.2	70.4
Rent/borrow	24.6	22.5	29.8	29.6

Housing. Between 1977 and 1987, the difference has decreased between the sectors with respect to dwelling type—mainly due to lack of improvement in the economic conditions of the formal sector. In 1977, Kim included dwelling type in her measure of "style of living" She found that sector did indeed tend to influence the type of dwelling in which the household lived. The 1987 data showed a similar relationship, but in the cases at both ends of the spectrum, the percentage living in shacks and percentage living in houses, the differences between sectors had decreased. The percentage in the informal sector living in houses jumped 26% while the percent in the formal sector increased only 16%; the difference between sectors in percent living in shacks decreased from 13.1% to

154

7.3%. This fits the overall pattern of a reduction in the gap between the economic position of the two strategies.

In the 1977 data, there is only a small difference in the percentage of owners in the two sectors (about 2%), but people in the formal sector were more likely to own their own dwelling. In 1987 this was no longer true, and, in addition, there was an overall decrease (about 5% to 7%) in the percentage of owners. The overall decrease appears to be a result of the crisis, and the deteriorating economic position of the formal sector accounts for the increasingly similar statistics in both sectors.

Migration. Given the ease of entry and relative freedom from regulation found in the informal sector, we would have predicted that the informal sector serve as a point of entry for many migrants into the urban economy. The data for 1977 showed this was not true in the city of Oaxaca. As noted in Table 5, there were more migrant heads of household (66%) than non-migrant heads of household (34%), but the percentages of migrants in the informal sector and the percentages of migrants within the formal sector remained within about 4% of the general population. Overall, there seems to be little correlation between migration and sector. The 1987 survey showed a slight increase in the proportion of migrants to non-migrants but there is little appreciable difference from the 1977 findings (again within about 4%).

Table 5
ORIGIN OF HOUSEHOLD HEADS (PERCENT)

	1977		1987	
	Informal Sector	All Households	Informal Sector	All Households
ORIGIN				
Non-Migrant	30.6	34.0	28.3	29.8
Migrant	69.4	66.0	71.7	70.2

Given the stability in the percent of migrants to the city in each sector of the economy, we would argue that the increase in the size of the informal sector in the city in the face of the crisis must be a result of an intra-city shift from formal to informal strategies, not an increase in migration.

Conclusions.

Our comparison of households in 1977 with those in 1987 indicates that some significant changes are occurring in Oaxaca's economy and that household economics, as well as level of living and demography are affected by those changes.

Economic sector: The proportion of formal/informal sector workers reversed from 60/40 to 40/60 between 1977 and 1987. This change is even more dramatic for women, reflecting a restructuring of the service economy in Oaxaca, eliminating job security for those women in the tourist industry.

Income: Neither median income nor the differential between formal and informal sector employment changed. Mean income fell by more than half in both sectors, indicating a reduction in salaries at the upper end. Formal sector incomes were the hardest hit by the crisis and, consequently, the gap between the two sectors is decreasing.

Worker dependency ratio: The worker dependency ratio has gone up in both sectors between 1977 and 1987. The overall increase in the number of people each worker supports is a result of the shrinking job market. As formal sector opportunities disappear, many households are forced into an informal strategy; this, in turn, makes entrance into the informal sector more competitive, thus keeping younger, less experienced workers out of the job market all together.

Dwelling type: The difference between the sectors with respect to dwelling type has decreased between 1977 and 1987 mainly due to lack of improvement in the economic conditions of the formal sector. This fits the overall pattern of a reduction in the gap between the economic position of two strategies.

Ownership: The percentage of owners has decreased in both sectors between 1977 and 1987 while the gap between the formal and informal sectors virtually disappeared. The overall decrease appears to be a result of the crisis, and the deteriorating economic position of the formal sector accounts for the increasingly similar statistics in both sectors.

Migration: The increase in the size of the informal sector in the city in the face of the crisis must be a result of an intra-city shift from formal to informal strategies not an increase in migration.

The most important change in Oaxaca over the past ten years has been the dramatic rise in the percentage of households in the informal sector of the economy. The rise in the percentage of households with no worker in the formal economy is an indication that new employees are not being given long-term contracts leading to a stable job, and that established heads of households, who represented the largest single group in the formal sector in 1977, have been bumped out of the formal into the informal sector of the economy. We would argue that this pattern suggests a fundamental restructuring of Oaxaca's service economy. With households falling out of the formal and into the informal sectors of the economy the differences which existed between them are being reduced or eliminated.

References.

Bromley, R.
1978   The Urban Informal Sector: Why is it Worth Discussing? World Development 6: 1033-1039.

Davies, R.
1979   Informal Sector or Subordinate Mode of Production: A Model. In Ray Bromley and Chris Gerry, eds., Casual Work and Poverty in Third World Cities. Chichester: John Wiley and Sons, pp 87-104.

Eckstein, S.
1967   The Rise and Demise of Research on Latin American Poverty. Studies in Comparative International Development 11: 107-126.

Geertz, C.
1963   Peddlers and Princes. Chicago: University of Chicago Press.

Hart, K.
1973   Informal Income Opportunities and Urban Employment. Journal of Modern African Studies 2: 61-89.

International Labor Office
1972   Employment, Incomes, and Equality: A Strategy for Increasing Productive Employment in Kenya. Geneva: International Labor Office.

Kim, M-H.
1982   The Informal Sector in the City of Oaxaca, Mexico. M.S. thesis. Athens: University of Georgia.

Murphy, A. D.
1979   Urbanization, Development, and Household: Adaptive Strategies in Oaxaca, a Secondary City of Mexico.

Unpublished Ph.D. dissertation. Philadelphia: Temple University.

Roberts, B.
1978 Cities of Peasants: The Political Economy of Urbanization in The Third World. Beverly Hills CA: Sage Publications.
1990 The Informal Sector in Comparative Perspective. In M. Estellie Smith, ed., Perspectives on the Informal Economy. Lanham MD: University Press of America, pp. 23-48.

Winter, Mary, E. W. Morris, A. D. Murphy
1987 Participation in the Informal Economic Sector: Causes and Outcomes. Paper presented at the Annual Meetings of the Sociey for Applied Anthropology, April 11. Oaxaca, Mexico

THE NEED FOR A RE-EVALUATION
OF THE CONCEPT "INFORMAL SECTOR":
THE DOMINICAN CASE[1]

Martin F. Murphy
Department of Anthropology
University of Notre Dame

Introduction.

In the 18 years since the term "informal sector" was made popular in academic and international development circles (International Labor Office 1972), thousands of pages have been dedicated to describing and analyzing this phenomenon. However, most authors continue to view simply as "other" those economic activities which do not fit into neat categories of what an urban dependent capitalist economy "should be," or whatever is the opposite of the ideal.[2] All these activities are placed under one basic rubric with little concern for their diversity. They are described using a compound term which juxtaposes them with the norm. Whether we call these activities "informal" or, now, "nonstructured" (International Labor Office 1986), we begin our description and analysis of these phenomena as the opposite of what is supposedly desirable or even acceptable. A novel twist to this approach, but with a similar result, is found in the definition presented to us by Alejandro Portes and Saskia Sassen-Koob (1987: 31). "The informal sector can be tentatively defined as the sum total of all income-

---

[1]The author wishes to acknowledge the contributions made by Franc Báez Evertsz and Leo Despres through their comments to a draft version of this work, and Isis Duarte for sharing unpublished data. The author is grateful also for the thoughts shared by Bryan Roberts and Robert Hunt during the conference. Of course, the author assumes all responsibility for any errors in this work.
[2]Although this term is also used to describe certain economic activities in highly industrialized capitalist economies and socialist economies, here we limit our discussion to its use in the description of dependent capitalist economies.

earning activities with the exclusion of those that involve contractual and legally regulated employment."

This dualism has restricted our perceptions of what it is that we are describing and analyzing in any particular urban context. Many authors have decried the two-sector approach. Nonetheless, most tend to fall into the same trap even while they criticize it. Ray Bromley's (1978) introduction to a series of key articles concerning the informal sector is an excellent example. He argues that the two-sector approach is based on fallacious assumptions and then uses the approach in a modified form in the same article to explain what he believes to be the nature of urban economic organization. Or, in a later work, Bromley (1982) includes street criminal activity in the same category as street retail distribution because both take place in the streets, are not licensed, controlled or monitored by the State, and are therefore different from the formal sector.

Through the present work I wish to demonstrate the nature and characteristics of a particular economic activity at two determined points in time and within the context of the capital city of Santo Domingo, Dominican Republic. This longitudinal study describes and interprets the activities, strategies and tactics of a group of mobile retail produce vendors in 1982 and 1987; it analyzes the demographic characteristics of the vendors; and it locates them and their activities within the larger contemporary Dominican context. At first glance, this economic activity meets all the traditional criteria for inclusion in the category "informal sector." However, through the following review of the basic tenets of the three principal schools of thought concerning the informal sector and comparison with the field data, we see that none of these schools can interpret these activities adequately.[3]

The formal history of the Structural Surplus Labor Force (SSLF) school begins in the early 1970s with the publications of Keith Hart (1970, 1973) and the International Labor Office's analysis of particular urban economic activities in Kenya (1972). This

---

[3]The review presented here owes an intellectual debt to the recent work by Vanessa Cartaya F. (1987).

theoretical approach was then modified and adapted to Latin America primarily by PREALC researchers (1974, 1978, 1983) and by PREALC Director Victor Tokman (1978, 1987a, 1987b; Souza and Tokman 1976). As its title implies, this school sees the informal sector as composed of a surplus labor force which is created by structural limitations placed on its incorporation into the formal sector. The SSLF approach claims that the origin of the informal sector is to be found in the modernization and industrialization schemes applied to dependent capitalist economies, especially in Africa and Latin America. According to adherents of this position, these schemes have produced fabulous urban growth while at the same time relying heavily on capital, rather than labor intensive industry which is unable to absorb significant numbers of workers from the growing urban population. The recent migrants and displaced workers find it impossible to secure employment in the private or public sectors and therefore generate their own employment opportunities.

Although there is a debate in this literature concerning the autonomous/complementary, benign/exploitative, nature of the relationship between the formal and informal sectors of urban economies, the division of economic activities into two parts is not seriously questioned. The former sector is modern, structured and large scale, the latter is the opposite. The SSLF school attributes seven essential characteristics to informal activities.

(1) The State has little or no control over these activities in terms of licensing, regulation or monitoring.

(2) The activities may be autonomous from or complementary to the so-called formal sector.

(3) Informal operations are small-scale in relation to the formal sector (smaller amounts of investment and operating capital, a small number of employees per operation, limited production and sales). The operations are characterized by relatively unsophisticated technology, little technical division of labor, and intensive use of labor.

(4) The owner of the means of production works directly in the production process and, when needing additional labor, this owner/worker relies primarily on family members, who may or may

not receive a wage. Family and friends replace impersonal sources for financing, technical preparation, and acquisition of the means of production.

(5) In the purchase of inputs and sale of products or services, these operations tend to buy at high prices and sell at low prices, relative to the formal sector. The reason given for this behavior is that they cannot compete with the purchasing power of the formal sector in the purchase of inputs or products, and must keep their margins of profit low in order to compete for sales.

(6) Because of their low profit margins and limited volume these operations seldom have surplus capital to reinvest; their economic state and that of their owners is precarious.

(7) Participants in these economic activities are poor.

Although neo-Marxists (often called "the political economy school") assign a different label to informal sector participants— "reserve army of unemployed"—they too see this phenomenon as a structural problem and are in general agreement with many of the characteristics that the SSLF school has used to describe these economic activities and their participants. However, the two clearly part ways on one essential point: For the neo-Marxists the informal sector is neither autonomous nor complementary to the formal sector; rather, it is subordinate and exploited by the latter. It is— according to such theorists as Moser (1978) and Portes and Walton (1981)—manipulated and dominated by the capitalist formal sector to reduce production costs through the reduction in remuneration. The informal sector is part of the continuum of the dependent capitalist system, not separate from it; it exhibits certain characteristics similar to the economic relations between the metropole and satellite countries, as adherents to dependency theory claim (cf. Nun 1969; Quijano 1974). Like the SSLF scholars, the neo-Marxists view the informal sector as a vehicle which perpetuates poverty.

The neo-liberal approach offers a simplistic definition of the informal sector, romanticizes the actions and roles of the participants, and projects, contrary to the two previously discussed approaches, a most optimistic future. This theoretical position defines "informal" as all economic activities which are not controlled or regulated by the State, i.e., activities that are extralegal and illegitimate—but not illicit. Using this broad, legalistic definition the leading spokesperson for this approach, Hernando de Soto (1986), denies the heterogeneity of economic activities as he lumps together such diverse groups as home owners with no legal title to their lots, street vendors, and professionals who "work off the books." The only characteristic that these actors share is the extralegal condition of some aspect of their economic activities and relations. But that is all that is necessary for the neo-liberals.

This approach, which can best be described as an exercise in State bashing, sees formal sector participants as victims of excessive and unnecessary government controls in matters concerning the establishment of an enterprise, property rights and regulation of labor. In turn, the informal sector participant is one who strikes out independently, operates outside of government interference, acts rationally and is glorified as the bearer of free capitalism.

The neo-liberals maintain few common features with the SSLF or neo-Marxist schools in their views concerning the origin of these types of economic activities or their characteristics. Along with some adherents of the SSLF school, but in clear opposition to the neo-Marxists, the neo-liberals see these activities as complementary and separate from the formal sector. However, they do not see the origin of this phenomenon in the exclusion of labor by the formal sector. Excessive regulation by the State is the culprit. In other words, the structure of the economy is not the problem, rather it is the limitations put on it by counterproductive State regulation. Implicit in this position is the notion that an unhampered, *laissez faire* economy will provide adequately and justly for all.

This approach, although not as influential in academic and intellectual circles as the other two principal positions, is of extreme importance because of the supporters that it has recruited. Based on a simplistic definition, an optimistic interpretation, and ideological underpinnings in style in many quarters, this position is supported by many of the most economically and politically powerful national and international agents of change in the so-called third world countries.

165

The Dominican case.

The present work is based on research performed in the Dominican Republic in 1982 and 1987.[4] It deals with a specific set of urban economic activities which are considered by the three schools discussed above as representative of the informal sector (they are not regulated or controlled by the State, and no taxes are paid). The intention of this work is to demonstrate that these theories are incapable of interpreting this phenomenon either within the larger Dominican or international contexts, and it is proposed that most other activities categorized within the informal sector in the Dominican Republic cannot be understood fully through the use of either of these theories.

Often the poor fortune of the research subjects is the good fortune of the researcher. This is the case here. A descriptive and explanatory study was undertaken in late 1982 with a specific informal sector population. A primary goal of the study was to determine if these participants in the informal sector maintained a distinct income advantage over many formal sector workers. In 1984, the most serious inflationary process of this century began in the Dominican Republic and continues until today (cf. Murphy 1987). In 1987, it was appropriate to perform the same study, using the same universe, to determine what differences could be noted under conditions of historically unheard of inflation and restructuring of the economy.

The following, therefore, is a description, analysis and discussion of the results of both research projects and a comparison of the two sets of results. The general hypotheses that guided this work are: (1) under specific economic and labor conditions so-called informal sector workers may maintain significant advantage in terms of income to their formal sector counterparts; (2) the former

---

[4]The first study was funded by the Museo del Hombre Dominicano, Santo Domingo. Students from the Departamento de Historia y Antropología, Universidad Autónoma de Santo Domingo (UASD) assisted in the field data collection. The 1987 study was funded by a grant from the Institute for Scholarship in the Liberal Arts, University of Notre Dame. Students from the Departamento de Sociología, UASD assisted in the field data collection phase of this study as well.

recognize this advantage; (3) based on recognition of the advantage, participants in this activity prefer their present situation to that of their formal sector counterparts; and (4) under conditions of rapid inflation, the participants in certain activities can better protect their real wages than the formal sector wage worker.

Lechugueros are mobile retail produce vendors who sell as many as 20 different types of vegetables and fruits. Their name comes from the principal product that they sell—a number of varieties of lettuce. The most adequate manner to describe their merchandise is to note that they sell the basic fresh seasonings, ingredients for salad, and other items for the traditional Dominican midday meal. It is estimated that, in the capital city of Santo Domingo, there are 500-600 *lechugueros* and virtually all purchase their perishables daily at the city's principal market. Their day begins at about 5-6 AM when they congregate at the *Mercado Nuevo* (the New Market) and begin to haggle prices with the market vendors. They spend two hours purchasing, cleaning, washing and arranging the produce on their carts. Some time around 7-8 AM, they leave the market and each heads for specific residential areas where, in turn, the produce is sold directly to the consumer.

Their mode of transportation, which is also their "store," is a cargo tricycle—a vehicle best described as a push cart mounted on a heavy duty bicycle frame. These vendors will travel as many as 20 kilometers round-trip, seven days a week. The neighborhoods where they sell their merchandise are set, as is their clientele.

Lechugueros represent one of many types of tricyclists in Santo Domingo. There are an estimated 5000 cargo tricycles working the streets on any given day. The operators sell perishable products, prepared foods, buy used bottles from consumers for resale, hire out as cargo handlers, gather discarded materials for resale, etc. Comparing data gathered through these samples with those collected in a study conducted in 1986 of all types of tricyclists, *lechugueros* are representative in terms of demographic characteristics and incomes (cf. García and Mejía 1987).

The principal hypotheses guiding this work assume that there is a basis for comparing the *lechugueros* with minimum wage workers because the two groups share common demographic characteristics (age, formal education, migration histories, marital status). There are two reasons why minimum wage workers were chosen as a reference group. First, as we will see below, the average *lechuguero* exhibits general demographic characteristics similar to those expected for individuals who generally fill jobs labelled as unskilled and semiskilled in dependent capitalist economies. Secondly, in the Dominican Republic, minimum wage workers represent the largest single category of unskilled or semiskilled workers in the so-called formal sector.

Unfortunately, there are no available studies which present these data for a minimum wage worker population in Santo Domingo. There are studies of industrial sector workers in the city (e.g., Duarte 1987). However, these projects group together industrial workers at widely divergent salary and skill levels, and there is no way to isolate the demographic data for minimum wage workers, nor for those who earn even more. Further, there are a number of studies addressing the characteristics of workers in duty free industrial zones throughout the country (cf. CIPAF 1986). Although the lion's share of these workers are minimum wage earners, they represent a very different population than the *lechugueros*. All work in cities other than Santo Domingo and the study populations are exclusively female. Because they are located outside Santo Domingo and because of the clear gender preference shown by the employers, these jobs are not comparable and not an option for the *lechuguero* population. The latter all reside in Santo Domingo and all are males.

Unpublished data provided by Isis Duarte from samples of industrial sector workers in Santo Domingo (1981) demonstrate, however, that on the variable of formal education, the only demographic variable isolated, workers in semi-skilled and unskilled positions exhibit formal education levels similar to the *lechugueros*. It may be affirmed also that the average tricyclist in Santo Domingo would not leave his present position for a minimum wage job, or even one that pays substantially more. This is demonstrated through the data gathered in the present studies and the field results presented by García and Mejía (1987: 165) which note that in 1986 the average tricyclist in Santo Domingo would not leave his present work for a monthly net salary of less than RD$369.40, 160% more than the net monthly minimum wage income at that time.[5]

The 1982 study found that the average *lechuguero* is 34 years of age and lives in one of the poor or working class neighborhoods near the central market. He is a male (100%), was born outside the capital (97%), and has lived in Santo Domingo for almost 14 years. His formal education level is less than four years and his colleagues' educational levels range from illiterate to high school student. He has worked various jobs but generally was an agriculturalist on his father's land until adulthood and then migrated to the city and began working as a day laborer. He lives with his spouse (79%) to whom he is not legally married (90%). Including himself, there are 4.68 persons in his household and he is the principal (100%) and the only income earner (89%) of that household.

He has worked as a tricyclist for more than seven years. He works only at that activity (98%), 6.5 days a week and almost eight hours a day. He invests RD$32.37 a day in products that he will sell, but his colleagues invest anywhere from RD$10.00-120.00. His gross receipts are RD$42.95 (range RD$19.00-150.00). His net income per day, after tricycle rental payment or overhead on his own vehicle and loan payments for daily operating capital, is RD$9.26. His monthly net income is RD$259.28 as compared to RD$120.62 for the minimum wage worker at the time of research, and he prefers his present work (69%) to that of minimum wage work with health insurance and retirement pension.

In demographic terms the *lechuguero* in the 1987 study is comparable to that of the 1982 study. He is 36 years old, lives in the same neighborhoods, migrated to the capital (93%) 15 years ago, has less than five years of formal education, previously worked as an

---

[5]In the three examples that follow the exchange rates were as follows: In mid-1986, US$1.00 = RD$3.40; in late 1982, US$1.00 = $3.25; in mid-1987, US$1.00 = RD$3.75.

agriculturalist on his father's land, as a day laborer, or never held another job (78%). He lives with his spouse (81%) but is not legally married to her (80%). His household is composed of 5.65 members and he is the principal (100%) and only (85%) income earner. His work as a tricyclist is his only job (93%) which he works 6.53 days a week, seven hours a day. He invests daily RD$85.44 in produce (range—RD$30.00-200.00) for which he receives after sales RD$107.74. After paying for the rental of the tricycle or overhead on his own and daily loan payments to loansharks, his net daily income is RD$20.74. His net monthly income is RD$580.72 as compared to RD$231.00 for the minimum wage worker. He prefers his present job (82%) to that of the minimum wage worker because, as he claims, he makes more money and has more independence.

Both the 1982 and 1987 samples show that these informal sector participants maintain significant advantage in terms of income to their formal sector counterparts. They recognize this advantage and prefer their present self-generated employment to wage work. Although they were reminded through the test instrument that their counterparts were legally entitled to health insurance and retirement benefits which they do not have, they still viewed their employment situation more favorably. Only 1% claimed to be working as a *lechuguero* because there were no employment opportunities in the formal sector.

Based on the income differences between the *lechugueros* and their counterparts, the economic strategy of the former is a rational one. They are, and also see themselves as, maximizing opportunities. But their analysis is not of the formalist or neo-classical schools. As we will see, their economic strategy is chosen within structural parameters.

In the Dominican case, we must ask if these produce vendors are earning such fabulous sums that the minimum wage job is not attractive to them; or is the minimum wage job is so poorly paid, supplementary benefits (health insurance and retirement) and working conditions so poor, and job security so tenuous, that they prefer their present situation? We may demonstrate through the use of certain data and observations that the latter scenario appears to be the case. In other words, the *lechugueros* opt for their jobs because the minimum wage position is unattractive to them.

In defense of this claim, we note that the average incomes of the *lechuguero* are not high in an absolute sense nor in relation to the prices of basic consumer goods and services, but only relative to the minimum wage. The Department of Economic Studies of the Central Bank of the Dominican Republic (Banco Central 1988a) developed a model in November 1984 to determine the costs of basic goods and services (food, housing, education, health services, recreation) for a typical low income family of five. Calculations that I have made based on these data and subsequent unpublished data for 1987 (Banco Central 1988b) demonstrate that a low income family needed RD$514.41 to meet these needs. In the summer of 1987, the average *lechuguero* earned 113% of this sum. Therefore, in mid-1987 the average informant was earning slightly more than the typical low income, or poor, family needed. On the other hand, the minimum wage worker at the time of the study had a net monthly income of RD$231.00 or 45% of the sum that the average low income family needed per month to maintain their 1984 standard of living. Therefore, it can be concluded that although the average *lechuguero* earned 246% more than the minimum wage earner in 1987, he did not exhibit an excellent income; rather, the other worker received an extremely poor wage.

Although the supplementary benefits offered to formal sector workers could not make up for this tremendous difference in income between the two groups, their importance still must be analyzed. Mandated by law, all minimum wage workers are entitled to a complete health insurance policy (clinic visits, hospitalization, and medication) by the State Instituto Dominicano de Seguros Sociales (IDSS). However, the health insurance policy is not as attractive as it first appears: If the employer is in arrears in payment to the institution—a very common occurrence—the worker is denied these services. Only the worker himself is covered completely under this plan. A legally-recognized wife is covered during pregnancy and for one year after the birth of their legitimate child and the child is covered for the first year of life. Since less than 13% of the *lechugueros* in the samples included in the study are legally married, the vast majority would be the only family members covered by health insurance.

Monthly retirement and disability benefits for minimum wage workers through IDSS are so low—less than RD$40.00—that the "advantage" to this category of worker is virtually insignificant. The national labor code in effect was written in 1951 under the dictatorship of Rafael Trujillo who was also the principal employer in the nation. The code offers few protections to the worker in terms of job security and working conditions. Even worse, the few formal protections offered to the worker are seldom effectively applied or enforced. Therefore, on this account the formal sector worker does not maintain a significantly advantageous position *vis-à-vis* the self-employed worker.

The self-employed worker represented in this study also maintains a significant economic advantage over his salaried counterpart in times of inflation. Dominican legislation does not provide for automatic, periodic adjustments to workers' incomes. Only through legal decrees by the executive and legislative branches are minimum (and most other) wages adjusted. At the time of the 1982 study, the stipulated gross monthly minimum wage was RD$125.00. From that year until the period of the 1987 study, there was only one salary adjustment; to bring the gross minimum wage to RD$250.00 per month, a 100% adjustment was made in 1985. However, the official cumulative inflation rate between 1982 and 1987 was 102.18% (Banco Central 1988c). The monthly net income of the average respondent to the 1982 study was RD$259.28 versus the net monthly minimum wage income of RD$120.62, or 215% higher. The results of the 1987 study are RD$580.72 versus RD$236.00, and 246%. Further, the increase in the *lechuguero's* average income 1982-1987 was 124%.

These data demonstrate three tendencies: In times of inflation, the informal sector worker maintains his advantage over his counterpart; the advantage has grown by almost 15%; and the increase in the average *lechuguero's* income was significantly greater than the official cumulative inflation rate.

Also important but not demonstrated in these data is that these self-employed workers make periodic adjustments to their income which allow them to keep up with inflation, even on a daily basis. Their counterparts must wait for decrees to adjust already eroded real wages. In this manner, if he loses at all, the informal sector worker does not lose as much as his counterpart during periods of price inflation.

If the conditions for a *lechuguero* are so superior to those for employees with equivalent backgrounds, why is it that workers remain in the formal sector? The answer is simple: Although the average *lechuguero's* net monthly income in 1987 was superior to even some professionals, social and cultural norms prohibit those with professional credentials from working in this area. Still, the typical minimum wage worker has none of these sociocultural restrictions. But entry into the informal sector is limited by occupation-specific knowledge, investment and operating capital or access to loans, and the lack of entrepreneurial skills. To be a *lechuguero* one must learn the market and retail prices of the products that are traded. One also must have respected contacts associated with the business to secure credit from loan sharks and the tricycle rental garages. And finally, one must develop a clientele and the entrepreneurial skills essential to the trade.[6]

These observations help us to understand, at least partially, why "no opening" signs are virtually permanent fixtures outside Dominican factories. Their presence tells us two things. First, industrial jobs are seldom filled through the application process but rather through personal contacts. Secondly, minimum wage jobs never go unfilled. Therefore, the maintenance, even growth in the number, of non-industrial jobs, have not affected the market for minimum wage workers. Further, the growth of the so-called informal sector, under present conditions, is not without limits as the neo-liberals imply.

---

[6]The informants claim that it takes the typical *lechuguero* 12 months to develop his business. The study data demonstrate that those with less than 12 months experience exhibit average earnings of less than 60% of those with more experience.

The results of this two-part study have demonstrated the validity of the four principal hypotheses that were posited. The results also tell us much about the non-applicability of many of the tenets of the three major schools concerning the informal sector.

First, we note the flaws in the Structural Surplus Labor School as it is applied to this Dominican economic phenomenon.

(1) Although the operations of the *lechugueros* are small scale as compared to legally constituted corporations, the amount of capital necessary to start up and operate as a *lechuguero* is prohibitive for many who might wish to work in this field.

(2) The activities of the *lechuguero* obviously do not demand the same technology of a supermarket or other large scale produce distribution units. Still, technology is an important factor in the trade. For example, an historical sketch of mobile retail produce sales in Santo Domingo demonstrates how *lechugueros* have replaced two other groups through technological advances that were made in response to the growth of the city. At the turn of the century mobile retail produce vendors, many of whom were Oriental immigrants, walked the streets with their produce in large baskets connected by a yoke. They were replaced in the second quarter of the century by women who sold their products from burros, a more efficient manner to cover a larger area and carry more. The *lechugueros* then replaced the burro-mounted vendors in the 1960s and 1970s with a much faster and larger capacity means of transportation—the cargo tricycle.

(3) The *lechuguero* does not compete with the supermarkets and other retail distribution units in terms of the prices that he commands for this produce. He sells at higher prices but offers fresher, higher quality produce at the customer's door. He competes in terms of quality and service rather than price.

(4) The *lechugueros* may be poor by the standards of some but their incomes are more than double that of the minimum wage workers and higher than even many salaried professionals in their principal jobs. Low profit margins and limited sales volume do not restrict the *lechuguero* from reinvesting and expanding his business. Rather, the major obstacle to expansion is his extended family. The *lechuguero* is often the most well-off of his extended family and, in

the Dominican cultural context, this implies a responsibility to the rest of his family.

The neo-Marxist approach with an emphasis on the domination of economic actors such as the *lechugueros* by large-scale capitalist enterprises is simply erroneous in this case. The price that the *lechuguero* demands from the consumer is significantly higher (average 20%) than that of the retail distribution units. He is not part of a system which reduces cost. He is, however, a petty merchant operating within a specific context who attempts to maximize profit and minimize loss.

The *lechuguero* does meet all the necessary criteria of the neo-liberal approach. He operates outside government control and regulation and therefore is involved in an extralegal economic activity. However, because they include almost all economic activities, the neo-liberals explain none of them. In dependent capitalist countries, virtually every economic activity, even many which take place within the government dependencies themselves, has some aspect that the neo-liberals can point to and thereby claim that these activities are of the informal sector. Using this approach as a theoretical base to analyze and understand the activities of *lechugueros* only obfuscates important similarities and differences among this group and others.

Conclusion.

There are two general conclusions to this work. First, because all three principal approaches that we discussed place paramount importance on the extra-legal, non-government regulated, status of economic activities such as those studied here, we are trapped in an intellectual quagmire. Regardless of the criticisms levelled against previous attempts to analyze these types of economic activities, the critics only offer new variants of the dualistic model. These activities are seen as autonomous from, complementary to, or dominated and exploited by another supposedly homogeneous set of economic activities—those of the formal sector. However, we recognize the heterogeneity of this latter group of economic activities in all our analyses of it when we do not consider "other" economic activities. We readily note the differences between agriculture and manufacture, commerce and finance, and so forth. Why do we not consistently recognize the differences between non-government regulated commerce (e.g., mobile retail sales) and finance (e.g., loan sharking) when we recognize these differences when examining department stores and banks? The answer is to be found in the inordinate emphasis placed on the non-regulated nature of these former activities and the real or presumed poverty of the participants in these activities.

In order to build an appropriate body of theory to explain the origins, characteristics, and roles of these activities and their participants within the larger national context, we must study these phenomenon and the actions of their participants on their own terms. Through this inductive, empirical research strategy we will see that certain existing theoretical statements have explanatory merit in our study of some activities and not others. As an example, the works of Portes and Walton (1981) and Portes and Sassen-Koob (1987) are essential for our understanding of national and international programs of subcontracted manufacture but confuse our understanding of mobile retail vendors (*lechugueros*) in Santo Domingo. We must describe and explain all economic activities within their specific historical, social, cultural, political and economic contexts.

Secondly, in the Dominican case we see that the levels of exploitation (in terms of wages, fringe benefits, working conditions and job security) for all wage earners are so extreme that self-generated employment is a desirable alternative for many. Now, in the 1980s, with the restructuring of the Dominican national economy and the general restructuring of the international economy, these levels of exploitation are increasing. As a consequence, the differences between the relative advantages of work in the informal and formal sectors are assuming even greater significance. Although country-specific data for the Dominican Republic are not included among those presented for the Latin American economies studied by PREALC (1987), we note that, in these Latin American economies, informal sector employment has increased by 6.8% annually while the urban formal sector has increased by only 2% in this decade (cf. Roberts, this volume).

Apparently, this same trend is occurring also in the Dominican Republic. Obviously, modernization and dependency theories so popular in the 1950s through 1970s have limited explanatory power for this decade. Will our study of the type of urban economic activities addressed here help us develop appropriate macrolevel theory to explain the world economy of the 1980s and 1990s? I believe the exercise is worth the effort.

References.

Banco Central de la República Dominicana.
1988a Canasta Nacional de Bienes y Servicios de Primera Necesidad (Base November 1984). Santo Domingo: Banco Central.
1988b Precios de los 25 Primeros Artículos de la Canasta Familiar de Bienes y Servicios de Primera Necesidad. (Unpublished data from the Depto. de Estudios Económicos, prepared February 2 1988).
1988c Indice Nacional de Precios al Consumidor y Tasas de Inflación Anual Acumulada. (Unpublished data from the Depto. de Estudios Económicos, prepared March 9 1988).

Bromley, R.
1978 Introduction. The Urban Informal Sector: Why is it Worth Discussing? World Development 6: 1033-1039.
1982 Working in the Streets: Survival Strategy, Necessity, or Unavoidable Evil? In A. Gilbert with J. E. Hardoy and R. Ramírez, eds., Urbanization in Contemporary Latin America. New York: John Wiley and Sons, pp. 59-77.

Cartaya F., V.
1987 El Confuso Mundo del Sector Informal. Nueva Sociedad 90: 76-88.

CIPAF (Centro de Investigación Para la Acción Feminina).
1986 Cuando Trabajar es un Infierno, Volumes I, II. Santo Domingo: Ediciones Populares Feministas (CIPAF).

De Soto, H.
1986 El Otro Sendero: La Revolución Informal. Lima: Editorial. El Barranco.

Duarte, I.
1981   Estudio Sobre Industrialización y Fuerza Laboral en Santo Domingo. (Unpublished study data).
1987   Trabajadores Urbanos. Santo Domingo: Taller.

García, B. and M. Mejía.
1987   Análisis Socio-cultural del Triciclero de la Super-población Relativa. (Licenciatura thesis, Depto.de Sociología, Universidad Autónoma de Santo Domingo).

Hart, K.
1970   Small Scale Entrepreneurs in Ghana and Development Planning. The Journal of Development Studies 6(4): 104-120.
1973   Informal Income Opportunities and Urban Employment in Ghana. The Journal of Modern African Studies 11: 61-89.

International Labor Office
1972   Employment, Incomes and Equality: A strategy for Increasing Employment in Kenya. Geneva: International Labor Office.
1986   Fomento de las Pequeñas y Medianas Empresas. Geneva: International Labor Office.

Moser, C.
1978   Informal Sector or Petty Commodity Production: Dualism or Dependence in Urban Development? World Development 6: 1041-1064.

Murphy, M.
1987   The International Monetary Fund and Contemporary Crisis in the Dominican Republic. In R. Tardanico, ed., Crises in the Caribbean Basin. Political Economy of the World-System Annuals 9: 241-259. Newbury Park CA: Sage Publications.

Nun, J.
1969 Superpoblación Relativa, Ejército Industrial de Reserva y Masa Marginal. Revista Latinoamericana de Sociología 2: 178-235.

Portes, A.
1983 The Informal Sector: Definition, Controversy, and Relation to National Development. National Development Review 7: 151-174.

Portes, A. and S. Sassen-Koob.
1987 Making it Underground: Comparative Material on the Informal Sector in Western Market Economies. American Journal of Sociology 93: 30-61.

Portes, A. and J. Walton.
1981 Labor, Class, and the International System. New York: Academic Press.

PREALC
1974 El Problema del Empleo en América Latina: Situación, Perspectivas, Políticas. Santiago: PREALC.
1978 Sector Informal: Funcionamiento y Políticas. Santiago: PREALC
1983 Movilidad Ocupacional y Mercados de Trabajo. Santiago: PREALC.
1987 Ajuste y Deuda Social: Un Enfoque Estructural. Santiago: PREALC.

Quijano, A.
1974 The Marginal Pole of the Economy and the Marginalized Labor Force. Economy and Society 3: 393-428.

Souza, P. and V. Tokman.
1976 The Informal Urban Sector in Latin America. International Labor Review 114: 355-365

Tokman, V.
1978   An Exploration into the Nature of the Formal-Informal Relationship.World Development 6: 1065-1075.
1987a   El Sector Informal: Quince Años Después. El Trimestre Económico, Mexico: Fondo de Cultura Económico.
1987b   Desarticulación Social en la Periferia Latinoamericano. (Paper presented at the Colloquium El Sistema Centro-Periferia: Presente y Perspectivas, Madrid, 4-19 May, 1987).

COMMUNITY GROWTH VERSUS SIMPLY SURVIVING: THE INFORMAL SECTORS OF CUBANS AND HAITIANS IN MIAMI

Alex Stepick
Department of Sociology and Anthropology
Florida International University

Introduction.[1]

This paper examines the case of the informal sector in Miami, Florida.[2] It finds an extensive informal sector of activities that escapes government regulation or violates labor law and that has expanded notably in the past 25 years. Miami's largest informal sector activity is, probably, the importation and distribution of illegal drugs but, because of their clandestine and often violent activities, research in this area is difficult. Thus, this paper does not focus on illegal drugs or the related area of money laundering but, instead, examines Miami's two more licit and distinct informal sectors. One is closely linked with the broader Cuban enclave economy and the other is mainly isolated from the same broader

[1]An earlier version of this paper was presented to the Conference on the Informal Sector organized by the Program in Comparative International Development of The Johns Hopkins University and held at Harpers Ferry, West Virginia, October 1986. Many people helped contribute to this paper. They include Alejandro Portes, Robert Lamothe, Annette Williams, Marie Ade, Sophonie Milien, Maria Patricia Fernandez-Kelly, Max Castro, Oliver Kerr, Carlos Velez-Ibanez, Yves Colon, and Andy Banks. Carol Dutton Stepick's editorial comments have greatly improved the readability of this paper. Research support was provided by the National Science Foundation (Grant #SES-8215567), the Ford Foundation, Florida International University Foundation, School of Arts and Sciences at Florida International University, and the Haitian Task Force.

[2]The term "Miami" can have a number of referents. Most narrowly, it means the City of Miami. It also can refer to the broader urban area encompassed by Dade County or the Miami SMSA. In some cases, it even loosely refers to all of South Florida, including Fort Lauderdale, and further up Florida's east coast. In this paper, I use "Miami" to refer to the contiguous urban area in Dade County.

economy and consists of Haitian immigrant survival strategies. The existence and growth of both informal sectors is attributable to both immigration and ethnic antagonism. Cuban immigration greatly contributed to those informal sector activities linked to the broader economy, while Haitian immigration accounts for the creation of an isolated informal sector. In both cases, inter-ethnic and racial antagonism and the broader economy's rejection of immigrants formed part of the foundation of each informal sector. After a brief discussion of the paper's methodology, I present a description of the evolution of Miami's overall economy and its immigration history, followed by synopses of the Cuban and Haitian informal sectors.

Theoretical framework and methodology.

I borrow my definition of the informal sector from Portes and Sassen-Koob: "...the sum total of income-earning activities with the exclusion of those that involve contractual and legally regulated employment" (1987:31). From an historical perspective, the formal economy and not the informal is both the more recent and the more atypical. However, the informal cannot be understood without reference to the formal since the characteristics of the informal economy are not inherent in economic activities themselves. Rather, they reflect the relationship of the economic activities to the State. Moreover, as the State has evolved, so has the distinction between informal and formal economic activities. What is informal today may have been formal a decade ago. Similarly, what is informal in one place may be formal in another place with another State.

The informal sector is thus heterogeneous, but not randomly so. It specifically includes at least five different types:
(1) Independent entrepreneurs isolated from the formal sector (Hart 1973; Bairoch 1973);
(2) entrepreneurs who exist in the formal sector's interstices;
(3) disguised wage laborers who appear to be independent entrepreneurs, such as garbage pickers in Cali, Colombia (Birbeck 1979);
(4) a "super-exploited proletariat," the "reserve army" of labor who work but receive less than minimum wage and are subjected to other abuse (Amin 1976; Bromley 1978);

(5) an enclave economy in which co-ethnic minority workers and their bosses are tied together by overlapping economic and social ties (Portes and Sassen-Koob 1987).

Each of these different types of informal economic activities has different causes and consequences for both informal workers themselves and the resultant class structure. In brief, isolated entrepreneurs, disguised wage laborers, and the "super-exploited proletariat" are all likely to have low standards of living and to be involved in survival strategies. In contrast, those who are entrepreneurs and exist within the formal sector's interstices may have relatively good standards of living. Whether owner or worker, the former are likely to prefer their positions in the informal sector because of what they perceive as greater opportunities for socioeconomic mobility.

Analysis of the informal sector must therefore delineate the historical development of the relationship between the formal and informal sectors, concretely situate both sectors in a particular locale and time, and examine the processes of the economic activities and their relationship to the State.

Miami's economic growth and immigrant history.

Miami has been characterized by some as the vortex of the Caribbean (Garreau 1981), even of the entire Latin American, economy (Levine 1985). This role is rooted in the arrival, beginning in the 1960s, of hundreds of thousands of Cubans. It is reflected in the increasing roles in the economy of transportation, import and export businesses, and diverse services, particularly international finance. Miami International Airport is the ninth busiest airport in the world in passengers and the sixth largest in air cargo tonnage. Among U.S. airports, Miami ranks second only to New York's Kennedy Airport in international passengers and cargo. Moreover, the Port of Miami provides a base for over 85 steamship companies and is the largest cruise ship port in the world. By 1982, Miami stood second only to New York as an international banking center (Mohl 1983: 76; Luytjes 1983). Miami also has the largest free trade zone in the United States where export-import companies

185

can store, process, manufacture, assemble, display, or re-export goods from abroad without first paying tariffs. It is the undisputed drug capital of the U.S. and tons of newspaper publicity and millions of dollars spent on federal anti-drug task forces have done little to abate the influx of drug dollars.

If, as claimed, Miami is capable of being examined as the core of the entire regional economy of Latin America, the role must be seen as a new one. Fundamentally unlike the other U. S. cities with large informal sectors—e.g., the New York metropolitan area (Sassen-Koob 1986) and the southwestern U.S. (Fernandez-Kelly and Garcia 1989)—Miami is not a city formed by a long-developed, industrial-sector dependency on massive waves of foreign immigration . Not until recently have immigrants played a central role in Miami's economy.

Miami's Cuban enclave informal economy.

A good portion of Miami's economic growth and particularly the focus of the economy on Latin America has been attributed to the immigration of Cubans into Miami (Jorge and Moncarz 1980). By 1985, there were at least 750,000 Hispanics in the area, approximately 40% of the entire metropolitan population (Metro-Dade, 1987). Cubans have been an extraordinarily successful immigrant group and, for every measure of family income, Cubans score higher than the U.S. Hispanic population and only slightly below the total U.S. population (Perez 1986: 9). The bases for this success are multiple, but one of the Cuban community's outstanding characteristics is its peculiar form of economic adaptation, the enclave economy (Wilson and Portes 1980; Portes 1981; Portes and Bach 1985, chapter 6; Haug and Portes 1980). Nearly 15% of the Miami Cubans who came in the past decade are self-employed and over one-half of the most recent Mariel arrivals work in Cuban-owned firms (Portes, Clark, and Manning 1985).

The Cuban community has a number of advantages in forming ethnic businesses. First, they were initially warmly welcomed by the U.S. government. While virtually no early Miami Cuban entrepreneurs utilized the Small Business Administration, they did

186

benefit from general support for refugees. Even more importantly, many came from the middle and upper classes in Cuba and their families owned businesses or they themselves had worked in firms before coming to the U.S. It was not unusual for some of the younger adults to have attended elite universities in the U.S.

Their timing was also fortunate. As one of the cities in the so-called "sunbelt" of the southern half of the nation, Miami expanded throughout the 1960s and 1970s (excluding a period during the nation-wide 1973 recession). Because of the influx of Cubans and relocated "snow birds" (those from the "frost belt" in the northern half of the continent who winter in Florida), housing and business construction boomed. Cubans also arrived in Miami just as transportation links to Latin America were expanding. They self-consciously and effectively utilized their cultural background to grab a good share of the rapidly expanding Latin business. In the early 1970s, Cubans began to gain some influence in the world of local finance, first, by becoming secondary level bank officers but, within a few years, by holding top positions in the Cuban banks that began to appear. Both steps eased access of capital to Cuban entrepreneurs since, despite ostensibly greater risks, such institutions were willing to loan on the basis of a Cuban applicant's reputation (rather than a borrower's current equity).

All of these factors combined to encourage Cuban entrepreneurship. Cuban enterprises grew from just over 900 in 1967 to.the approximately 25,000 that presently exist. By the early 1970s, Cuban-owned construction companies were putting up at least 35% of all Dade County's new buildings (Portes and Bach 1985: 89) and by the mid-1980s they erected more than 50%.

What has not been recognized so far is the role that the informal sector has played in contributing to the development of the Cuban community. Most Cuban workers are still wage laborers and the presence of a large, low wage work force greatly contributes to the success of the Cuban businesses. However, workers voluntarily accept inferior working conditions because they hope to become entrepreneurs themselves. Thus, much of the area's economic growth has been underwritten by the expansion of informal labor practices incorporating low wage immigrant workers and through this process has emerged a distinct informal sector, a Cuban enclave economy.

Table 1
RECENT CUBAN AND HAITIAN REFUGEE EMPLOYMENT (PERCENT)

	1974-76 Cuban refugees	1980 Cubans	1980 Haitian refugees
Unemployed	14.0	26.8	58.5
Unemployed males	14.0	25.8	38.8
Self-employed	8.0	13.2	0.1
Working in Cuban firms	31.2	42.0	10.0
Secondary sector	--*	24.9	47.7
Informal sector	--*	31.4	33.4

*Data unavailable

As Table 1 shows,[3] nearly one-third of the most recent Cuban arrivals work in informal enterprises and over 40% work in Cuban owned enclave enterprises.

The Cubans participate, as both owners and workers, in the informal sector activities that are closely integrated with the broader economy, especially in the apparel industry, restaurants, and construction. In Miami, the most common types of labor law violations, according to the U.S. Department of Labor, are the falsification of employee records to avoid paying overtime, home work in the apparel industry, and the exploitation of child labor. Most common violators are those in the apparel and construction industries, and hotels/restaurants, together constituting 16% of Miami's labor force in 1980 (see Table 2).

---

[3]Portes and Stepick 1985 discuss the labor market incorporation of recent Cuban and Haitian refugees. In this case, "informal "was defined as: (1) workers paid in cash or without tax deductions; or (2) domestic servants and kindred; or (3) the itinerant self-employed such as odd-jobbers and street vendors; or (4) workers whose hourly wages are below 80% of the minimum.

Table 2
EMPLOYMENT AND ETHNICITY (PERCENT)*

	1960**		1970			1980		
	W	B	W	B	H	W	B	H
Apparel	94.4	5.6	17.8	3.7	78.5	10.4	7.08	2.6
Construction	80.1	19.9	60.1	19.4	20.5	43.8	16.6	39.6
Hotels	83.8	16.2	77.5	14.1	18.4	37.3	22.9	39.8
Restaurants	90.7	9.3	61.7	12.9	25.4	60.5	9.3	30.2

Whites=W; Blacks=B; Hispanic=H

*Sources: U.S. Censuses, Florida, 1960, 1970, and 1980. Numbers represent the percent of a particular ethnic group for that industry in each of the three censuses. For example, in the textile industry in 1960, 94.4% of the work force was White and 5.6% Black.
**The 1960 U.S. Census did not distinguish Hispanics. In the 1970 and 1980 U.S. Censuses, Hispanics are not mutually exclusive with either Blacks or Whites. Miami has relatively few Black Hispanics and the table assumes they are mutually exclusive. The figures for Whites were determined by subtracting the Hispanics and Blacks from 100%.

Apparel. Behind tall fences and barren walls in the Northwest section of Miami are many small apparel firms, the epitome of Sunbelt industry. No smokestacks. No old grimy buildings. Just low lying concrete block rectangles joined by acres and acres of pavement covered with thousands of automobiles. Inside the block buildings is the Sunbelt's most attractive economic asset: abundant, non-union, low wage labor. In Miami, nearly 25,000 women, mainly Cuban, cut and sew the latest fashions, primarily in women's and children's clothes.

Miami's apparel industry has its roots in a diversification of the local economy that began in the 1940s. Its biggest boost, however, came in the late 1960s when many New York manufacturers, primarily Jewish, relocated in Miami. They were attracted by waves of Cuban immigration into South Florida, labor that offered an alternative for companies in the face of threatening unionization in the Northeast. In marked contrast with the degeneration of the industry in other parts of the U.S., overall rates of employment in the apparel sector have held steady in Miami for the past 20 years. Miami's firms are almost all small, family-owned enterprises. Of the nearly 750 firms, only 20% have more than 20 workers and the average number of employees is 30.

While overall employment has been steady, ethnicity of workers has changed dramatically. As Table 2 indicates, 25 years ago nearly 95% of employees were White; and many, although by no means most, were unionized. Today, 85% of the apparel workers are Hispanic women and far fewer shops are unionized.[4]

Miami manufacturers claim that they have had difficulty finding new workers to replace their aging and retiring female Cuban workers. The economic success of the Cuban community permits the second generation of Cuban women to forsake the low wages of the apparel industry, while the virtual elimination of Cuban immigration has eliminated new supplies of workers. Central and South Americans supply a partial, but inadequate answer. Haitians and Black Americans provide a potential solution, but manufacturers have been reluctant to incorporate them. In 1960, when the industry in Miami was still gestating, 5% of the workers were Black. Twenty years later, the proportion had climbed only to 7%. In the early 1980s, Haitian women began to work in the apparel industry, but after the falsely-based AIDS scare (Cooley 1983, Durand 1983, Laverdiere et. al. 1983) Haitian employment plummeted. Currently, a typical factory of 20-25 workers is likely to have only one or two Haitians. Owners claim that Hispanic workers create a culturally closed shop making others feel unwelcome. Haitian workers retort that Hispanic supervisors favor Hispanic workers over Haitians. Regardless of the psychological and social motivations, the effect is racist exclusion. Blacks, both native and foreign, are not

---

[4]U.S. Census, Florida, 1960. Incidentally, Miami epitomizes the difficulties in making ethnic distinctions in the U.S. The majority of Miami Cubans are of Spanish descent and many resent being contrasted with "Whites." Conversely, many in Miami's dominant White population resent being identified by the residual category, "Non-Hispanic White." Some also reject the category "Anglo" because of its ethnic specificity which implicitly excludes Jews and numerous European ethnic groups. Blacks of Caribbean descent also frequently object to being lumped with American Blacks.

incorporated into the local apparel industry in proportionately significant numbers.

While the Cuban work force is retiring and owners refuse to replace them with Blacks, Miami's apparel industry has felt increasing competition from foreign imports and New York City's Chinatown apparel district. The response has been the informalization of work practices. Miami firms have divided themselves into three types: (1) legal firms with factories obeying all or most labor laws; (2) factories in which labor laws are avoided whenever possible; and (3) firms that specialize in putting-out or home work.

The legal firms in the first category have been hit the hardest by foreign competition and New York City's Chinatown apparel district. A number of large firms have closed shop in Miami, some totally ceasing operation, some resettling abroad. Union membership, which was concentrated in the largest firms, fell from 5000 in 1978 to 1000 in 1986.

Firms in the second and third categories are, however, still surviving and even thriving. In 1980, the U.S. Department of Labor, stating that Miami was swiftly becoming one of the sweatshop capitals of the U.S., formed a strike force which found labor violations in 132 firms. The violations represented $180 million in owed wages to over 5000 workers (Risen 1981). A good portion of the violations consisted of home work, illegal in the U.S. apparel industry, which is estimated to incorporate between 30%-50% of local production. The U.S. Department of Labor claims Miami homeworkers actually earn at least the minimum wage. It is also asserted that apparel workers prefer home work. Whatever the case, this part of the informal sector forms an important component of the Cuban contribution to Miami's economy.

Construction. As in other sunbelt cities, construction has boomed in the postwar era in Miami. Between 1940-1960, Dade County's population increased by nearly 90% each decade. Between 1960-1980, the rate declined but still showed a significant 30% per decade. From the 1960s until the mid-1970s, local unions refused to accept Cuban workers. Until the late 1960s, unions controlled 90% of all housing construction in Miami. As Cuban immigrants began creating their own non-union firms and competing for housing contracts, unionized construction workers focused on higher paid jobs building condominiums in Miami Beach and office buildings in downtown Miami. The breakthrough for Cuban workers came during the 1973 recession.; the severely depressed construction industry, impelled many White construction workers to abandon Dade County.

When the unions finally recognized their mistake, it was too late. The number of unionized workers declined from a high of 10,000 to a nadir of 3000 in the late 1970s. By the mid-1980s, Cuban firms controlled more than 50% of all Dade County construction and nearly 90% of new housing. Larger, non-Hispanic White-controlled construction firms have virtually abandoned Dade County with the exception of constructing large high rise office buildings in the city center. The ethnic composition of the labor force, seen in Table 2, further reflects this transformation. The proportion of Hispanic construction workers doubled in the decade 1970-1980, from 20% to nearly 40%. Hispanics achieved this relative growth primarily at the expense of Whites whose numbers declined from 60% to 44%.[5]

When Cubans first began penetrating the construction industry, in the 1960s, informal practices predominated in Cuban construction firms. Then, small scale entrepreneurs operated out of the back of their trucks, accepting payment in cash and, in turn, paying their workers with cash. As the industry and the number of Cuban firms grew through the 1970s, work relationships became regularized. Larger firms began subcontracting with smaller Cuban firms. Most larger firms now pay by check—as do many of the subcontractors who also generally pay all the workers' contributions and take all the appropriate deductions. Wages are lower than union wage scale, approximately by one-third, but they remain far above

---

[5]While the proportion of Blacks dropped from 19.4% in 1970 to 16.6% in 1980, the absolute numbers of both Blacks and Whites increased as the total construction labor force grew (U.S. Census, Florida 1970, 1980).

the minimum wage. In short, the Cuban construction industry started informally and then became formalized.

More recently, however, informal labor practices have re-emerged. In the wake of the 1980 Mariel influx, small scale subcontractors exploited the new, unemployed immigrants by offering lower wages, hovering near the minimum wage, and payment in cash without any deductions. Since 1980, many subcontractors, especially smaller ones, no longer pay time-and-a-half for overtime, and they falsify records to conceal the true number of hours worked.

Unlike the apparel industry, the construction industry's strength was achieved before the influx of immigrants and, again unlike the apparel industry, established firms refused to incorporate Cuban workers. Anti-immigrant prejudice in the construction industry assumed a different form from the apparel industry. In construction, it worked against the short term interests of the early Cuban immigrants. But, because of the gradual emergence of the Cuban enclave and the utilization of informal economic practices, Cuban construction workers obtained jobs despite the unions excluding them. Again, informal practices have underwritten Cuban success and contributed to the broader Miami economy.

Hotels and Restaurants. Though tourism is a declining industry in Miami, hotels and restaurants, are still important, especially in their contribution to the informal economy. Many attempt to lower costs by violating labor laws, e.g., paying less than the minimum wage, not paying time and a half for overtime, making illegal deductions (such as for breakage), deducting fees for workers' uniforms from the latters' wages, and not meeting health and safety standards. These practices exist throughout the industry, but they are most common in restaurants, especially those owned by Cubans.

Large restaurants concentrate their resources up front, in style and decor. The shadows and doors to the kitchen obscure the savings achieved by violating health and safety standards. Unlike labor violations in the apparel and construction sectors, however, these practices have not increased because of the influx of Cuban workers.

Rather, the historical weakness of organized labor in this industry meant that firms did not need the vulnerability of new immigrants to engage in informal labor practices.

Further, it is such smaller firms that are far more likely to maintain informal labor practices. They have also been more deeply affected by immigration. Little Havana, Miami's largest and most well-developed ethnic neighborhood, is dotted with small restaurants in which the waiters, waitresses, busboys, and dishwashers may be Mariel Cubans or undocumented Central American workers who receive sub-minimum wages. Mariel Cubans have fulfilled the functions of a new wave of low wage, exploitable immigrant labor. They are willing to work as dishwashers for $200 a week, cash—payments off-the-books with no deductions or employer-contributed benefits; Cubans who arrived earlier will not settle for less than $300 a week. While most of these restaurants' patrons are Cubans, Cuban restaurants are becoming increasingly popular with the broader Miami population. Thus, again informal practices have contributed to both the Cuban community and the broader Miami economy.

Haitian informal sector survival strategies.

The Miami Haitian experience, including the nature and function of its informal economy, contrasts starkly with that of the Cubans. Rather than a welcome, they have experienced rejection at every turn. The U.S. government has conducted a resolute and consistent policy of discouraging their arrival and encouraging their return to Haiti (Miller 1984; Zucker 1983; Loescher and Scanlan 1984; Stepick 1982, 1987). Although boat arrivals in South Florida total less than one-fifth the number of Haitians in New York, they have been the object of much publicity. The first detected Haitian boat arrived in Miami in 1963; the second did not come until 1973. It was not until 1977 that Haitians began arriving regularly. Between 1977-1981, between 50,000 and 70,000 Haitians arrived by boat in Miami. Another 5000-10,000 came by plane, and a smaller number resettled in Miami after living in New York, Montreal, or some other northern metropolitan area.

Those moving from the north are likely to have desired skills and be absorbed easily into the local economy. Others, however, have had more difficulty. As Table 1 reflects, unemployment is nearly 60% , more than three times that of the general Miami population. In contrast with the Cubans, less than 2% report being self-employed and even fewer report working for other Haitians. Over one-half of the Haitian refugees in Miami who do manage to find work, work for non-Haitians in secondary sector jobs and another one-third work in informal enterprises (Table 1 and Portes and Stepick 1985).

While a small Haitian business community has formed, it compares poorly in every way with the Cuban business community. Sales are low; the businesses provide little employment beyond the entrepreneur-owners; and the rate of failure is very high (Stepick 1984).

Table 3
ESTIMATED INCOME FOR INFORMALLY
SELF-EMPLOYED HAITIANS*

	Monthly	Yearly
Dressmakers and Tailors	$ 65-200	$2,500- 9,000
Construction	150-400	4,000-10,000
Automobile Repair	85-500	6,000-12,500
Transportation	40-100	4,000-12,500
Beauty and Barber	30-500	6,000-12,500
Petty Commerce	50-200	2,500- 6,000
Restaurants	200-600	4,000- 8,000

*Estimates of monthly income refer only to the particular informal sector activity. Estimates of yearly income, however, refer to the individuals' total income including other employment or receipt of government benefits.

With the partial exception of hotels and restaurants, the economic activities discussed in the previous section do not incorporate Haitians. Rather, the modal form of labor market incorporation for recent Haitian refugees is lack of incorporation, i.e., unemployment. Yet, most are not maintained by welfare.

Instead, they are casually self-employed in a variety of enterprises. Unlike many recent descriptions of Third World informal enterprises (Portes and Sassen-Koob 1987), their incomes are low (see Table 3), generally below the poverty line which in 1984 was just over $8000 for a family of three. Most self-employed informal entrepreneurs drift back and forth between working for someone else in a secondary or informal sector job and their own informal activity. Generally, they do not leave a wage labor job voluntarily in favor of their own business. Rather, informal businesses provide supplements, not substitutes, to wage labor. Usually, they become full-time informal sector entrepreneurs only when they have no choice—when they lose or cannot obtain wage labor employment. Moreover, unlike Cuban business folk in the apparel, construction, and hotels/restaurant sectors, Haitian informal entrepreneurs do not have any employees working for them.

The most common Haitian informal activities are dressmaking and tailoring, petty commerce, food preparation, child care, transportation, and the provision of semi-skilled services such as construction work, automobile repair, and electronic repair.

Those who make a living as dressmakers or tailors in the U.S. were also dressmakers and tailors in Haiti. They serve what is, virtually, an exclusive Haitian market. As in many Third World countries, the sewing trades flourish because of the relatively high expense of ready-made clothes and the low cost of labor. Such trades persist in the U.S. partially because of cultural tradition, a preference for tailor-made clothes, but also because the informal sector labor provided by these dressmakers and tailors remains cheap. In Little Haiti, a custom-made woman's dress may be had for less than $15. An item of children's apparel may cost less than $10. Correspondingly, dressmakers' and tailors' earnings are low. The highest yearly income reported was $9130—but most earn closer to $2500, which they supplement by part-time, temporary work in the formal sector or stretch through sharing within the household (see Table 3). While many of the women have worked in the apparel industry, frequently cycling in and out of jobs, I found no Haitians actually engaged in home work contracted out by a factory.

Even more common than sewing (at least for females) is petty commerce. Women frequently use a small ($15-$50) store of capital, to become petty merchants. They go door-to-door or set up makeshift stands that appear on corners and empty lots—a few during the week, many more on the weekends. However, the preferred form of petty commerce is to go to a local flea market where sellers may offer Haitian food products such as yams and spiced pickled cabbage, ready-made clothes, or goods from Haiti such as toiletries and decorative ceramic goods. With the exception of the latter category, most commodities are purchased at retail price in downtown, usually Cuban-run stores. The clientele of the petty entrepreneurs is exclusively Haitian, and mostly those of the same social class as the vendor. Haitian door-to-door vendors are not likely to venture into middle class neighborhoods and affluent Haitians are more likely to shop in mainstream stores than flea markets.

Another common informal activity among women, food preparation, is well known within the Haitian community but invisible to non-Haitians. Women turn home kitchens into food preparation centers for informal restaurants and use, say, the back yard or the living room as the dining area. A high proportion of the single men in Little Haiti either do not know how to cook or don't wish to prepare their own meals They rely almost exclusively upon restaurant food. These informal sector restaurants usually charge about $3 for a meal, about $1-$2 less than the Haitian formal sector restaurants. The women who run these restaurants estimate they make about $500 a month or about $6000 a year.

Finally, an important female informal activity is child care. While walking the streets of Little Haiti, one frequently encounters houses spilling over with children. They are not, as some assume, large overflowing families living in objectionably crowded conditions. Rather, the children are likely to be in informal day care. The earnings of most working Haitians are too low to afford State sanctioned commercial day care and public facilities do not even begin to address community needs. Many women have stepped into the breach and offer low-cost day care. Most of their clients earn no more than the minimum wage. Many do day work in agriculture and average even less than the minimum wage. Accordingly, day care fees are rock bottom, varying between $2-$5 per day per child.

Men are less likely to engage in informal self-employment than women. For those who are so engaged, activities are, again, petty businesses similar to or the same as those worked in Haiti, directed at the Haitian market and, in Miami, low income generating.

The most visible male activity focuses around the public transportation needs of the community. Cabs are usually older American cars, which individuals purchase for between $500-$1500. Primarily, drivers cruise around the grocery stores that serve Little Haiti. Full-time drivers make around $100 a week while those that operate only on week-ends earn about $40. Other forms of informal transportation are the vans and aged school buses used to transport people between Miami and the agricultural fields as well as between cities. The vans are usually much newer and in better condition than the independent ("gypsy") cabs—as they must be for the longer trips they make. They require an investment of at least a few thousand dollars but some are new and cost $10,000 plus. The decomissioned school buses require a smaller initial investment but, as might be expected, have higher maintenance costs. Regardless, the investment is well worth the cost. The owners have a captive market since there are no alternative forms of transportation easily accessible to the Haitians. Trips to the agricultural fields bring only $4-$5 per person, but the work is steady and the vans usually run full. The substantial money, however, is earned on the weekends when the vans go between Miami and the agricultural towns such as Belle Glade, a 1-1/2 hour drive apart. For this type of a trip, van owners can charge up to $25 per person and can easily earn $250 a week (about $12,000 a year).

A slightly less visible but even more common male activity is the provision of semi-skilled services, e. g., construction, electronics and auto repair. Like the dressmakers and tailors, individuals involved in these activities usually have had previous experience and training in these trades in Haiti before coming to the U.S., many having worked in similar firms, usually at low wages. They begin by setting up a small business on the side while still working for wages, usually devoting full attention to the business only when they lose their job. For example, Haitian auto mechanics working on the street provide affordable repairs since, while prices are usually set by the task, the effective wage for auto mechanics hovers close to the minimum wage. As with the other Haitian informal activities, the clientele of these men is almost exclusively Haitian.

Increasingly, Haitians are also becoming homeowners in Little Haiti. Frequently, they take advantage of the housing shortage for Haitians by becoming landlords and (illegally, of course) remodeling single-family homes into rooming houses or apartments. The tasks of remodeling are undertaken by informal Haitian construction workers who earn close to the minimum wage.

In sum, Haitians have constructed a significant informal sector based upon casual self-employment. Clearly, these activities are survival strategies and are neither inherently preferable to wage labor employment nor disguised wage labor for firms in the broader economy. Instead, Haitian self-employment in informal activities forms an enclave antithetical to that of the Cuban enclave. It displaces no individuals or firms in the broader economy. It is not in the interstices of the broader economy. It produces goods and services consumed exclusively within the Haitian community, although it also sells goods produced outside the community. And it provides an income close to the poverty threshold.

Conclusions.

The first and most obvious conclusion from our survey of Miami's informal sector is that it is diverse. It consists of two fundamentally different components: On the one hand, we have the informal activities of the Cuban enclave that have become integrated with the broader economy; on the other hand, there is the informal sector of the Haitians—independent, isolated, and consisting of survival activities segregated from that same broader economy within which the Cubans operate so effectively.

Moreover, each segment is itself internally diversified. The first section of this paper delineated five different types of informal sectors: isolated entrepreneurs, interstitial entrepreneurs, disguised wage laborers, "super-exploited" wage laborers, and an enclave sector. Miami has four of these five types: Informalization in the apparel industry, particularly through homework, is disguised wage labor; the parts of the hotel industry which are informal can best be described as "super-exploited" since workers receive lower wages and benefits than those mandated by law; the construction and restaurant industries in the Cuban community form a significant part of the Cuban enclave economy; and the Haitians constitute an informal sector of isolated entrepreneurs.

The creation of the Cuban enclave economy has added a peculiar dynamic to Miami's informal sector, a co-ethnic alliance and solidarity, instead of conflict, between capital and labor in which workers voluntarily submit to increased levels of exploitation in return for paternalistic care and frequently, especially in construction and restaurants, assistance in subsequently establishing and maintaining their own businesses. Informal practices have created a vital, dynamic sector that has contributed to rapid socioeconomic advancement of Cubans compared to other immigrant groups (cf. Portes and Bach 1985; Portes and Stepick 1985).

In contrast, in response to rejection by those in the larger economy, Haitians have created their own informal sector which closely resembles the original descriptions of informal work in Third World cities—casual self-employment isolated from the broader market. Though contemporary analyses of third world informal sectors tend to emphasize their articulation with the formal sector, at this point, the Miami Haitian informal sector remains apart. It is not a deliberate attempt by capital to increase competitiveness. On the contrary, it is largely isolated from the broader market and little utilized by it. Perhaps, with more time, the opportunities for exploitation and the longer-term needs of the overall economy for low wage, unprotected labor will overcome the deterrence of racism thereby transforming the survival strategies of Haitians into backward capitalist informal relations.

References.

Amin, Samir
1976   Unequal Development, An Essay on the Social
        Formations of Peripheral Capitalism. New York:
        Monthly Review Press.

Bairoch, Paul
1973   Urban Unemployment in Developing Countries: The
        Nature of the Problem and Proposals for its Solution.
        Geneva: International Labor Office, 1973.

Birbeck, Chris
1979   Garbage, Industry, and the "Vultures" of Cali,
        Colombia. In R. Bromley and C. Gerry, eds., Casual
        Work and Poverty in Third World Cities. New York:
        Wiley, pp. 161-83

Bromley, Ray
1978   Organization, Regulation, and Exploitation in the So-
        called "Urban Informal Sector": The Street Traders of
        Cali, Colombia. World Development 6
        (September/October): 1161-1171.

Cooley, Martha
1983   Haiti: The AIDS Stigma. NACLA: 47-48.

Durand, Guy
1983   AIDS: The Fallacy of a Haitian Connection. Bulletin
        de l'Association des Medecins Haitiens a l'Etranger 19:
        17-20.

Ferdandez-Kelly, Patricia and Ana Garcia
1989   Informalization at the Core: Hispanic Women, Home
        Work and the Advanced Capitalist State. In A. Portes,
        M. Castells, and L. Benton, eds., The Informal Sector
        in Advanced and Developing Countries. Baltimore
        MD: The Johns Hopkins University Press, pp. 60-77.

Garreau, Joel
1981   The Nine Nations of North America. New York: Houghton Mifflin.

Haug, Madeline and A. Portes
1980   Immigrants' Social Assimilation: An Analysis of Individual and Structural Determinants. Duke University, manuscript.

Hart, Keith
1973   Informal Income Opportunities and Urban Employment in Ghana. Journal of Modern African Studies 11: 61-89.

Jorge, Antonio and Raul Moncarz
1980   The Cuban Entrepreneur and the Economic Development of the Miami SMSA. Manuscript. Department of Economics, Miami International University.

Laverdiere, Michel, J. Tremblay, R. Lavallee, Y. Bonny, M. Lacombe, J. Boileau, J. Lachapelle and C. Lamoureaux
1983 AIDS in Haitian Immigrants and in a Caucasian Woman Closely Associated with Haitians. Canadian Medical Association Journal 129: 1209-1212.

Levine, Barry
1985 The Capital of Latin America. Wilson Quarterly Winter: 46-69.

Loescher, Gilbert and John Scanlan
1984   Human Rights, U. S. Foreign Policy, and Haitian Refugees. Journal of Interamerican Studies and World Affairs 26: 313-356.

Luytjes, Jan
1983   International Banking in South Florida: Analysis and Trends. Miami FL.: Bureau of Business Research, Florida International University.

Metro-Dade County Planning Department
1987   Profile of the Hispanic Population. Miami FL:
Research Division, Planning Department, Metro-Dade
County.

Miller, Jake C.
1984   The Plight of Haitian Refugees. New York: Praeger.

Mohl, Raymond
1983   Miami: The Ethnic Cauldron. In R. M. Bernard, R.
M. and B. R. Rice, eds. Sunbelt Cities: Politics and
Growth Since World War II. Austin: University of
Texas Press, pp. 71-89.

Perez, Lisandro
1986   Immigrant Economic Adjustment and Family
Organization: The Cuban Success Story Reexamined.
International Migration Review 20: 4-20.

Portes, Alejandro
1981   Modes of Structural Incorporation and Present
Theories of Labor Immigration. In Mary M. Kritz, C.
B. Keely, and S. Tomasi, eds., Global Trends in
Migration. New York: The Center for Migration
Studies of New York, pp. 279-297.

Portes, Alejandro and R. Bach
1985   Latin Journey. Berkeley: University of California
Press.

Portes, Alejandro, J. Clark and R. Manning
1985   After Mariel: A Survey of the Resettlement
Experiences of 1980 Cuban Refugees in Miami. Cuban
Studies 15: 37-59.

Portes, Alejandro and S. Sassen-Koob
1987   Making It Underground: Comparative Material on the
Informal Sector in Western Market Economies.
American Journal of Sociology 93: 30-61.

Portes, Alejandro and A. Stepick
1985   Unwelcome Immigrants: The Labor Market Experiences of 1980 (Mariel) Cuban and Haitian Refugees in South Florida. American Sociological Review 50: 493-514.

Risen, J.
1981   Sweatshops Pervasive in Miami. Miami Herald May 18: C1

Stepick, Alex
1982   Haitian Boat People: A Study in the Conflicting Forces Shaping U.S. Refugee Policy. Law and Contemporary Problems, Duke University Law Journal 45: 163-196.
1984   The Business Community of Little Haiti. Dialogue 32, Occasional Papers Series, Latin American and Caribbean Center, Florida International University.
1987   Haitian Refugees in the U.S. London and New York: The Minority Rights Group (second ed.).

Sassen-Koob, Saskia
1986   New York City's Informal Economy. Paper presented at the Conference on the Informal Sector, Harpers Ferry, West Virginia.

U.S. Bureau of the Census
1963   Census of Population, 1960. vol. I, part 11 Characteristics of the Population, Florida. Washington D. C.: U.S. Government Printing Office.
1970   Census of Population, General Social and Economic Characteristics, Florida, Final Report Population Census. Washington, D. C.: U.S. Government Printing Office.
1980   Census of Population, General Social and Economic Characteristics, Florida, Population Census 80. Washington D. C.:U. S. Government Printing Office.

Wilson, Kenneth and A. Portes
    1980   Immigrant Enclaves: An Analysis of the Labor Market
           Experiences of Cubans in Miami. American Journal
           of Sociology 86: 295-319.

Zucker, Naomi F.
    1983   The Haitians versus the United States: The Courts as
           Last Resort. Annals of the American Academy of
           Political and Social Science 467: 151-162.

ECONOMIC CRISIS AND THE INFORMAL STREET MARKET SYSTEM OF SPAIN

Anthony Oliver-Smith [1]
Department of Anthropology
University of Florida
and
Joaquín Beltrán Antolín
María Angeles Lorenzo Quintela
María Victoria Martínez Saez
María Teresa Pedruelo Pedruelo
María Dolores Rosell Vaquero
Department of Social Anthropology
Universidad Complutense de Madrid

Introduction.

Among the most common sights on Spanish highways today are tan/cream-colored vans and trucks of all makes, shapes and sizes, always with an "80" (kilometers speed limitation) stamped on the back. They belong to the *vendedores ambulantes* (traveling vendors) of Spain's system of outdoor flea markets. They are in evidence

[1] The research on which this article is based was carried out together with five senior students in the Faculty of Political Sciences and Sociology, Universidad Complutense de Madrid. The research was part of the activities of the course in field methods that I taught during a visiting professorship at the institution. The project was partially funded by a grant from the Ayuntamiento del Distrito de Tetuan (Madrid), which Dr. Jose Lison Arcal (Department of Social Anthropology, Universidad Complutense de Madrid) and I wrote jointly. I carried out research on the *rastro* system as a whole while the students undertook the ethnographic study of the Tetuan *rastro*. Most of the information in this article on the Tetuan *rastro* is drawn from the final research report prepared by the students (Beltrán Antolín et al., 1985). Their participation in the project as a whole as well as their contribution to this article specifically is a major one and is gratefully acknowledged.

207

everywhere, from the remote mountain roads of Picos de Europa of Cantabria to the highways of bustling coastal tourist areas, traveling within and among the networks of informal periodic street markets of Spain's villages, towns and cities. Over the last 15 years, these markets, marketing systems, and traveling vendors have become increasingly important in the economic life of the nation; they provide gainful activities to the recently unemployed as well as reasonable price alternatives to consumers caught in the grip of Spain's prolonged economic crisis.

Travelling vendors and the *rastro* complex.

Markets and traders have been of greater or lesser importance in Europe since antiquity (open air market places are seen in remains of early urban settlements) to the present, their fortunes rising and falling with those of the State and the city (Bienefeld 1979: 29-30). Although a feature of Spanish life in the Roman era and even before, Madrid's famous Rastro, the prototype for the markets of the modern system, originated only in the 17th century.

The *Rastro* began in an area along the street called Ribera de Curtidores (Riverbank of the Tanners), not far from the main slaughterhouse of the city. The literal meaning of *el rastro* is "path," referring in this case to the path left by sheep dragged between the corrals and the slaughterhouse (Corral Raya and Sanz 1953: 89). At one end of Ribera de Curtidores in the Plaza de Coscorro, the scraps and leavings of the slaughterhouse were sold to the general public. Eventually, a general foodstuffs market, including fruit and vegetable vendors, cheese sellers and wine merchants as well as rag-pickers, coalesced there.

By the early 20th century, with the location of municipal urban food markets in the various neighborhoods of Madrid, the role of the *Rastro* as a food market had diminished, but its function as a flea market where used goods of all sorts, ranging from clothing and tools to building materials, antiques (including art from buildings demolished in the urban development of the city), had greatly expanded (Campos Romero n.d.: 135). Today, the *Rastro* is an enormous, sprawling outdoor street market, encompassing not only

Ribera de Curtidores but 13 other streets and the Plaza del General Vara del Rey in a 25-block area of old Madrid. Although the *Rastro* is primarily a Sunday morning event, it operates on a smaller scale during the week and, as a whole, the area contains more than 500 permanent retail establishments which are active on a daily basis as well as Sundays.

The *Rastro* of Madrid is the prototype for a nation-wide complex of urban periodic street markets, known variously as *mercados*, *mercadillos*, and *rastrillos*, which now predominantly retail new merchandise as well as some foodstuffs. In effect, the entire nation is a mosaic of regional networks of these markets in towns and villages that are cluster around a major regional capital where many of the traveling vendors live. The village and town markets, as well as the neighborhood (district) *rastrillos* of the larger cities, constitute a system only in that they are linked by the choices of individual vendors to attend them. Vendors' choices of location are based on assessments of local demand, competition and local market charges.

Estimates from informants place the number of "professional" (i.e., formally registered) traveling vendors, also known as *ruteros* ("route people") at close to a quarter of a million people for the whole nation, although such a figure remains to be substantiated by more comprehensive research. I refer here to estimates of formal registration, a seeming contradiction, because the Madrid office of the Treasury Department lists only approximately 300 formally registered vendors—which would account for those the Tetuan district *rastrillo* alone. Thus, given the unreliability of formal statistical sources for formally registered vendors, we must rely on informants' estimates.

Moreover, in addition to those formally registered, an incalculable number of informal vendors also make their living in the market system. For example, formally registered travelling vendors for the Madrid area are estimated at some 3500, but as many as 7000 other unregistered *advenedizos* (literally, upstarts) may make at least part of their living by selling in the Madrid system (de las Herâs

1984: 22). Other informal sources place the count considerably higher.

The *rastro* system, therefore, is the context for both formal and informal enterprises whose activities intersect and whose personnel interact and interrelate in a wide variety of relationships.

Formality and informality.

The fact that the *rastro* system is a context in which both formally registered vendors and a larger number of "upstarts," *domingueros* (Sunday sellers), and others make or supplement their incomes doing essentially the same thing in the same institutional context is a clear demonstration that we cannot speak of a clear formal/informal division regarding people or activities. The *rastro* system confirms Bromley's assertion (1978: 1035) that people may work in the informal and formal sectors at different times of the day, year or life cycle in activities which may be performed in both formal and formal enterprises.

The formal/informal distinction was a valuable but somewhat crude first step in the attempt to come to grips with what is basically a form of individual adaptation to constrictions on economic life and well-being brought about by global and national economic forces and institutions. To speak of "informal personnel" is to obscure the existence and activities of the "moonlighter" or "Sunday person" who is formally employed during normal business hours, throughout some if not all of the regular work week. And to speak of "informal activities" denies the fact that virtually identical products may be sold or services performed by both formal and informal enterprises. Again, following Bromley's lead, I would maintain that the formal/informal distinction is only appropriate and useful when applied to an enterprise which is a cluster of relationships between people and things organized for commercial purposes. The formality or informality of an enterprise is a function of its relationship to the State.

Our discussion of the *rastro* system of Madrid will focus on people, services, products and activities of different kinds of

210

enterprises defined by their relationship to the State. In effect, there is nothing in and of itself which is informal (or formal for that matter). The informal sector does not come into being until the formal sector exists—which does not happen until the State attempts to capture the economy, that is, when its personnel move to appropriate some measure of the generated surplus for State maintenance. State personnel implement various means of regulation and taxation, using as justification the State's own maintenance and the delivery of services to the population it governs. In the State's attempt to control and manage the economy, it enters into relations with the population that are characterized by tension/accommodation and compe-tition/symbiosis, dyads at once complementary and contradictory, which are generally expressed in relationships between administrative elements and enterprises as well as formal and informal enterprises. The *rastro* system of Madrid is one context in which such relationships are being forged out of the tensions in Spain's regional, national and international economic life.

Economic miracle and economic crisis.

The increase in *rastro* system formal and informal parti-cipants, as well as the expansion of the informal sector in general (sometimes called the "submerged economy" in Spain), may be traced to economic changes which took place between 1959 and 1974, the era often referred to as the "Spanish Economic Miracle" (Harrison 1985). While it is neither possible nor necessary in the present context to describe in detail the processes which resulted in both the so-called miracle and the crisis it precipitated, it is appropriate to present a brief summary of the major economic forces at work and, in particular, their socioeconomic consequences for the population.

Prior to 1959, protectionist policies and the oft-stated goal of economic autarky of the Franco regime (cf. syndicalism), limited organizational and technological innovations developed elsewhere prolonging the life of archaic structures and practices in both agriculture and, especially, industry which was characterized by the predominance of small enterprises (Lieberman 1982: 19). The Spanish economy in the 1950s has been described as "close to bankruptcy," in part brought about by slow post-civil war recovery and equally slow development of its industrial sector caused by scarcities in raw materials, foodstuffs and energy supplies (Lieberman 1982: 22, 199). Rural and urban areas suffered severe underemployment and displayed almost Third World social conditions, including high rates of poverty, malnutrition, illiteracy, and morbidity.

Mindful of these conditions and of the social unrest they engendered, Spanish officials in 1959 radically altered the course of policy and implemented a set of reforms known as the "Stabilization Plan." The two major objectives of the plan were to (1) restore internal financial stability through fiscal and monetary measures designed to restrict demand and limit inflation and (2) liberalize external trade and encourage foreign investment (Harrison 1985: 146). The steps taken included: (1) reducing inflation by limiting public sector spending; (2) devaluating the peseta (Pta.); (3) dismantling a restrictive structure of quotas and tariffs on imports; (4) offering substantial incentives and guarantees to foreign investors; (5) accepting US$420 million in loans and credits from foreign banks (Harrison 1985: 146-148).

Although the initial impact of the plan aggravated existing conditions, by 1961, the reforms of the stabilization plan had stimulated an unprecedented era of economic growth. Between 1961-1973, Spain's gross domestic product (GNP), calculated in constant 1970 prices, grew at an average annual rate of 7.5% and national income between 1959-73 rose by 156%, from Ptas.1,162,348 to Ptas. 2,971,081 (Harrison 1985: 144). This growth was accompanied by major expansion of foreign trade, the rates of both import and export gross domestic product (GDP) more than doubling. With increased competition from abroad, long dormant Spanish industries were forced to modernize and expand, creating thousands of jobs and accelerating the transformation of the traditional agricultural economy to that of a modern, industrialized nation. Between 1959-1973, the percentage of the active labor force employed in agriculture fell from 5.12 million (41.9%) to 3.3 million (25.3%) as people migrated from the countryside and small towns to cities such as Madrid, Barcelona, Bilbao, San Sebastian and

Vitoria, as well as their growing industrial environs (Harrison 1985: 145).

Between 1964 and 1972 the average increase in industrial hourly wages was 287.9%. Placed against a 69.9% rise in the cost of living, the real hourly industrial wages increased 218% (Lieberman 1982: 238-239), triggering substantial improvements in the living standards of a higher proportion of the population than ever before in the nation's history. The period is fondly recalled today as *la época de las vacas gordas* (the time of the fat cows).

Essentially, Spain's "economic miracle" was due to three major factors: (1) The increasing availability of capital from foreign investment; (2) the abundance of a cheap labor force; and (3) a booming tourist industry, the latter alone capable of underwriting the nation's foreign exchange deficit (Salmon 1985). In the mid-1970s, however, the dependent nature of the "miracle" became shockingly clear with the world-wide economic recession and the generalized contraction of international commerce, triggered by OPEC's decision to raise oil prices. Spain was particularly vulnerable to the energy crisis since, in this period, almost three-quarters of her energy requirements were petroleum-derived (Harrison 1985: 171). GDP rates fell by more than two-thirds those of the "miracle" years. Oil prices primarily accounted for the reduction of a $557 million surplus to a $3.3 billion deficit. Although tourism increases helped offset these losses, it also led to tripling inflation rates that placed pressure on Spaniards who, at the same time, faced massive cutbacks in employment. Between 1974 (the beginning of the recession) and 1984, the official jobless rate rose from 2.94% to 20% (398,000 to 2,639,800 people) (Harrison 1985: 176; *El País* 1984: 12). The "miracle" was truly over; the *vacas gordas* were dead.

The *rastro* system of Madrid today.

The *rastro* system of Madrid today consists of a network of approximately 40 periodic street markets, meeting on different days of the week within a radius of roughly 50 kilometers from the city. As mentioned earlier, these markets constitute a network only in that

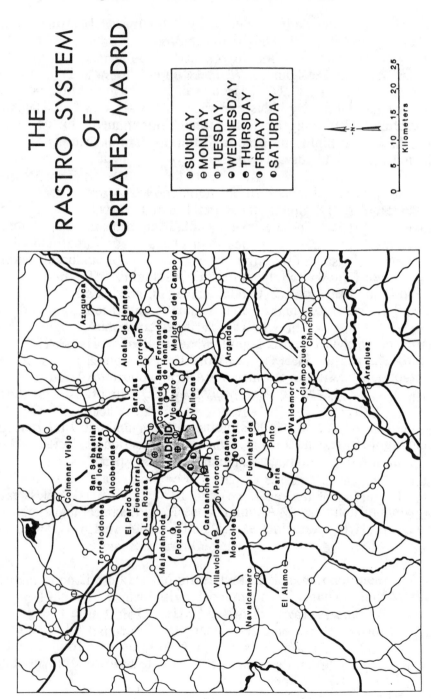

THE
RASTRO SYSTEM
OF
GREATER MADRID

⊕ SUNDAY
⊖ MONDAY
◐ TUESDAY
◑ WEDNESDAY
● THURSDAY
○ FRIDAY
◉ SATURDAY

they are most frequented by sellers living in and operating from greater Madrid (see Map 1). This does not mean that, on occasion or even regularly, Madrid vendors will not sell in more distant markets if conditions are appropriate. Nor does it mean that vendors from other regions distant from the capital will not sell in Madrid if the market merits the effort and expense. Indeed, some markets vary in their conditions on a seasonal basis. For example, the market of the suburban community of Villalba provides an adequate clientele for travelling vendors during the fall, winter and spring months of the year. However, since many people from Madrid have vacation houses or apartments there, the summer market in Villalba expands spectacularly. The reverse situation obtains in the bustling urban *rastrillo* of the Madrid district of Tetuan which suffers a 50% decline in the summer months of July and August. In addition, some vendors like to reserve one or two days a week for those small towns in the region that lack markets. A town without a formal market will charge a vendor a small fee to set up a stand to sell in the plaza on a given day. Such a decision involves balancing little or no competition against a reduced buying public for the merchandise.

Thus, all travelling vendors must individually calculate factors of demand, competition (from other sellers and local retailers), travel costs (fuel, food, lodging), and the amount/structure of market charges (see below) in their decisions to sell in one market or another. Since travelling vendors may live in Madrid proper or in any of the surrounding suburban communities of the city and return home after a day's selling, a route does not necessarily involve a series of markets that are linked in any geographical sequence. This relative freedom from geographical constraints is due to the increased ability to purchase cars and trucks that were afforded the working classes by high wages during the "miracle" years. Older informants narrate tales of hardship and restriction in travelling sales in the days following the civil war. Before and after the war, vendors travelled from town to town by foot, horse cart, train and, only occasionally, motor vehicle. The practice was to form groups of four or five vendors to share expenses. Together, they bought food and stayed in *posadas* (inns) where, at a small cost in addition to their lodging, the *posadera* (innkeeper) would cook their foodstuffs for them. In each town, they would simply set up their stands in the plaza, pay a few "reales" to the town official, and sell what they could. Today, if their trips take them overnight, they carry food or eat in restaurants and sleep in their vans; thanks to the availability of individually owned motor transportation, most formally registered travelling vendors eat at their own tables and sleep in their own beds at night. They may start off to market in the early hours before dawn but, in most cases, they are home by late afternoon, after which they may go to a factory or other supplier for the next day's or week's goods, or have free time for other activities.

The *rastrillo* of Tetuan.

To understand the way the market system is working in the context of current economic conditions in Spain, it is useful to examine in some detail a *rastro* within the system. The *rastro* which will be examined is that of Tetuan, one of 18 districts of the city of Madrid.

Commerce (especially street vending) has always been present in Tetuan. In the late 19th century what was then the suburban town of Tetuan de las Victorias had both daily markets and daily street vending. This lasted until 1929 when the main street, la Calle O'Donnell, became an important throughway for greater Madrid. That led to the relocation of vendors of fruits, vegetables, and used goods to a side street called Marqués de Viana. The construction of a permanent marketplace was paralyzed by the outbreak of the civil war in 1936. The marketplace itself disappeared during the civil war but the black market which flourished in Madrid during these unsettled years became centered here and became the principle economic activity of the district.

In the hard times of the 1940s, the marketplace reappeared on Marqués de Viana Street where vendors or *rastreros*, as they were known, sold old and used goods every day of the week. The street soon became the location of 30% of the ragpickers as well, and constant buying, selling and barter of these types of merchandise took place. Indeed, in this context we can speak of a type of marginalized goods exchanged between marginalized vendors and buyers, operating with little interference and only nominal charges by the district authorities.

In the 1950s, the *rastrillo* of Tetuan began to evolve away from its focus on used and old goods to a market that also included a mixture of new goods, foodstuffs and used goods. At the same time, it ceased to be a daily *rastro,* limiting its activities to Sundays and holidays. This trend continued through the 1960s into the 1970s as new goods and fresh foodstuffs began to predominate in the market. As these latter commodities began to penetrate the *rastro,* travelling vendors began to aspire to a less marginalized image—at the same time that greater control on market activities began to be exercised by district authorities. From the latter half of the 1970s to the present, the Tetuan market has experienced a rapid increase in participation by both buyers and sellers of a widely varied selection of merchandise. The market today occupies 12 blocks of Marqués de Viana Street every Sunday morning from roughly 9:00 AM to 3:00 PM. The Tetuan *rastrillo* is one of the major Sunday markets in the Madrid circuit, including El Rastro, Vallecas, and Hortaleza (see Map 2).

Actually, market activities begin much earlier than the hour at which customers begin arriving. Vendors, both men and women, arrive at dawn, driving down Marqués de Viana street to their habitual or formally assigned spaces, marked in two-meter segments along the curb. They first unload and assemble the steel rod structures and plywood sheets or folding tables which make up their merchandise stands. After the merchandise is arranged on the stand, the vehicles that clogged the street are moved and parked on side streets. If there is time, vendors may grab a quick breakfast at one of the more than a dozen bars and taverns along the 13 blocks of Marqués de Viana street (all but one of which survives solely because of the business done on *rastro* day). Soon, the vendors return to take up their places in front of their stands to await the first customers between nine and ten in the morning. By noon, the initial trickle of customers has become a veritable avalanche of people and the *rastro* is a swarming hive of activity.

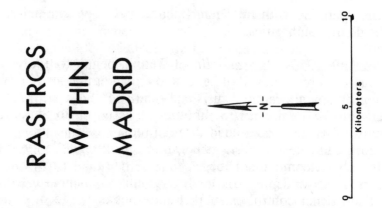

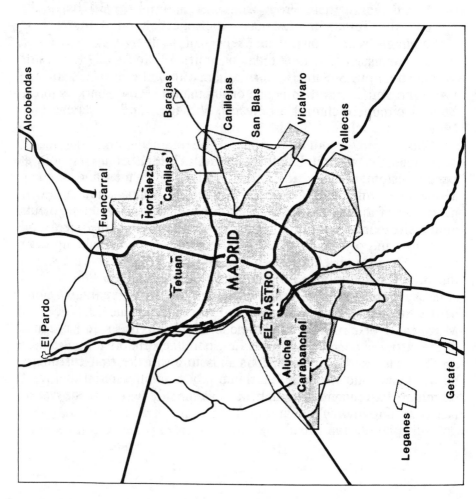

Despite all this regularity, it is still somewhat difficult to speak of a fixed schedule for the *rastrillo* since, in this outdoor context, sellers and buyers must contend with climate and seasonal variation. In summer the stands are set up earlier and the customers arrive earlier to avoid the devastating Madrid afternoon heat. In winter, everyone comes later to avoid early morning cold. In all cases, the vendors are dependent on the attendance of customers; cold, rain, or excessive heat can keep the public away and occasion serious losses for the vendors. In addition, as mentioned earlier, seasonal population movements can cause one market to expand and another to contract considerably. Those Spanish holidays that fall within one day on either side of a weekend (*puentes*, bridges) also cause major reductions in the number of marketers; summer vacations reduce the Tetuan market by half.

The vendors, just as the market, may vary seasonally or even weekly according to climate. Indeed, a major feature of the Tetuan or any other *rastro* is its variability. The variability and flexibility which tend to favor both vendors and clients is also a major issue of conflict with town and district administration, a point which will be discussed below. Thus, the vendor population of any given market— and, consequently, the array of goods which are offered for sale— will vary considerably over a year's time.

There are 307 formally registered travelling vendors in Tetuan *rastrillo* on Marqués de Viana street. The street has been divided into 581 two-meter sections allocated in various lengths to 268 vendors. The remaining 49 vendors, most of whom sell fruits and vegetables or second-hand goods, are located on side streets or at the conjunction of Marqués de Viana and the Paseo de la Dirección.

Formally registered vendors are all those who have established their credentials with the national and district authorities and who pay taxes and the stipulated charges on a bi-annual basis (see below). The great majority of these professional vendors are *ruteros* who sell in different *rastros* on different days. The legal requirements for travelling vendors are many and complicated. They must possess a Ministry of the Treasury license for public sales which they must present with a copy of their identity card and an application to the district offices to obtain a vending permit. The permit costs roughly $40 per two-meter segment of stand occupancy, is payable on a bi-annual basis, and stipulates the type of product which may be sold as well as the quantity and location of vending space. In addition, there is a daily charge of US$2.30 to sell in the *rastro*. Other costs incurred by formally registered vendors include merchandise costs, storage, transport (public or vehicle maintenance and gas), insurance, and, occasionally, wages.

However, there are many more formally registered vendors than appear on the administration's books, and there are many more vendors than those who are formally registered. The illegal or informal vendors may sell in the *rastro* on a regular or sporadic basis—but always under the slight risk of being fined, having their merchandise confiscated, or both. It is the informal vendors who maintain the traditional image of the *rastro*; they sell a congeries of goods ("junk"), e.g., used tools, books and magazines, handcrafts and novelties of all sorts, and second hand clothes. Although some vendors may assemble stands and pass unnoticed by the police in the throng of buyers and sellers, others will carry their goods and stroll through the crowd, with a wary eye out for the authorities. A brief observation in the Tetuan *rastrillo* might reveal mobile vendors hawking lemons, garlic, children's books, candies, watches, puppies, jewelry, "musical" balloons, artificial flowers, thread and plastic tablecloths. The great majority of these vendors are either very young or very old but, generally, are the very poor who subsist on whatever they can make in the *rastro*. Many claim that, upon application, they were denied formal status despite the fact that they have been selling in the *rastro* for some time. Informal vendors may be either *ruteros* or *domingueros* who sell only in the Tetuan *rastro* on Sundays because they have other work during the week.

Although we know the data supplied by the district authorities is incomplete, it does permit the construction of a profile of 60.73% (307 of 489) of the licensed vendors in the Tetuan *rastro*. According to the district data, 76.55% of the vendors are men and 23.45% are women. There seems to be no correlation between the type of product sold and the age or sex of the vendor in the Tetuan *rastrillo*. Men outnumber women in the work force three to one and the most numerous age groups are those between 20-60 years old. Licensed female vendors in the market are concentrated between the ages of 30-49 years of age but a group between 20-24 years years of age is also notable (13.33%). The size of this younger group is due to various factors, most importantly, the impact of the economic crisis on young people finding jobs in the shrunken employment market. Males are numerically concentrated between the ages of 35-59 years of age, and tend to be *ruteros* with considerable tenure in the profession. It is also important to note that the size of the group over 60 years of age (15% of the men and 8% of the women) is another manifestation of the economic crisis; for them, *rastro* vending is now the only source of employment and income.

The majority of licensed *rastro* vendors—71.91% of the men and 63.64% of the women—are married. There are no widowers but widows constitute 7.57% of the latter percentage. Marital data is significant in this context since individual vending licenses are *de facto* family licenses. Direct observation reveals that, while the license may be held by a man, the stand often is run by someone else, a spouse, child or parent. Indeed, stands that are operated by a single individual are in the minority. Most stands have both men and women hawking goods to the public; this makes for a more balanced ratio between the sexes in the market than is indicated by the formal statistics. The observation also correlates highly with the family-based organization of *rastro* vending.

Origin and residence are two important facets of the profile of *rastro* vendors. In light of the fact that Madrid is one of the principle migration targets of the nation, it is not surprising that fully half the *rastro* vendors are from other regions of Spain. It is also important to point out that the majority of the vendors come from rural areas.

Almost two-thirds (66.11%) of the formally registered vendors live in Madrid. Nearly 40% come from Tetuan district itself and the vast majority of the rest from such working class districts as Vallecas, Hortaleza, Fuencarral, Villaverde and Carabanchel. Essentially, these are the districts that have been most seriously affected by the economic crisis. The other one-third of the vendors live outside the municipality of Madrid, in dormitory cities such as Parla, Fuenlabrada, Alcorcón, Leganes and Alcobendas that have engulfed the little villages that originally ringed the capital.

The articles that are sold in the 489 stalls of the Tetuan *rastrillo* in would represent the stock of a major cut-rate store. A full listing of the products fills six, two-column, single space pages. However, the products may be divided into three basic categories—new goods, used goods, and food.

Other than fruits, vegetables, and occasionally animals, there is little spatial organization by product within the market. Only a few vendors, other than those selling fresh or dried fruits and vegetables, specialize in just one kind of product. A stand might have a variety of electronic items such as calculators, batteries, and cassette recorders mixed with sewing materials, stationery, and knickknacks. The variability of the products is also a function of the season as well. In the summer, such articles as sandals, sunshades, bathing suits, tanning lotions, and fans will be plentiful; in winter boots, overcoats, school materials, umbrellas and scarves abound; as Christmas nears, there is a major increase in toy vendors. This variability indicates that vendors are not constrained by the product category listed on their licenses but adjust their merchandise to the season as would any retail merchant. Table 1 lists the categories of merchandise, the number of vendors, and the percentage of the total the number represents.

The *rastro* system and the current economic crisis.

It is clear that, as with many aspects of the Spanish economy today, the *rastro* system is involved in a process of relatively rapid evolution. There are essentially three major dimensions in which these processes of change and their accompanying tensions are most evident; these dimensions correspond to those areas where the *rastro* system plays its most important roles in the current economic crisis in Spain. First, there is the *rastro* system's economic importance to participants, both vendors and clients; secondly, the symbiosis/competition between formal and informal sectors—both

Table 1
RASTRO COMMODITIES AND VENDORS

	PRODUCT Number	VENDORS Percentage
Antiques and used goods	70	14.31
Birds and cages	18	3.68
Books and magazines	33	6.75
Cassettes and records	19	3.89
Ceramics and folk art	16	3.27
Cleaning materials	5	1.10
Clothing	107	21.88
Cosmetics	6	1.15
Dishware, plastics	16	3.27
Eyeglasses	1	.20
Flowers and plants	14	2.86
Fresh/dried fruits, vegetables	52	10.63
Furniture	8	1.64
Hardware	18	3.68
Jewelry and trinkets	20	4.09
Knickknacks	26	5.32
Leather goods	23	4.70
Mattresses	3	.61
Prints and paintings	5	1.05
Product publicity	1	.20
Radios and watches	3	.61
Raffles/lotteries	2	.41
Toys (new and used)	23	4.70
Total Number of Stalls	489	

within the *rastro* system as well as between the latter and the wholesale/retail sectors; and, thirdly, the tension between the State and the *rastro* system over formalization.

The economic importance of the *rastro* system to its participants, vendors and clients alike, is manifest in two major innovations in the system since 1973. In the first place, the *rastro* has shifted from being a marketplace for used goods, antiques and "junk" to a primary emphasis on retailing new merchandise for individuals and households at accessible prices. The competitive pricing system generally permitted by low overhead has meant that the *rastro* offers an attractive economic alternative to standard retailers for buyers who have felt a severe impact due to the economic crisis. While product quality may be lower, *rastro* clients are far more concerned with stretching strained welfare and unemployment benefits or inflation-diminished paychecks than high quality purchases. Though some vendors may offer credit or lower prices to known customers, client loyalty is tenuous, vendor competition is fierce, and price tends to be the deciding factor in any purchase in the *rastro*.

Perhaps even more important is the extent to which the *rastro* system is a source of income to the many left without jobs in the crisis. Indeed, were it not for the informal or submerged economy in general, economic conditions (and, by extension, political unrest) would be considerably worse in Spain. With official statistics for unemployment running at 20% at the time of the study, an editorial in *El País* (1984: 12), the country's major daily newspaper, claimed that a distinction had to be drawn between official unemployment and real unemployment. The editorial convincingly argues that, in large measure, the submerged economy is responsible for the maintenance of relatively peaceful conditions as well as the continued evolution and development of democratic political structures in Spain (1984: 12).

Evidence that the *rastro* system has absorbed many unemployed people comes in part from the national identity cards of formally registered vendors which included the holder's occupation. Very few vendors have listed their occupation as *vendedor ambulante* (traveling vendor); in addition to other skilled trades which have suffered in the crisis, the most frequently mentioned occupations are textile worker, glass worker, printer, carpenter, and silver worker.

During the boom years, it became possible for many workers to make purchases that a few years before would have been unthinkable. Through credit and time purchases, many workers acquired small cars such as Fiats, Seats, Renaults, Avias and other small European models. By the time the crisis hit, many of these cars had been paid off. When the massive lay-offs hit industry, many workers invested their severance pay in merchandise which, with their cars, enabled them to join the *rastro* circuit as a means of making a living. This fact reinforces the position that work in the informal sector often requires considerable resources and is not entirely a situation of free entry (Pahl 1987: 46). In effect, the boom and bust sequence of the Spanish economy between 1961-1975 created conditions which favored entry into the *rastro* system as an adaptation to the crisis.

The *rastro* system also serves an important symbiotic function in the total economic system; it competes with the formal retail and wholesale sector. *Rastro* vendors obtain their wares from both the formal and informal sectors of the wholesale and retail trade. Their contacts with representatives of these sectors, however, are jealously guarded information lest a price or volume advantage be lost.

Goods from the formal sector may come from various sources. Factory or product representatives are used only occasionally because such representatives tend to distrust vendors and their prices tend to be high. Another source of goods is wholesale warehouses, some of which specialize in stocking goods for travelling vendors. Although we found no one who does it on a regular basis, some vendors do, occasionally, purchase their stock from other vendors. Some vendors buy directly from producers—factories, workshops or farmers—and this involves traveling to the locations. Generally speaking, vendors who avoid middlemen by buying directly from producers, purchase goods in larger quantities, sometimes only five or six times a year. Larger purchases entail larger amounts of capital, plus larger and more efficient storage facilities, all of which are beyond the range of most travelling vendors. Most vendors, lacking capital and storage capacity, buy frequently, sometimes even on a daily basis, in small lots. Some vendors purchase their stock from the retail sector. As one informant told us, a vendor will go to the elegant stores on the Gran Via or Serrano (Madrid's 5th Avenue) and buy their recent, after-season goods, usually shoes and clothing. Fashion being the changeable creature it is, these goods (as an informant told us) now have a zero value for the stores so the retailer is willing to move them under cost in order to make room for the current season's stock. In effect, the retailers are selling something that has had its value reduced to zero for much more than zero.

In addition, there are various informal sources of stock for traveling vendors. Clandestine factories, producing everything from sports clothes (complete with designer logos and labels) to bootleg cassette tapes (with black and white photocopies of original covers), as well as shoes, tools, automobile parts and countless other items, are sources of stock for travelling vendors. Used goods, of course, generally circulate through informal circles. And, finally, while it is difficult to prove, it is understood that, certainly, a part of the merchandise sold in any *rastro* may be stolen.

In the last analysis, the strategy pursued by most vendors is to have more than one fairly constant supplier. This strategy, however, does not mean that one will not seek and take advantage of resources found outside one's regular suppliers. Although we cannot speak of formal bookkeeping, vendors are completely aware of the condition of their operations, including inventory, profit margins and competition. Generally, both suppliers and vendors prefer to pay in cash because they like to "keep the books daily."

The *rastro* vendors also compete with the formal retail sector for the poorer market. Relations between retail establishments and the *rastro* vendors may be quite tense, particularly in the area of the *rastro* itself. In attempts to offset the economic advantage which *rastro* vendors enjoy due to low overhead, retail establishments often pressure local authorities to relocate the *rastro* vendors or increase their regulation—the latter usually involving imposing more and higher fees. Formal sector merchants, the most hostile to the *rastros*, have been largely fruit and vegetable stores; they have charged *rastro* vendors with selling contaminated foods, thus causing outbreaks of poisoning. Conflicts between formal sector merchants and *rastro* fruit and vegetable vendors have occasionally become violent.

At present, there is considerable tension between the *rastro* system and the State over the issue of formalization, and there is division among vendors themselves over the degree of formalization appropriate for *rastro* vendors. The State, in the form of city and district governments, has essentially two motives to regulate the *rastro* system. On one hand, the State's somewhat protectionist attitude toward its permanent retail establishments creates policies which tend to diminish the competitive edge which the *rastro* system holds. On the other hand, government—no matter if national, city or district—perceives the *rastro* system largely as a source of revenues in the form of fees, licenses and income taxes. Traditionally, and until as recently as 1975, the *rastro* vendors and system operated relatively independently of governmental control. Sellers went wherever they thought the market would be best and they were charged nominal amounts (though this sometimes consisted of a small fine paid to the police for "occupying public space") to sell in the *rastro*.

The situation in the *rastros* of Spain is much changed today. For many vendors, their greatest current worry is not competition or inflation but the degree of regulation that towns and districts are attempting to impose on them. In the early 1970s, when the government of Madrid adopted a policy designed to rid its streets of vendors, the latter formed a clandestine association to defend their interests. With the return of democracy in 1978, the new legal status of the organization allowed it to expand rapidly. In the 1980s, however, economic troubles and weak leadership have rendered the organization ineffective, and it is now in danger of expiring through lack of member participation. It has offered only occasional resistance to government policies of formalization and regulation.

To sell in any *rastro* today it is necessary to have a license (Ptas.10,000-25,000, roughly US$65-$165), a transport license ($15) plus $1-$2 per day for each market. The license to sell in the *rastro* lasts from six months to a year. As one vendor told us:

> This business of having to buy the license ahead of time is ruining many vendors because it means that the vendor has to commit himself to one route for the whole year. And if a market turns out to be poor, it's very difficult to change because you lose the money you spent on the license and you have to pay the same amount to another *rastro*. This factor is inhibiting competition between vendors and markets and, in the long run, it will hurt the consumer because without competition prices won't be self-regulating and they will go up.

It is also worth mentioning that the average vendor is paying roughly $50 a month in daily rental fees which, coupled with the long term fees and license charges, adds significantly to the overhead, thus driving up prices.

Another dimension of the formalization process involves the payment of income taxes (Mingione 1983). In order to obtain a Treasury Ministry license, which is necessary to obtain the municipal vending license, a vendor must register with the *Ministerio de Hacienda* (Treasury Ministry). Once formally on the government books, the vendor is liable for payment of income taxes and is obligated to keep some form of records to substantiate income levels over time. The ability of those in the submerged economy to evade payment of national income taxes is one side of a general dilemma faced by the government. On the one hand, with some estimates (Tamames 1985) placing it as high as 33% of GDP (1981), the informal economy is large enough that it represents a significant loss of income to the government in unpaid taxes. On the other hand, attempts to regulate this sector may drive some individuals out of business, thereby reducing the difference between official and real unemployment. The closer real unemployment gets to official unemployment, the greater the probability of serious political unrest becomes. Regarding the *rastro* system, the government seems to

228

vacillate between greater incorporation into and regulation of those within the formal sector versus permitting relative ease of access for informal vendors and, for the public, to the goods/services provided.

The vendor population of the *rastro* system is also divided over the issue of formalization. Indeed, there is some conflict within the system itself between the formally registered vendors and the unlicensed vendors. There are both material and ideological concerns at work in this conflict. The licensed vendors pay the series of fees already mentioned, and the unlicensed vendors either do not pay at all or they pay only the day rent. The licensed vendors believe this lack of payment constitutes an unfair advantage. In general, the unlicensed vendors are the poorest in the *rastro*—old ragpickers, young people out of work, Gypsies, and others dealing on an occasional basis in either used or, perhaps, seasonal goods. In short, unlicensed vendors tend to be those who cannot afford to or do not understand why they should pay for a whole year's license. Ideologically, the licensed vendors object because they see themselves as legitimate businessmen who are being grouped in the public eye with the unlicensed vendors who are portrayed as marginal, as thieves, "hippies," and Gypsies. Indeed, the licensed vendors, many of whom have been selling in the system for years, have suffered from and are fully aware of the image of marginality with which they are perceived. This image notwithstanding, one informant spoke for vendors from both groups when commenting:

> It is better to sell, even without a license, than to rob and become part of the crime problem....Then, even though it makes competition tougher, it's better to let someone who has no other way to live sell in the market.

Conclusion.

Many people are selling in the *rastro* because they have no other alternative and will leave the *rastro* system the moment they find other work. Lozano (1983: 349) notes a similar tendency among vendors in a California flea market. Although licensed vendors extoll the virtues and freedoms of being independent, many do not wish their children to follow in their footsteps because of the negative imagery connected with the work. They urge their children to study, to find other work, knowing that if things do not go well they can always come back to the *rastro*, despite the low prestige it holds in the public eye.

In essence, the conflict that exists between the licensed and unlicensed vendors is a product of the policies of the authorities. Although we deal explicitly with the Tetuan *rastro*, currently this conflict is appearing in almost all *rastros*. The attempts to formalize and regulate the *rastro* has limited the number of licenses awarded at precisely the time at which the demand for licences is increasing because of economic need. In Tetuan, for example, in a period of three months some 80 people applied for licenses and only 17 were granted them. The logical consequence, therefore, is for the number of unlicensed vendors in the *rastro* to increase. Over and above those who are refused licences are those who do not even apply, largely because the small amounts they earn in the *rastro* to live on would not be enough to pay for their licenses. These are the *lumpen* (literally, "trash") of the *rastro*, the ragpickers, the vendors of used and unusable goods, in effect, those who represent little competition for the professional licensed vendors who sell new merchandise.

The conflict between licensed and unlicensed vendors when it appears is due as well to the lax attitude of enforcement of policies in the *rastro*. Generally, strolling through the *rastro* on Sundays, the police don't bother the unlicensed vendors, asking only those who they are sure have licenses to present them. Occasionally, they will "invite" an unlicensed vendor to leave and the hawker will obligingly retire, only to reappear within minutes as the police continue their *paseo*. Other illegals—generally those whose "stall" consists of a crate of small items (e.g., garlic, lemons, nail polish, key rings) placed in the middle of the street between the lines of stalls—can disappear and reappear quickly enough to avoid even the modest "invitation" of the police to abandon the *rastro*.

Thus, in the context of the economic crisis in Spain the *rastro* system plays out its role as a major supplier of economically accessible goods to the working poor and as an important source of employment and income for those most victimized by current conditions. As an early element of the informal sector, the *rastro* currently is enmeshed in both symbiotic and competitive relationships with the formal sector but itself is experiencing the tension between formal and informal sectors in the context of governmental attempts at regularization. The government, in turn, must be cautious to balance its needs for income in the form of unpaid taxes and fees against the very real possibility of major social unrest ensuing from higher levels of unemployment which could result from its policies of regulation of the *rastro* system and the informal sector in general.

References.

Beltrán Antolín, Joaquín, María Angeles Lorenzo Quintela, María Victoria Martínez Saez, María Teresa Pedruelo Pedruelo, María Dolores Rosell Vaquero
1985   Estudio socio-antropológico de la venta ambulante en el rastrillo de Tetuan. Manuscript.

Bienefeld, Manfred
1979   Urban Unemployment: A Historical Perspective. In R. Bromley and C. Gerry, eds., Casual Work and Poverty in Third World Cities. Chichester: John Wiley and Sons, pp. 27-44

Bromley, Ray
1978   Introduction. The Urban Informal Sector: Is it Worth Discussing? World Development 6: 1033-1039.

Campos Romero, Maria Lourdes
n.d.   Estudio geográfico del rastro Madrileño. Madrid.

Corral Raya, J. and J. M. Sanz Garcia
1953   Madrid es así. Madrid.

El Pais
1984   El paro, la pobreza, y la economia sumergida. June 3: 12. Madrid.

Harrison, Joseph
1985   The Spanish Economy in the Twentieth Century. New York: St. Martin's Press.

de las Herâs, Jesus
1984   El Ayuntamiento ha olividado el control del mercado libre, sequin vendedores del Rastro. Madrid: El País March 28: 22.

Lieberman, Sima
1982   The   Contemporary   Spanish   Economy: A   Historical
       Perspective. London: George Allen and Unwin.

Lozano, Beverley
1983   Informal   Sector   Workers: Walking   Out   the   System's
       Front Door?   International Journal of Urban and
       Regional Research 7: 340-362.

Mingione, Enzo
1983   Industrialization, Restructuring and the   Survival
       Strategies of the Working Class.   International Journal
       of Urban and Regional Research 7: 311-339.

Pahl, Raymond E.
1987   Does Jobless Mean   Workless?   Unemployment and
       Informal Work. In L. A. Ferman, S. Henry, and M.
       Hoyman, eds., The Informal Economy. The Annals of
       the American Academy of Political and Social Science
       493: 36-46.

Salmon, Keith
1985   Spain. National Report No.103. International Tourism
       Quarterly. London: The Economist Publications Ltd.

Tamames, Ramon
1985   The Spanish Economy: An Introduction. New York:
       St. Martin's Press.

BLACK MARKETS AND WELFARE IN SCANDINAVIA: SOME METHODOLOGICAL AND EMPIRICAL ISSUES

Gunnar Viby Mogensen
Program Director, Economist
Rockwool Fondens Forskningsprojekt

Introduction.

The phenomenon commonly labeled as the "black" economy has played an increasing role in the public debate in many industrialized countries recently—sometimes under other headings (e.g., "informal economy," "black work," "underground economy," or "moonlighting").[1] At the same time, the phenomenon has attracted only minor attention from the social sciences in Scandinavia.

Exceptions to this rule are, for Norway, studies by Isachsen and Strøm (1982) and Isachsen et al (1985); in Sweden, several studies by Hansson (1982); and, in Denmark, works by Bonke (1986), Viby Mogensen (1985), Stetkär (1983), and Aage (1984).

These last Danish studies, based on interviews carried out by the Danish Central Bureau of Statistics and the Danish National Institute of Social Research, within representative samples of the adult population, have been repeated (1986) and extended (on-going in 1988).

This report will focus on the methodological and theoretical issues that have emerged in the course of the Danish research. It is stressed that some of these issues presumably can be dealt with best by the interaction between economists and anthropologists—of the

---

[1]As I will note below, these terms usually apply to a broader range of phenomena than will be addressed here.

sort demonstrated, for instance, at the Society for Economic Anthropology meeting in Knoxville in 1988.

Concept and methodology.

Danish studies have concentrated on the informal markets for goods and services, excluding illegal activities. The basic subject of the studies therefore are productive activities that should be included in the Gross National Product (GNP) but are usually left out because the activities are not statistically tracked or available to the tax or customs authorities.

Figure 1
CONCEPTS SURROUNDING "THE BLACK ACTIVITY" AS MEASURED IN THE DANISH INTERVIEW STUDIES 1980-1988

Formal (declared economy)	Household: Goods		Measured in practice in the GNP	Total (theoretical) GNP
	The declared part of the market economy			
Informal economy (non-declared economy)	The non-declared part of the market economy	"Usual under declaration" (full price)	Partly measured in practice in the GNP	
		Black activity (less than full price)		
	Households: Services		Not part of the GNP	

As shown in Figure 1, a further subdivision of categories has been carried out, splitting "the non-declared part of the market economy" in two, depending on whether a full price is paid—as when a shopkeeper gets his normal price for a basket of goods, says goodbye to the customer, and places the money directly in his wallet; or, alternatively, when both parties to the transaction know about the lack of declaration, split the money spared from income tax, value added taxes, and possibly expenses of the firm which usually performs the job or activity in question. Black markets or the black economy thus defined are, therefore, only a part of the informal sector, which also includes normal one-sided tax and customs cheating—and, of course, the service production inside the households. Do-it-yourself-work falls outside the concept used here.

The main reason for concentrating our research on this (perhaps) rather narrow concept is, first, that only this part of the non-declared economy has a clear relevance in the field of labor market research. While full-price under-declaration usually will have no effect on the demand side of the market, and be without clear effect on the supply side, non-declared activities at less than full price will create their own, new markets, including labor markets. When both seller and buyer in the transaction know or assume that the activity will remain undeclared, a special price is formed, giving both a lower cost for the buyer (thus creating a special demand) and a higher net payment to the seller (thus calling forth a special supply). Secondly, the non-declared markets with a special, lower price level, seem to have been growing much faster than the rest of the non-declared part of the GNP, at least in Denmark in the last 10-20 years.

It should be stressed that the definition chosen raises several questions. The main problem is that a distinction between "black activity" and "unusual declaration" can be made only on the basis of a registration of the knowledge or assumption on both sides of the market of the lack of declaration, i.e., a registration which the usual administrative and statistical registers cannot give the researcher. Interviews or participant observation are the only methods available, and their results cannot be compared to the data used by the National Accounting Office in the Central Bureau of Statistics. In distinguishing between "black activity" and the category of services produced in the household, which includes services provided one's family and do-it-yourself activities, one encounters at least two serious problems: (1) There is a possible element of non-reciprocated gift giving in an activity; (2) how to define "household." When is the person performing an undeclared activity to be excluded from the category of "black activity participant," because the individual must be reckoned a member of the household that receives the output of the activity?

With regard to gifts, in the Danish interview studies, any undeclared activity of economic value crossing the borderline of "the household" was included—even if the so-called payment was simply the expectation of some reciprocity. Interviewers were instructed to accept answers from the respondents relating to activities as gifts—e.g., free services "just done because we're friends"—only after probing and only if the argument for "no economic value in the transaction" was very strong. The instructions to the interviewers included an example of an activity of economic value, chosen from one of the pilot studies. This involved a farmer, who took full care of a horse for a neighbor and, as well, daily transported the neighbor's children to and from school. On the other hand, daily shopping for a seriously handicapped relative was used as an example of activities without economic value in the sense of the project.

With regard to the household concept, an undeclared economic activity of the respondent was counted as "do-it-yourself" if it was performed for somebody from the family living at the same postal address as the respondent. If it is performed for any other person (or firm), it was judged as an activity of the black economy.

It should be stressed that the statistical "solutions" chosen with regard to the concept "gift" (and also, perhaps, the concept "household") raise several serious methodological questions. One problem is that the threshold for a transaction being judged as having "no economic value" might be very different among respondents in different social and geographical groups. Thus, even a trained, professional corps of interviewers, thoroughly instructed by the researcher, cannot ensure the application of a uniform concept of "gift." These methodological questions are good examples of the need in present research (mentioned above) for further interaction between the theory and methodology of economics and anthropology.

A survey institution with highly qualified interviewers and high response rates was sought to collect the data. In 1980, 1984, 1986 and 1988 the combined interviewer section of the Central Bureau of Statistics and the Danish National Institute of Social Research was asked to include questions in its multipurpose questionnaire to representative samples of Danes aged 16 and older relative to participation on the seller's side of the black markets for goods and services. The section in the questionnaire starts:

> The next questions are related to different extra incomes, including that from what is usually called black activity. Many things indicate that a large part of the population accepts black activity. It could be tax evasion in the form of "moonlighting without tax," but it could also be exchanges of services between friends, neighbors and members of the family (except for those living with you). When you answer the questions, remember to include this last type of undeclared activity.[2]

The interviewers then stressed that we were looking for cases, where buyer and seller were aware of or assumed a missing declaration. They then asked whether the respondent had been engaged in this sort of activity within the last 12 months, and whether cash was involved in the payment. Up to and including 1986, the only other information at hand for the study were the usual background variables (e.g., sex, age, education, job type, income). In 1988, the respondents also were asked to give information on type, cost (e.g., of materials), duration, and income from the undeclared activity, as well as detailed information on the effects of this extra income on the consumption pattern of the household.

In 1983, the same institution asked a series of questions on activities as buyers on the black market: Type, price, form of payment, total expense, satisfaction with the activity performed, and opinion on the cause of buying in the informal sector and alternatives, if this special market had not been available.

---

[2]My translation.

In the series of projects running 1980-1986, the size of the sample has varied—between 2000 and 3100 interviews obtained, with a response rate of 75-85%. As the sample is drawn from the rather well-developed Danish administrative data registers, the characteristics of respondents and non-respondents are known. The group of non-respondents is typical for Danish surveys: Metropolitan, outside the work force, or unskilled labor. If this group had answered as did the respondents of the same sex, age and marital status, the frequency for average participation on the black market would have been raised in 1984 by 0.2%, though less in the other years.

Interviewing in April and October 1988 was carried out by telephone interviewing utilizing two multipurpose questionnaires. Three thousand interviews were expected although a slightly decreasing willingness in the population over the last several years to give answers to structured questionnaires have reduced this number somewhat.

Survey data.

The share of positive answers regarding sales in the black market rose from 8% (1980) to 13% (1984) and 14% (1986). In all three cases, the results must be evaluated as the minimum levels. Based on data on numbers of hours worked on the black markets from a somewhat similar survey in 1982, relative to the known total number of registered hours worked in Denmark in the same year, the frequency for 1986 corresponds to a black market in Denmark equivalent to about 3.9% of the GNP. The other, non-analyzed part of the black sector, the average or "usual" underdeclaration can presumably be estimated as, at least, a further 1.6% of the GNP. This gives a total Danish non-declared sector of at least 5.5% of the GNP.

Concerning the buyers' side of the black market in the 1983 survey, 19% of the respondents said that they had been buyers of black work within the last 12 months. Of the work performed, 46% belonged to the building sector, with repair work (especially painting) as the most dominant group. Services such as child care, garden work, cleaning, and hairdressing amounted to 29%, while the rest of the black work market was dominated by repair work (especially on cars) and activities of trade, e.g., marketing meat from farms. The average payment for the transactions on the black market was 770 Dkr. (c. US$120 dollars), for goods and services that would have cost about 1400 Dkr. on the normal market.

With regard to the payment procedure, the data showed that cash was used in 40%-50% of the cases. The exact figure varies with the method of measurement. In most of the rest of the cases the payment consisted of bartering services, delivered immediately or later.

Using log-linear and other statistical tests, it was found that the variables with the strongest effect on the probability of participating in the black market as a buyer were: ownership of a dwelling, length of working hours, and, to some extent, age. In 1983, the typical consumer on the Danish black market was a person in the age group 20-40 years, a dwelling owner, and worked long weekly hours.

Though respondents gave a range of answers, the main reasons given for buying in the informal sector were: (1) The high tax level[3] mentioned by 51% of the respondents; (2) the high costs of hiring a skilled worker from a firm for repair work (41%); (3) stagnant or falling real disposable income.

On the seller's side of the market, the 1986 survey showed that age and occupational group especially play a role. The number of respondents who had performed black work within the past year fell significantly with rising age. The frequency was, for instance, 31% for persons below 20, 15% for persons in the age group 30-39, and 5% for persons between 60-69 years.

---

[3]According to OECD figures, in 1981-1985, the tax level was c.55% in Denmark and the other Scandinavian countries, compared to c. 45% in Western Germany, and just over 30% in the United States.

With regard to occupational status it turned out to be important to include persons from outside the work force. Those attending school and university have very high frequencies—18% for university students and 30% for secondary school children. Inside the work force, participation in the black market was present in all groups. But the frequency is especially high for skilled workers (30%), and rather low for self-employed outside agriculture (13%) and white collar workers (10%).

Relative to the probability of being a seller in Denmark's black market, variables other than age and occupational status play a minor role—though women have a somewhat lower frequency than men (10% against 17%). Further, frequency of involvement rises slowly, depending on the degree of urbanization and geographic variables—ranging from 11% in Copenhagen in eastern Denmark to 23% in rural districts in western and northern Jutland.

The Danish results from the interviews cannot be directly compared to data published for Norway and Sweden, as the latter data are gathered by using a concept equivalent to "the total non-declared sector," unfortunately minus non-cash incomes (both countries). The best documented study (for Norway, Isachsen et al 1982) refers only to labor incomes. In this study, the authors found that 18% of 877 adult persons, representing a response rate of 73% on mail questionnaires, answered "Yes" to a question about cash income from non-declared work within the last 12 months. While, the exclusion of non-labor incomes has lowered this Norwegian figure somewhat, the figure must have been increased substantially by the inclusion of "usual underdeclaration," i.e., undeclared, full-priced activities.

On the other hand, a rough comparison between the Scandinavian countries is not totally impossible. If one accepts the attempt above to supplement the Danish data with an estimate of "the usual underdeclaration," where the minimum estimate given is based on reasonably reliable statistical information, the Danish results indicating a total non-declared sector of "at least 5.5% of GNP" can be compared with "between 4 and 6%" in Norway cited by Isachsen and Strøm (1985), and figures from Hansson for Sweden within the same interval. This rather identical Scandinavian level of around 5% of the GNP can then be compared with what appear as qualified estimates for West Germany (Kirschgässner 1983) and the United States (Simon and Witte 1982) of 4%-12% of GNP, and percentages for southern Europe well above 20%.

It should be stressed that a Danish non-declared sector of 5.5% or more of GNP is not equivalent to a similar underestimation of the Danish GNP figures (cf. Stetkär 1983). As indicated in Figure 1 above, part of the non-declared sector is, in practice, already measured in the Danish GNP. The main reason is that most intermediate consumption in the non-declared sector has already been included in the GNP through the production or the import statistics. We are able to suggest an interesting thesis if the following three assumptions are true: First, the not unusual relation between wage and other expenditures of 2:1 in the building sector of the non-declared market is general for the market; secondly, the effects of some respondents in the surveys presented here not to report actual off-the-books activities; and, finally, the attempts of the national accountants to adjust for the non-declaration more or less cancel out each other. If these are valid premises, the following conclusion may be drawn: The underestimation of the Danish GNP would amount to around two-thirds of the figure for the total non-declared sector—or approximately 3.5%. At the beginning of the present decade, the similar measure would have been around 2%.

The black market and welfare in Denmark.

One of the most serious welfare problems in Denmark in the last ten to fifteen years has been the very high level of unemployment. It might be a reasonable question to ask whether society could convert all or part of what appears to be a rapidly increasing amount of black activity to "normal" activity—with a consequent decrease in unemployment? Or is the problem artificial since, in reality, many of the unemployed are employed as workers or sellers in the black economy?

If the approximately 200 million hours of work in the black sector in Denmark in 1984 could be converted to work for the unemployed, 100,000 new full-time jobs would have been created, and an unemployment rate of 10.8% would be reduced to about 7.8%. Such a possibility would, however, be very difficult to implement. In order to remove the causes for undeclared work, it would be necessary to reduce the difference in price between the black and the normal market, e.g., by reducing the rates in the income tax. The analysis in the study indicates that such a reduction actually could have some effect. But the effect is reduced by the fact that the difference in price in Denmark seems very considerable. For example, in 1983 the normal price level often was found to be 80%-100% above the price actually paid on the black market. At the same time, many buyers in the latter sector stated in the surveys that, for them, the alternative to the black market is not necessarily the normal market. Instead, 34% would have covered their needs by do-it-yourself work, and 30% simply would have delayed the solution of the problem.

A large part of the literature on the informal economy presumes that among the unemployed the frequency of participation on the seller side of the markets is significantly higher than average (cf. for Norway, Isachsen and Strøm 1985; for Western Germany, Petersen 1982; for the United States, Gutmann 1978; and Simon and Witte 1982; and, for the industrialized world generally, OECD 1981).

In most cases, the data behind this presumption are scattered. Thus, some of the conclusions may be a result of the material available or the way it is analyzed rather than social reality. The U.K., for example, appears to be an exception to one of the basic assumptions about the informal economy—that it serves as a magnet for the under- and unemployed. Pahl's (1984) research has shown that in the U. K. the informal sector appears to attract employed workers more frequently than unemployed.

The 1980 Danish results also defied the general assumption; in this country, too, the frequency of informal sector participation was the same for the population overall as for the unemployed. In studies done in 1984 and 1986, however, the frequency for participation by the unemployed moved up to 17%, i.e., slightly above the average of 13%-14%. If the frequency stays close to the average for the population, one reason could be that Denmark has one of the world's highest levels of unemployment compensation (up to 90% for unskilled workers). Another reason could be the rather efficient bureaucratic control system. Finally, it may be that long-term unemployment, often seen as a strong cause for an especially high frequency of black work among the unemployed, is less prevalent in Denmark than in most other industrialized countries.

Another dominant problem in the discussion on welfare policy in Denmark is the intention to stop what is usually called the increasing discrepancy between rich and poor in the personal income distribution. In fact, measured in any statistical reliable way, the discrepancies have been decreasing or stagnant for several decades as well as in recent years (cf., e.g., Egemose 1985). This trend has not influenced the political decision to try to use a still higher and progressive personal income tax in an attempt to solve what is considered a problem of increasing income polarization.

Figure 2
INCOME MATCHED TO EXTENT OF
BLACK MARKET BUYING

Income in Dkr[4]	% admitting to buying on the black market 1987
0-59,000	15%
60,000-99,999	22
100,000-149,999	25
150,000 and over	27

To the extent that the personal income tax has a responsibility for the seemingly strong growth of the black economic sector, this part of the Danish welfare policy seems to be nearing a dead end.

---

[4]In July, 1989 the Danish krone (Dkr.) was priced at $.0728; thus, 100,000 Dkr.would equal about US$13,731.00.

The results from the research here have shown that the frequency with which sellers of goods and services participate in the informal economy is practically constant through all the income intervals; within the population above age 25, the frequency rises with higher income. This last tendency is found also on the buyer's side of the market. This, of course, means that the possibility of getting the goods and services cheap—and thus the possibilities for increasing the consumption on the normal market—are increasing for the better and best placed groups in the population, the very social segment for whom the tax policy was assumed to reduce the consumption possibilities.

Conclusions.

As has been noted by all who have attempted to study the black economy, there are many difficulties in arriving at any sound conclusions about its size, its structure, participants and their participation—in short, practically every element of the sector. Not the least problematic are the assumptions and the models that analysts bring to bear on those scattered and (unfortunately) questionable data that *are* available. I have tried to clarify these aspects from the economic perspective for, in particular, Denmark in order that those who approach the question may have an enlarged understanding of the issues confronting those concerned with the more practical issues of, say, government budgeting and policy-making.

References.

Bonke, Jens
1986   Husholdningsøkonomi. En teoretisk og empirisk belysning af husholdningsproduktionen. Memo No. 157. The Economic Institute, University of Copenhagen.

Egmose, Sven
1985   Udviklingen i den personlige indkomstfordeling. In Sven Egmose, Lisbeth Egmose, Gunnar Viby Mogensen og Hans Aage, Uligheden, politikerne og befolkningen. København: Social forskningsinstituttets publikation No. 139, pp. 38-90.

Grazia, R. D.
1984   Clandestine Employment. The Situation in the Industrialized Market Economy Countries. Geneva: International Labor Office.

Gutmann, P. M.
1979   Are the Unemployed, Unemployed? Financial Analyst Journal Sept/ Oct.: 26-27.

Hansson, I.
1982   The Underground Economy in a High Tax Country: The Case of Sweden. In V.Tanzi, ed., The Underground Economy in the United States and Abroad. Lexington KY: D. C. Heath, pp. 233-243.

Isachsen, A. J., J. T. Klovland and S. Strøm
1982   The Hidden Economy in Norway. In V. Tanzi, ed., The Underground Economy in the United States and Abroad. Lexington KY: D. C. Heath, pp. 209-231.

Isachsen, A. J. and S. Strøm
1985   The Size and Growth of the Hidden Economy in Norway. The Review of Income and Wealth 31: 21-38.

Kirschgässner, G.
1983   Size and Development of the West German Shadow
        Economy, 1955-1980. Zeitschrift für gesamte
        Staatswissenschaft 139: 197-214.

Organization for Economic Cooperation and Development (OECD)
1981   The Hidden Economy in the Context of the National
        Accounts. Mimeo. Paris: OECD.

Olwig, Karen Fog, S. Sampson.
1986   Danmarks anden økonomi og kultur. Uden regning.
        Charlottenlund: H. Rosinank.

Pahl, R. E.
1984   Divisions of Labor. Oxford: Basil Blackwell.

Petersen, Hans-Georg
1982   Size of the Public Sector, Economic Growth and the
        Informal Economy. The Review of Income and
        Wealth 28: 191-215.

Simon, C. P. and A. D. Witte.
1982   Beating the System: The Underground Economy.
        Boston: Auburn House.

Stetkär, K.
1983   Den sorte sektor i nationalregnskabs-sammenhäng.
        Samfundsøkonomen 2: 18-24.

Tanzi V., ed.
1982   The Underground Economy in the United States and
        Abroad. Lexington KY: D. C. Heath.

Viby Mogensen, Gunnar
1985   Sort arbejde i Danmark. Copenhagen: [With ques-
        tionnaires and an English summary]. Study No. 9,
        Institute of Economics, The Copenhagen High School
        of Commerce: Nyt Nordisk Forlag Arnold Busck.

Aage, H.
1984   Makroøkonomiske virkninger af uformel økonomi.
        Økonomi og Politik 58: 294-305.

SELF-EMPLOYMENT VERSUS WAGE EMPLOYMENT IN HONG KONG: A RECONSIDERATION OF THE URBAN ECONOMY

Josephine Smart
Department of Anthropology
University of Calgary

Introduction.

Street trading is one of the most studied informal economic activities since Hart (1973) first introduced the concept of an "informal sector" more than two decades ago.[1] The majority of such studies are conducted in developing countries in Africa, Latin America and Southeast Asia. There are several reasons for this pattern of regional localization. First, street traders exist in vast numbers in developing countries, partly due to the increasing participation of primary producers in the cash economy and partly due to the limited employment opportunities in urban centers for the rapidly growing population of rural migrants and urban natives. People concerned with economic development, poverty and survival strategies by the poor in Third World countries are naturally drawn to the dynamics of informal activities (Bairoch 1973; Banerjee 1982, Bromley 1982; Bromley and Gerry 1979; CUSO 1987; Fapohunda, et al. 1978; Hart 1973; IDRC 1975; Joshi, et al. 1976; Lessinger 1985; Lomnitz 1977; McGee 1973; McGee and Yeung 1977; Peattie 1982; Remy 1982; Rogerson and Beavon 1982; Tse 1974).

---

[1] There is a long standing debate and criticism of the analytical utility of the concept of "informal sector" (see Bromley 1978; Davies 1979; Drakakis-Smith 1981; Moser 1978; Sinclair 1978). At the 1988 Society for Economic Anthropology (SEA) Conference on The Informal Economy, there were many outstanding discussions of the ongoing evolution of conceptual approaches in the study of the informal economy in developing and developed countries.

Secondly, developing countries are ideal testing grounds for the study of the articulation of modes of production, in particular that between capitalism and non-capitalist forms of production such as street hawking and petty commodity production. The focus of these studies is structured around the concept of domination and subordination (Chevalier 1982; Foster-Carter 1978; Long and Richardson 1978; Moser 1978). It is suggested that the petty commodity producers—such as garbage pickers in Cali, cottage industrialists in Peru and commission hawkers—are dominated by capitalist enterprises that control their level of return to labor, their access to the market for the commodities they produce, and their access to capital. In effect, the capitalist domination imposes significant constraints in the process of capital accumulation and economic expansion in petty commodity production (Scott 1979; Birkbeck 1978; Bromley 1978).

There is a widespread conception that informal activities are marginal economic endeavors undertaken by people who are "forced" into it by unemployment and poverty. This image is compatible with the observed economic situation in many developing countries (CUSO 1987). However, it is open to debate whether this simplistic relationship between participation in the informal economy and unemployment holds true in all societies each with its specific history of economic development. If unemployment is the fundamental cause in the emergence and persistence of street trading activities, then one can expect the level of street trading to decline as wage employment opportunities open up. Recent evidence suggests that such is not the case. Lessinger's (1985) study of market traders in Madras indicates that many rural migrants turn to street hawking to escape the insecurity of casual wage labour. Similarly, Rogerson and Beavon's (1982) study in Soweto reveals that many African Blacks resort to street trading in order to escape the marginality of low paying wage employment. Their findings suggest that resistance to proletarianization, rather than unemployment, may be a significant factor in people's decisions to enter street hawking in some situations.

The purpose of this paper is to explore the complexity of the phenomenon of resistance to proletarianization in the specific context of Hong Kong's development 40 years ago from a non-industrialized *entrepôt* to the highly successful export economy it is today. In doing so, it provides a framework for a better understanding of the forces contributing to the persistence of a thriving street hawking economy in contemporary Hong Kong despite its consistently low unemployment rate and strong economic performance in manufacturing, financing and trade. This paper is part of a larger study which involved two periods of research in Hong Kong from May to August 1982, and from September 1983 to April 1985.[2]

Hong Kong: The economic miracle.

Hong Kong was little more than a barren, rocky island when it was ceded to Great Britain in 1842 after the Opium War. The harbor, its only redeeming feature at that time, has since developed into one of the most active on the international scene, and the busiest container port in the world. Hong Kong is now recognized as a major manufacturing, financial and trading center which, in 1986, provided employment for nearly all its available work force of 2.5 million (*Hong Kong* 1987).

As recently as 40 years ago, the small British Colony was besieged by underdevelopment and increasing an number of refugees and returnees from China after 1949 and the end of the Japanese occupation in 1945. At that time, the large pool of unemployed labor was a liability. Later, the same liability became one of the major assets in Hong Kong's economic development. The export-oriented manufacturing sector is the cornerstone of Hong Kong's economy. It produces a wide array of products to specification for overseas buyers—among them, textiles garments, toys, electronics, footwear, and a multitude of plastic products. Other than a short period of high unemployment (12%) during the oil crisis in 1973, Hong Kong has, since 1961, enjoyed near full employment, with low

---

[2]The research was made possible by an Ontario Graduate Scholarship (1983-84), a Social Sciences and Humanities Research Council of Canada Doctoral Fellowship (1984-85) and a grant-in-aid from the Center of International Studies at the University of Toronto. I would like to thank The Center for Asian Studies (University of Hong Kong) for its generous provision of facilities for the period 1983 to 1985.

unemployment rates ranging from 0.7% in 1961 to 2.2% in 1986 (Woronoff 1980: 81-83; *Hong Kong* 1987: 52; Hopkins 1971).

Hong Kong's economic development has little to do with natural resources or agriculture. This British colony—an area of a mere 1070 square kilometers—is made up of the main island of Victoria, the Kowloon Peninsula, the New Territories, and 235 islands of varying sizes. Agricultural land is concentrated in the New Territories but there has been a decline of the local peasant economy as a result of the twin factor of industrialization (which pulls away labor from agriculture) and stiff competition from imported produce from China (the biggest supplier of Hong Kong's food products). In the developed zones of Hong Kong Island and in Kowloon, much of the area is land reclaimed from the ocean front, a symptom of the acute scarcity of land in the urban spaces (Lands Department 1984: 7). At the end of 1986, there were 5.59 million residents in Hong Kong, making it one of the most densely populated cities in the world (*Hong Kong* 1987: 291). While the overall density per square kilometer was 5192, many urban districts had a population density over 20,000 persons per square kilometer. A dramatic population growth in Hong Kong from 1.8 million in 1947 to 4.4 million in 1976 was largely a result of immigration, both legal and illegal, from China (Sit 1981: 3-8). Over 98% of the population is Chinese by origin.

The industrial revolution that began in Hong Kong in the 1950s was not a matter of choice or planning but, rather, a "fortuitous coming together of circumstances and a seizing of opportunities" (Hong Kong 1987: 4). First, the inflow of investment capital, technical know-how and skilled labor power from Shanghai after 1949 was instrumental in driving Hong Kong towards industrialization as the importance of the *entrepôt* trade declined (Brown 1971; Chen 1984; Cooper 1980: 12-13). The Shanghai textile industry found new roots in Hong Kong, followed by other lines of industries—metals, plastics, clothing, artificial flowers and electronics. Secondly, the cheap cost of production in Hong Kong helped it to find a niche in the world market by manufacturing to specification for industrialized countries. Hong Kong was one of the new frontiers of capitalism in the 1950s and, as with South Korea and China today, provided cheap manufactured goods to the Western countries. By 1969, the domestic exports of Hong Kong exceeded the total exports of India (Brown 1971: 3). Since the early 1970s, more than four-fifths of domestic production has been for export. In 1986, the domestic export value was HK$154 billion, an increase from HK$130 billion in 1985 and HK$138 billion in 1984 (*Hong Kong* 1987:323). Despite the world-wide stock market crash in October 1987, Hong Kong experienced a 13% growth in GNP for that year—a clear indication of the strength of its economy (Cottrell 1988: 85-86).

Hong Kong's success in the world market is not just luck; it is built upon a large amount of hardship and struggle. Paramount to the success of Hong Kong's export economy is the industry's extreme flexibility in meeting changes in the world market demand, its relatively cheap labor costs, and the continuing peaceful relationship between management and labor (Brown 1971; Lui 1984; Lin et al. 1979 and 1980; Rabushka 1979; Riedel 1974; Woronoff 1980). Of specific relevance to this paper is the issue related to the conditions of employment and relative low return to labor in industrial employment.

Table 1
LABOR FORCE PARTICIPATION RATES (LFPR) OF POPULATION AGED 15 AND ABOVE IN HONG KONG
(1981 Census)

YEAR	LFPR	
	Male	Female
1961	90.4%	36.8%
1971	84.7	42.8
1981	82.5	49.5

The remarkable features of the work force in Hong Kong are (1) its large size (2.5 million in 1986); (2) a high labor participation rate (see Table 1) which surpasses that of many industrialized countries (ILO 1984); and (3) its high productivity. Woronoff comments that, "Hong Kong's labor force works hard, long, well and productively" and "the average Hong Kong worker puts in twice as much time as the average Western worker" (1980: 84-85).

The hardship and exploitation experienced by the workers during Hong Kong's early stages of industrial development are well documented by England and Rear (1975). It is a familiar story of the structural and voluntary exploitation characteristic of the early stages of industrial development. The working conditions for the workers in Britain during the first Industrial Revolution as described by Marx, Engels, or Thompson were strikingly similar to the situation in early post-war Hong Kong. In some Hong Kong industries, the sweat shop image still exists today largely because space shortages make even adequate improvements difficult in factories located in high-rise industrial buildings, squatter areas and crowded, mixed-use urban districts. Some industries—particularly those in electronics and garment manufacturing where quality and guaranteed reliability are paramount—are offering air-conditioned working environments and higher wages in an attempt to keep their staff from leaving for better wages or working conditions in other enterprises. The lot of the proletariat in Hong Kong has improved significantly as a result of increases in real wages and a wide range of legislation introduced by the government to protect and promote workers' entitlement to various benefits. Most Western workers, however, would be less than impressed by the protection, e.g., maternity leave—without pay; a prohibition on child labor—defined as those under 14; paid sick leave—of one day per month; a mandatory vacation—of seven consecutive days a year; plus severance pay, restrictions on the length of the work day to eight hours, and the number of overtime work hours to no more than 200 hours a year (Woronoff 1980: 86-93). Due to the generally weak enforcement of labor legislations, the real improvement for the working class in Hong Kong is difficult to assess (Ng 1983).

One undisputed improvement is the increase in real wages. In the period 1960-67, real wages in industrial employment went up by an impressive 110%. But even more impressive is the 200% increase in labor productivity during the same period and the sharp rise in return to investment from 19.5% per year in 1960 to 47.4% a year in 1967 (Lin et al. 1980: 14). If not the only such locale, Hong

Kong is probably one of the few places in which investors can recuperate their investment within three to four years. In comparison, the increase in wage rate for manufacturing workers in 1986 was only 4.1% (*Hong Kong* 1987: 84). It must be stressed that the wage levels in Hong Kong for all sectors have gone up significantly over the years and the work situation is considerably better than in most developing countries. Certainly, it is better than it was a few decades ago when Hong Kong entered its industrial revolution.

Despite the rise in real wages and the increasing government intervention in promoting workers' interests, two salient factors about wage employment in Hong Kong remain. First, no minimum wage is legislated; wage scales in all private sectors are determined by the law of supply and demand, through personal negotiation between employer/employee, and based on qualification, experience, labor supply/demand, as well as the economic well-being of the particular enterprise. Workers are known to move from factory to factory as often as several times a year to follow offers of higher wages and better working conditions, no matter how small.

The rise and fall of wages is also governed by world market forces and Hong Kong's need to remain competitive in the world system. Wages can only go so high before the cost of production shoots past a critical point which will undermine Hong Kong's competitiveness considerably. There is already growing evidence that many Hong Kong manufacturers are moving their production into China to capitalize on the cheaper cost of labor and to solve the problem of recruiting workers in Hong Kong given the relatively low wages in industrial employment compared to service sector and white-collar employment.

The second salient feature of the working situation in Hong Kong is the lack of unemployment insurance and other structural security guarantees usually associated with wage employment in the industrialized countries. For instance, Western workers are entitled to unemployment insurance once they have worked for a certain period of time. People have a vested interest in seeking wage employment since it is a prerequisite for unemployment benefits. In

Hong Kong, however, institutional or structural security associated with wage employment is extremely limited.

In the industrialized countries, the switch from wage employment to self-employment entails the loss of various structural security components, e.g., company pensions, medical/dental plans, paid vacations and maternity leaves, as well as eligibility for unemployment insurance. In Hong Kong, the jump from wage employment to self-employment still carries a lot of risk, but it does not entail the same loss of structural security; it is not there in the first place.

In summary, wage workers in industrialized countries enjoy more job protection and other structural security than most Hong Kong wage workers due to the very different nature of the overall economic context in mature versus burgeoning countries. The dynamics of the Hong Kong export economy has its foundation in the ability of the system to: (1) restructure its labor force and production according to world market forces; (2) keep the cost of labor down; and (3) maintain the work force's commitment to efficiency and high labor participation by suppressing the same kind of structural security associated with wage employment that is common in industrialized countries.

Street hawking in Hong Kong.

The long history of street hawking in Hong Kong is attested to by the inclusion of street hawking as an occupational category as early as the 1872 census. At that time, Hong Kong had a population of 121,985 and the total number of hawkers listed was 2431. In the following years, the population of Hong Kong climbed steadily and so did the number of street hawkers. By 1931, the number of hawkers had risen to 16,285, while the population reached 849,751 (McGee 1973: 35). During the Japanese occupation of Hong Kong (1941-45), many people fled the Colony and returned to their home villages in China. There was, then, a sharp decline in street hawking activities, partly in response to the drop in population and partly due to the shortage of foodstuffs and other commodities.

After the occupation, returnees and Chinese refugees flooded the Colony. The influx of both legal and illegal immigrants from China between 1945-80 was the primary cause of an increase in population from 1.8 million in 1947 to 4.4 million in 1976, putting immense strain on housing and other public facilities in the urban areas of Hong Kong (Sit 1981: 3-4). Government officials were alarmed by the sharp increase in street hawking activities in the post-war years and its "disorderly effect on the city streets" (McGee 1973: 42). In 1947, the number of hawkers was estimated to be anywhere from 40,000-70,000.

The situation in Hong Kong immediately after 1945 bore a strong resemblance to the situations in many contemporary developing countries where people, many of whom are uprooted from their land base, migrate to the cities seeking employment opportunities. They frequently end up resorting to self-employment in order to get by. Though there is no analysis of the factors contributing to the rise in street hawking activities in Hong Kong in the post-war period, it is fairly reasonable to suggest that economic underdevelopment and uncontrolled population growth were the major causes.

The economic development of Hong Kong in the next few decades did not bring down the absolute number of street hawkers but the overall percentage of the population in street hawking declined considerably from 3% in 1947 to 1.5% in 1984. In the 1981 census, 63,000 people were identified as hawkers, of whom close to 40,000 were unlicensed illegal hawkers.

There is a great deal of controversy concerning the magnitude of illegal hawking. The latest government estimates are typically conservative, suggesting that there were 16,000-17,000 illegal hawkers in 1984 (*A Consultative Document on Hawker and Market Policies* [hereafter referred to as *Urban Services*] 1985: 14). Other sources give a higher estimate of 50,000-70,000. Whatever the real number of street hawkers is, they are ubiquitous in the urban areas of Hong Kong.

Legal and Illegal Hawkers. Street hawkers, known as *siu faan*[3] in the Cantonese dialect, are best described as self-employed petty retailers involved in the distribution of a wide range of locally produced and imported goods and produce. According to the *Hong Kong Public Health and Urban Services Ordinances 1960* (Hong Kong Urban Services Department 1960) a street hawker is:

(a) any person who trades in a public place—
    (i) by selling or exposing for sale any goods or merchandise; or
    (ii) by exposing samples or patterns of goods, wares or merchandise to be afterwards delivered; or
    (iii) by hiring or offering for hire his skill in handicraft or his personal services;
and
(b) any person who itinerates for the purpose—
    (i) of selling or exposing for sale any goods, wares or merchandise; or
    (ii) of hiring or offering for hire his skill in handicraft or personal services.

There are two types of hawkers by legal definition—legal and illegal. Illegal hawkers are differentiated from legal hawkers by two characteristics, each of which is independently sufficient to convict the person in question of the violation of the existing Hawker By-Laws. First, illegal hawkers are defined by their spatial context, i.e., the illegal use of public space for their economic activities. It makes no difference whether the person is a licensed or unlicensed hawker, one is defined as an illegal hawker so long as one is operating in a spatial position outside government regulated trading areas.

Second, an illegal hawker is someone who hawks without a license. There are 16 different types of hawker licenses according to commodity type or characteristics of hawking unit (e.g., mobile van,

---

[3]Cantonese words used in the text are italicized. They are romanized according to Sidney Lau's *A Practical Cantonese-English Dictionary* (1977), but without the tonal markers.

wall stall). The 1985 license fee ranged from $1530[4] for a fixed pitch license to $290 for an itinerant license. Licensed hawkers have to comply with a wide range of government regulations concerning their commodity type, location of work and hours of operation. Many licensed hawkers are known to violate one or more of these rules at some point. Since 1970, as a result of the government's decision to restrict license issuance, it has become almost impossible to obtain a hawker license.

Other than the legal definition, there is very little difference between the illegal and legal hawkers in their operational organization and function. The street hawkers' role in commodity distribution and their contributions to the economy are widely recognized (McGee 1973; Ho 1972). In 1983, street hawking contributed an estimated one billion dollars to the economy, representing roughly 11% of the value of the retail trade (Urban Services 1985: 15). In particular, they have a prominent role in the distribution of raw/cooked foodstuffs and other staples, locally produced and imported manufactured goods. Street hawkers provide a valuable service to the community by filling the gaps in the existing retailing structure. Thus, for example, the falling demand for hawkers who offer traditional services and handicrafts (e.g., dough sculpture, letter writing, laundry/ironing) has led to a declining number of such types. And, as pointed out by Portes and Walton (1981: 11, 86) and Frobel, et al. (1980: 30), street hawking and other informal activities lower the cost of subsistence by offering goods and services at low prices, keep the cost of labor down, raise the surplus value extracted by capitalist enterprises, and provide for all or part of the costs of the reproduction of new generations of workers for the capitalist system.

State Intervention. The positive contribution of street hawking to the wider economy was recognized as early as 1936 in a report by the Chairman of the Urban Council, Mr. R.R. Todd. He pointed out that street hawking provided a convenient service to the public, kept down the cost of living of the poorer classes, and provided a source

---

[4]All monetary figures are given in Hong Kong dollars, abbreviated "$" The exchange rate in 1985 was HK$7.8 to every US$1.00.

of social welfare for the old and weak (McGee 1973: 37-38). In the same breath, however, Todd also recommended that street hawking be eradicated in the view of its many negative aspects, such as obstruction, threat to public health, temptation "to the Asiatic Police as a source of squeeze," and unfair competition to formal retail outlets (McGee 1973: 38-39). Among Todd's successors, this extreme argument against street hawking has moderated over time; still persisting, however, is the central philosophy that street hawkers and their trading activities are not welcome in the urban milieu. The conflict between the government and hawkers in their perception of the proper use of public space deepens with ever-increasing urbanization and industrialization. Intensifying government intervention in restricting hawkers' access to public space reflects both the government's on-going perception of street hawking as an urban problem, and the hawkers' resistance to government intervention.

Despite a growing alliance between the government and capitalist interests in Hong Kong, there is no evidence to suggest that the government is involved in any sort of conspiracy or active attempt to preserve the hawking sector on the basis of its contribution to the well-being of the capitalist economy as mentioned by Portes and Walton (1981) and others. This dissociation between action and ideology is probably a product of two factors: First, the government cannot allow the hawkers to disrupt the spatial order in the city without compromising its moral obligation to protect the public's interest, however that is defined; secondly, the government does not understand the mutually beneficial relationship between capitalism and the street hawking economy in Hong Kong. This misunderstanding of the articulation between capitalism and non-capitalist form of production is apparent in a report by the Urban Council in 1963 which argued that:

> The unrestricted issue of hawker licenses is not in the best interests of the public; able-bodied persons ought not to be encouraged to hawk when they might be better employed in industry for the economic benefit of the community (Anonymous, n.d., HKRS 438, DS 1/8).

In response to this report, it was legislated in 1970 that itinerant licences would no longer be issued and hawker licences would be issued only to those who worked from a fixed location as assigned by the government. In effect, the government stopped issuing new licences, thus forcing all existing unlicensed hawkers and future newcomers to become illegal hawkers and therefore vulnerable to enforcement actions. By criminalizing street hawking, the government hoped to drive able-bodied hawkers into industrial employment. If it had worked as expected, the cheap services and goods offered by the hawkers would disappear as the hawking sector contracted; this, in turn, might drive up wages somewhat. However, such wage increases would undermine the competitiveness of Hong Kong products in the world market and that would be contrary to the interests of the local economy in general.

In any case, the above mentioned scenario never materialized and thus we are unable to assess the role of street hawking in keeping down the cost of living in Hong Kong. The fact that the 1970 legislation has not produced the expected results is indicative of the government's limited understanding of the dynamics of street hawking and its interrelationship with the Hong Kong specific capitalist development. By 1970, people were no longer forced into street hawking by unemployment. Mostly, they were hawkers by choice rather than by circumstances, attracted to the economic potential in street hawking *vis-à-vis* wage employment.

The present policies on street hawking reflect a shift in philosophy, a reluctant recognition that street hawking may be here to stay. Instead of a commitment to eradicate street hawking, the government now has a commitment to gain greater control over the operation of street hawking through licensing, daily raid-and-arrest operations to break up illegal hawking agglomerations, and relocating illegal hawkers into government regulated markets and Hawker Permitted Places (Smart 1986). The Urban Services Department, the licensing body as well as the biggest enforcement unit in hawker control, employs over 2000 people in its General Duties team to harass and arrest illegal hawkers daily between 8 AM and midnight in addition to other duties.

In response to government interventions which impinge on their economic well-being, hawkers adopt various operational strategies to avoid arrest and protect their economic interest. Most operations are kept small and mobile to enhance a hawker's chance to outrun pursuing enforcement agents. The small scale of hawking operations usually has little to do with under-capitalization or marginality; rather, it is a survival strategy in response specifically to the raid-and-arrest operations by government enforcement agents (Smart 1988). Some hawkers work only during a certain period of the day when enforcement actions are weakest; others move their operation to locations which attract less customers—but also less attention from enforcement agents. The wide range of responses reflects the high degree of differentiation among the hawkers according to the kind of resources they have at their disposal to organize their operation and to advance their ongoing struggle with the government over their use right of public space. While it is true that anyone can become a street hawker, given its low capital and skill requirement, it is quite a different matter to run a profitable hawking operation. A hawker must have the right connections and resources in order to gain access to a viable spatial position and commodity supply sources and credit—and, as well, be a very skillful and resourceful individual, able to evade state harassment effectively while running an active economic concern at an unsanctioned spatial position.

Economic strategies and opportunity structure. As noted earlier, street hawking is not a new phenomenon in Hong Kong. In the first two quarters of 1873 it was recorded that 1146 street hawkers took out a hawking ticket at the cost of 50¢ per quarter (Nacken 1968: 129). The number of people involved in hawking in the precolonial days is not known but it is fairly certain that there were always petty traders in Hong Kong. The proportion of the population involved in street hawking remains small: 1.9% in 1872 and 1931, 3.8% in 1947, 1.5% in 1986. Street hawking has never been a mainstream economic endeavor and, despite an almost threefold increase in population from 1.8 million to 5.5 million, the total number of hawkers in Hong Kong (c. 70,000) has remained relatively stable since 1947.

It is difficult, if not impossible, to generalize about the street hawkers because they are a highly heterogeneous group. But if one must make such generalizations, one can say that street hawkers are predominantly male, married, non-Hong Kong born residents with little formal education. Street hawking in Hong Kong has always been male dominated, a deviation from the female dominated situation in most African, Southeast Asian, and Caribbean societies (McGee and Yeung 1977). At present, the sex ratio in hawking is about 3:1 in favor of males.

The high proportion of China-born migrants in the Hong Kong population is reflected in the dominance of Chinese migrants from various ethnic origins in hawking. The three largest ethnic groups are those from Canton (including Macao), Sze Yap, and Chiu Chau—respectively making up 51.7%, 14.1% and 19.4% of the total hawking population (Census 1981a, b). In a study by McGee (1973), close to 20% of the hawking population were Hong Kong born. By 1981, the proportion of native-born residents in hawking decreased to 1.8%. This considerable decline indicates clearly that street hawking has become increasingly less attractive to the Hong Kong born. The key to this trend lies in the differential access to the opportunity structure in Hong Kong by the native born and the migrants.

Like rural migrants everywhere, the Chinese migrants in Hong Kong are often disadvantaged in their search for wage employment as a result of their peasant background, lack of knowledge of English, technological skills or other recognized academic qualifications, vocational training, and limited resources or connections. There are many sad stories about educated migrants who failed to cope with their demoted status in Hong Kong. Engineers and teachers end up in factories and restaurants. Prominent musicians and artists become casual workers. Most Chinese migrants, regardless of their previous occupation and training in China, find their employment opportunities restricted largely to low paying jobs with little prospects for advancement. Female migrants are usually better off than their male counterparts due to the high demand for female labor in the major industries.

For many migrants, their low-paying wage employment further marginalizes their position in the Hong Kong society. Their participation in street hawking is usually initiated by a conscious decision to capitalize on the greater income potential in self-employment in order to improve their socioeconomic position. Two earlier studies had established that many hawkers were engaged in wage employment before they went into street hawking. McGee (1973: 168) found that 77% of the surveyed hawkers in his study had previous experience in industrial and service sector employment. A 1979 survey of illegal hawkers by the Society for Community Organization (SOCO) indicated similar findings: 32% as laborers, 3%-7% as clerical workers and 10.8% as service workers. My own 1982-1985 study confirms that most newcomers in street hawking in the last two decades are relatively young, able-bodied men under 40 who had been actively employed before entering street hawking. Many admit that their savings from previous wage employment furnish their initial investment in self-employment. There are always the exceptions but, by and large, street hawking is no longer a refuge for the old and the destitute. Rather, the newcomers are mostly aggressive entrepreneurs who make a conscious decision to abandon wage employment for self-employment in order to realize their aspirations for greater socioeconomic mobility, knowing that they can always return to wage employment if it does not work out. Many survey respondents gave unemployment as a reason for entering street hawking (McGee 1973; SOCO 1979). In Hong Kong, however, the concept of unemployment must be examined critically since unemployment is usually temporary and part of the on-going restructuring process within the manufacturing sector to accommodate changes in world market demands. It is not unusual for a worker to change employers several times a year either because of layoffs or an individual initiative to go where higher wages are offered. Due to Hong Kong's strong economy, most people can get some kind of wage employment at any given time. Temporary unemployment is seldom a causative factor in people's decision to enter street hawking; rather, it acts as a catalyst to prompt people to consider self-employment as an alternative to wage employment and it is based on their understanding (received through friends and relatives in the street trade) of the demands and rewards in street hawking. In a Singapore study, it was found that over 90% of hawkers break into the work with the help of friends or relatives who were previously engaged in earning their living this way (Lim 1974: 38). Similarly, most newcomers in street hawking in Hong Kong are friends, relatives or within the immediate families of existing hawkers and shop owners at their location of operation; those who enter the business are fully aware of the costs and rewards in street hawking before they make their decision.

What exactly are the attractions of street hawking relative to low paying employment? What does it offer that justifies the hawkers' committed participation in street hawking despite increasing state intervention and harassment, the long hours of work, the labor intensiveness, the low social status associated with hawking, and the constant struggle to defend and maintain one's spatial position? The primary attraction is money: Street hawking can be highly lucrative, with an income potential higher than that from most industrial and service sector jobs, or even clerical jobs which require a fairly high level of formal education and at least some working knowledge of English. With the exception of a small number of truly marginal, low-income hawking units, most hawkers earn $2500 to $3000 per month after deductions for operation and reinvestment costs. The more successful hawkers can earn up to $5000+ each month. The income potential in street hawking is highly favorable and attractive in comparison to the median income of professional occupations ($3289), administrative and managerial jobs ($4638), clerical and related jobs ($1705), industrial employment ($1387), agricultural production ($1238) and employment in service sectors ($1396) as given in the 1981 Census.

The economic feasibility and attraction of street hawking is closely tied to the capitalist development and urbanization of Hong Kong. The increase in real wages and the security of full employment allows people greater consumption power. The underdevelopment of the formal retailing structure in Hong Kong ensures the continuing demand for the distributive function of street hawking. The high population density further contributes to the feasibility of street hawking, making it possible for hawkers to work from the same location in a permanent or semi-permanent manner, which is a primary issue of contention between the hawkers and the government.

In addition, self-employment offers a greater degree of autonomy, and in some cases greater security than wage employment. In Madras (South India), rural migrants are attracted to illegal street trading by its greater security relative to casual employment, its promise of a daily income, and because of the greater degree of personal autonomy it offers (Lessinger 1985: 317-318). Among the South African Blacks in Soweto, street trading promises to be a solution to income crises due to the absence of State social welfare and the low wages in formal employment (Rogerson and Beavon 1982: 259). In Hong Kong, McGee (1973: 176) finds that "independence," "being my own boss," "working with members of the family or friends," are important considerations in people's decision to enter street hawking. People's attraction to the greater autonomy in self-employment is an indication of a growing consciousness of the marginality of wage employment among workers in these societies. One of my informants sums up his feeling about wage employment as follows:

> I work even harder at street hawking than when I was a mechanic at a plastic factory. But at least I am my own boss; there is nobody to yell at me and order me around. They penalize you for being late, for missing work because of sickness, and for not working fast enough. If you dare to be late a few times, they will kick you out. I have been asked several times to work in a factory at attractive wages since I became a hawker, but I don't think I will ever go back to wage employment. I don't want to lose my freedom and independence.

In Madras, many traders share similar disdain for wage employment, which can be highly exploitative. In Lessinger's words (1985: 318):

> Traders vividly recalled the unfairness, maltreatment or humiliations they had experienced in other jobs, and they welcomed their present jobs which, if exhausting, at least

allowed them to arrange their own work schedules, to make their own decisions and to evade direct personal exploitation.

Clearly, people's resistance to wage employment must be seen in the context of their position in society, their access to resources, and the conditions of wage employment in the society in question. In his discussion of people's tendency to resort to mixed economic strategies along the continuum of wage employment, self-employment and non-wage work, Uzzell (1980: 47) suggests that,

> The lack of commitment to a single source of income is an adaptation to prevailing wages, hiring practices, and the social and political position of the workers...[and their] attempt to expand and diversify their economic activities.

I mentioned earlier that few local-born residents are attracted to street hawking. It would be erroneous to suggest that they are unmoved by the promise of higher income and better opportunities for socioeconomic mobility in street hawking. Indeed, it is often said that money is the single driving force behind the Hong Kong work force (though I suspect the same can be said for many societies). Why, then, when native-born residents make up over 50% of the total population, are they grossly underrepresented in hawking (1.8% in 1981), and why does their participation in hawking decline steadily over time?

I would suggest that native born residents are not attracted to street hawking because they have greater access to resources and opportunity for socioeconomic mobility than their migrant counterparts. Most Hong Kong-born residents have access to formal education at primary and secondary levels. Since formal education is one of the most important vehicles for occupational and social mobility, employment and advancement opportunities are generally higher for the better educated natives than recent migrants from China. In addition, English is a necessary requirement for the better jobs in both public and private sectors. Due to their lack of knowledge of English, many Chinese migrants are, relative to the locally born residents, in a greatly disadvantaged position in the competition for employment and advancement opportunities. As a result, recent migrants are likely to remain at the bottom of the pay scale in wage employment.

Many local residents are also working at low paying jobs in factories, offices, banks and shops, earning little more than $2000 a month, working eight to ten hours a day, six days a week. In comparison, however, they probably have a higher standard of living and greater disposable income due to their greater access to social and economic resources in Hong Kong. Local residents usually have a vast network of social/economic support from family and friends. For instance, many young people, single or married, share accommodations with their family and other siblings to reduce the costs of subsistence, and this, in turn, raises their disposable income. Local residents also have more social resources to obtain cheap baby-sitting services, news about jobs, labor exchange, low interest loans, and many other cost-saving devices. Recent migrants, on the other hand, are usually deprived of similar social supports in Hong Kong due to the dislocation from their social base in China. While they often resort to ties of *tong heung* (people from the same village) to gain access to housing, employment and marriage, they can count on limited social and economic assistance only from fellow migrants since the latter hold a similarly disadvantaged position in Hong Kong.

Local residents, given the benefit of various forms of social and economic supports from their existing networks in Hong Kong, often consider the social and psychological costs in street hawking too high in comparison to its economic rewards. Recent migrants, deprived of similar access to social and economic resources in Hong Kong, are highly attracted to the economic potentials in street hawking which they perceive as a means to: correct their disadvantaged positions in Hong Kong; satisfy their desire for material well-being; and secure their social and economic well-being in the long run. It is not surprising, therefore, that most street hawkers express a strong desire to remain in street hawking on a long term basis. Street hawking provides a way out of their occupational marginality in wage employment, a means to generate enough income for their economic well-being in Hong Kong, and a source of capital for investment in their children's education to secure their social mobility in adulthood. Street hawking is the best economic strategy given their limited access to various resources in Hong Kong.

Conclusion.

There is a widespread conception that people are forced into street hawking and other informal activities as a result of unemployment and poverty. While this image may be compatible with the observation in many developing countries, it does not accurately describe the situation in a significant number of other societies. Using Hong Kong as a case study, I have argued that a simple relationship between unemployment and participation in the informal sector is untenable. Most people who entered street hawking in the last two decades did so out of a conscious decision to resist the marginality of low paying wage employment because of greater opportunities for socioeconomic mobility offered by street hawking. It is not unemployment that drives most people into street hawking; rather, it is a case of active resistance to proletarianization by people whose aspiration for socioeconomic mobility is restricted by their marginal position in the society. In the specific case of Hong Kong, these people are mostly recent immigrants from China whose peasant background, limited formal education, lack of vocational training and limited access to social and economic resources in the host society are causes of their extreme vulnerability to the marginality of low paying wage employment. They find the higher income potential and greater autonomy in street hawking highly attractive—despite the increasing State intervention and harassment in street trade, the long hours of work, the labor intensiveness, the constant struggle to maintain one's spatial position and the many difficulties of running a profitable small business under conditions of almost perfect competition. Street hawking offers them a chance to achieve upward socioeconomic mobility. They may return to wage employment when the going gets rough in street hawking but, as long as its economic attractions outweigh those of wage employment, they would prefer to remain in street hawking. It is a rational economic strategy given the migrant's limited scope for advancement within the existing opportunity structure in Hong Kong.

References.

Anonymous
   n. d   Memorandum HKRS 438/DS, 1/8. Hong Kong Government Archives.

Bairoch, Paul
   1973   Urban Unemployment in Developing Countries. Geneva: International Labor Office.

Banerjee, Nirmala
   1982   Survival of the Poor. In H. Safa, ed., Towards a Political Economy of Urbanization in Third World Countries. Bombay: Oxford University Press, pp. 175-186.

Bertaux, Daniel and Isabella Bertaux-Wiame
   1981   Artisanal Bakery in France: How it Lives and Why it Survives. In F. Bechhofer and B. Elliot, eds., The Petit Bourgeoisie. London: Macmillan Press, pp. 155-174.

Birkbeck, Chris
   1978   Self Employed Proletarians in the Informal Factory: The Case of Cali's Garbage Dump Pickers. World Development 6: 1173-1185.

Bromley, Ray
   1978   Introduction. The Urban Informal Sector: Why is It Worth Discussing? World Development 6: 1033-1039.
   1982   Working in the Streets: Survival Strategy, Necessity or Unavoidable Evil? In A. Gilbert et al., eds., Urbanization in Contemporary Latin America. Chichester: John Wiley and Sons, pp. 59-77.

Bromley, Ray and C. Gerry, eds.
   1979   Casual Work and Poverty in Third World Cities. Toronto: John Wiley and Sons.

Brown, E. H. Phelps
1971   The Hong Kong Economy: Achievements and Prospects. In K. Hopkins, ed., Hong Kong the Industrial Colony. Hong Kong: Oxford University Press, pp. 1-20.

Canadian Universities Services Overseas (CUSO)
1987   The Informal Economy. Ottawa: Canadian University Services Overseas.

Chen, Edward K.Y.
1984   The Economic Setting. In D. Lethbridge, ed., The Business Environment in Hong Kong. Hong Kong: Oxford University Press, pp. 1-51.

Chevalier, Jacques
1982   There is Nothing Simple about Simple Commodity Production. Studies in Political Economy 7: 89-124.

Cooper, Eugene
1980   The Wood-carvers of Hong Kong. Cambridge: Cambridge University Press.

Cottrell, Robert
1988   Non-Intervention has a Negative Effect. Far Eastern Economic Review April 2: 85-86.

Davies, Rob
1979   Informal Sector or Subordinate Mode of Production? A Model in Casual Work and Poverty. In R. Bromley and C. Gerry, eds., Casual Work and Poverty in Third World Cities. Toronto: John Wiley and Sons, pp. 87-104.

Drakakis-Smith, David
1981   Urbanization, Housing and the Development Process. London: Croom Helm Ltd.

England, Joe and John Rear
1975   Chinese Labor Under British Rule. Hong Kong: Oxford University Press.

Fapohunda, L., J. Olanrewaju and H. Lubell
1978   Lagos: Urban Development and Employment. Geneva: International Labor Office.

Foster-Carter, Aiden
1978   Can We Articulate "Articulation"? In J. Clammer, ed., The New Economic Anthropology. Hong Kong: Macmillan Press, pp. 210-249.

Frobel, F., J. Heinrichs and O. Kreye
1980   The New International Divisions of Labor. Cambridge: Cambridge University Press.

Hart, Keith
1973   Informal Income Opportunities and Urban Employment in Ghana. Journal of Modern African Studies 11: 61-89.

Ho, Sek Fun
1972   Hawkers in Mongkok District: A Study in Retailing Geography. M. Phil. Thesis in Geography, University of Hong Kong.

Hong Kong Census and Statistics Department
1981a   Hong Kong 1981 Census Main Report. Hong Kong: Government Printer.
1981b   Hong Kong 1981 Census Basic Tables. Hong Kong: Government Printer.

Hong Kong Government
1985   Hong Kong Annual Report. Hong Kong: Government Printer.
1987   Hong Kong Annual Report. Hong Kong: Government Printer.

Hopkins, K.
1971   Hong Kong The Industrial Colony. Hong Kong: Oxford University Press.

International Development Research Centre (IDRC)
1975   Hawkers and Vendors in Asian Cities. Ottawa: International Development Research Center.

International Labor Office
1984   1984 Year Book of Labor Statistics. Geneva: International Labor Organization.

Joshi, Heather, H. Lubell and J. Moley
1976   Abidjan. Geneva: International Labor Organization.

Lands Department
1984   Town Planning in Hong Kong. Hong Kong: Government Printer.

Lau, Sidney
1976   A Practical Cantonese-English Dictionary. Hong Kong: Government Printer.

Leeming, Frank
1977   Street Studies in Hong Kong. Hong Kong: Oxford University Press.
1981   Kwun Tong: Community Within a Planned Industrial District. In V. Sit, ed., Urban Hong Kong. Hong Kong: Summerson Eastern, pp. 167-187.

Lessinger, Johanna
1985   Nobody Here to Yell at Me: Political Activism among Petty Retail Traders in an Indian City. In S. Plattner, ed., Markets and Marketing. Lanham MD: University Press of America, pp. 309-331.

Lim, Kim Char
1974   A Study of Hawkers in Singapore. B.A. dissertation, Nanyan University, Singapore.

Lin, Tsong-biau, Rance P. Lee and Udo-Ernst Simonis, eds.
1979　Hong Kong: Economic, Social and Political Studies in Development. New York: M. E. Sharpe Inc.

Lin, Tsong-biau, Victor Sit and Ying-ping Ho
1980　Manufactured Exports and Employment in Hong Kong. Hong Kong: Chinese University Press.

Lomnitz, Larissa A.
1977　Networks and Marginality: Life in a Mexican Shantytown. New York: Academic Press.

Long, Norman and Paul Richardson
1978　Informal Sector, Petty Commodity Production and the Social Relations of Small-scale Enterprise. In J. Clammer, ed., The New Economic Anthropology. Hong Kong: Macmillan Press, pp. 176-209

Lui, T.L.
1984　Urban Protest in Hong Kong: A Sociological Study of Housing Conflicts. M. Phil. Thesis in Sociology. University of Hong Kong.

McGee, T.G.
1973　Hawkers in Hong Kong. Hong Kong: Center of Asian Studies.

McGee, T. G. and Y. M. Yeung
1977　Hawkers in Southeast Asia. Ottawa: International Development Research Center.

Moser, C.O.
1978　Informal Sector or Petty Commodity Production: Dualism or Dependence in Urban Development? World Development 43: 336-341.

Nacken, J.
  1968   Chinese Street-Cries in Hong Kong. Journal of the Hong Kong Branch of the Royal Asiatic Society 8: 128-134.

Ng, Sek-hong
  1983   Women Workers in Industry and The Hong Kong Government's Role: Past and Present Attitudes. Hong Kong: Center of Asian Studies.

Peattie, Lisa R.
  1982   What is to be Done with the "Informal Sector"? A Case Study of Shoe Manufacturers in Colombia. In H. Safa, ed., Towards a Political Economy of Urbanization in Third World Countries. Bombay: Oxford University Press, pp. 208-230.

Portes, A. and J. Walton
  1981   Labor, Class and the International System. New York: Academic Press.

Rabushka, Alvin
  1979   Hong Kong. Chicago: University of Chicago Press.

Remy, Dorothy
  1982   Formal and Informal Sectors of the Saria, Nigeria Economy: An Analytical Framework with Empirical Content. In H. Safa, ed., Towards a Political Economy of Urbanization in Third World Countries. Bombay: Oxford University Press, pp. 231-248.

Riedel, J.
  1974   The Industrialization of Hong Kong. Tubingen: J. C. B. Mohr.

Rogerson, C. M. and K. S. O. Beavon
  1982   Getting By in the Informal Sector of Soweto. Journal of Economic and Social Geography 73: 250-265.

Scott, Alison McEwan
1979   Who are the Self-employed? In R. Bromley and C. Gerry, eds., Casual Work and Poverty in Third World Cities. Toronto: John Wiley and Sons, pp. 105-132.

Sinclair, S.
1978   Urbanization and Labor Markets in Developing Countries. London: Croom Helm Ltd.

Sit, Victor F. S.
1981   Post-war Population and Its Spatial Dynamics. In V. Sit, ed., Urban Hong Kong. Hong Kong: Summerson Eastern, pp. 2-25.

Smart, Josephine
1986   The Impact of Government Policy on Hawkers: A Study of The Effects of Establishing a Hawker Permitted Place. The Asian Journal of Public Administration 8: 260-279.
1988   How to Survive in Illegal Street Hawking in Hong Kong. In G. Clark, ed., Traders versus the State: Anthropological Approaches to Unofficial Economies. Boulder CO: Westview Press, pp. 99-118.

Society for Community Organization (SOCO)
1979   Report on Illegal Hawkers (in Chinese). Hong Kong: Society for Community Organization.

Tse, F.Y.
1974   Market and Street Trading: A Conceptual Framework. Hong Kong: The Chinese University of Hong Kong, Social Research Center.

Urban Council Markets and Street Traders Select Committee
1985   A Consultative Document on Hawker and Market Policies. Hong Kong: Correctional Services Industries.

Uzzell, J. Douglas
1980   Mixed Strategies and the Informal Sector: Three Factors of Reserve Labor. Human Organization 39: 40-49.

Woronoff, Jon
1980   Hong Kong: Capitalist Paradise. London: Heinemann Ed. Books.

HIDDEN DIMENSIONS OF
THE BURMESE[1] WAY TO SOCIALISM.[2]

Nicola Tannenbaum
Department of Social Relations
Lehigh University
and
E. Paul Durrenberger
Department of Anthropology
University of Iowa

Introduction.

Fried's (1967) definition of States as institutional forms to maintain unequal access to basic resources indicates that States are economic as well as political institutions. In all State societies, whether they be archaic empires, petty principalities, or modern socialist or capitalist States, economic relations are largely defined by policy. Economics is a discipline that defines official and public paradigms of economic life and the ideologies to support them. Economists define sets of cultural categories for governments to measure and the measurements provide the economists' data.

The concept of the "formal" or "first" economy is a cultural category which varies from time to time and place to place and labels officially measured phenomena. The work of housewives is not measured. It is "informal." The U.S. Department of Agriculture makes a number of measurements throughout the growing season of each major crop and issues crop predictions and reports. Measured

[1]Since General Saw Maung's coup a year ago, Burma has been renamed Myanmar.
[2]Tannenbaum conducted her research during 1979-1981 supported by a grant from the Midwestern Universities Consortium on International Activities and the International Fertilizer Development Center and during 1984-1985 supported by a post-doctoral fellowship from the Social Science Research Council. Durrenberger conducted his research during 1976-1977 supported by a fellowship from the Ford Foundation.

crops are part of the "formal economy." What is "in" and "out" of the formal economy depends on what governments elect to measure. Production and sales of alcoholic beverages are part of the formal economy of the United States today, but were not during Prohibition.

"Formal" and "informal" are not economic facts. They are categories relevant not to the working of economic systems, but to government measurement policies. When economists notice massive discrepancies among their measurements, as between value produced and deposits in banks, they account for them by reference to that which they neither measure nor theorize, a residual category they call the "informal." What is in the "informal" is what is not in the "formal"—and the latter is defined by government policy.

The two "sectors" change as policy does: When alcohol was prohibited in the U.S., its (illegal) production was not measured; but after repeal of that law, production was part of the formal economy because it was now tracked and accounted for. If agricultural productivity is measured it is part of the formal economy; if such production is ignored, it is part of the informal. The current classification of "unemployed" includes both those who do not have employment though they actively seek it and those who do not work and do not seek it. National policy defines both the formal and the informal, but measures only the formal. What is formal in one country may be informal in another; what is informal at one time may be formal at another. These are cultural categories, not economic facts.

Anthropologists, who work "on the ground" and confront "ethnographic realities" report many activities that economists and official statistical bureaus do not, as many of the papers in this volume document. Religious sects act as redistributive networks (Greenfield and Prust), Poles cultivate personal relationships to enhance their access to goods (Wedel), Spanish Gypsies and Irish Travelers lead an unmeasured existence (Kaprow and Gmelch), to indicate but a few examples. Mired in the mundane facts of everyday human existence, anthropologists who work in State societies notice that government measurements and policies do not address issues of importance to the people they work among, nor do economists embrace them in their paradigms.

We have done fieldwork among highlanders and lowlanders in Thailand's northwestern border area since 1967. From the first, we have seen and heard about a plethora of rebel armies, warlords, bandit gangs, and other armed groups. We have seen and heard about trading caravans going between Thailand and Burma. Sometimes, convoys came to the villages where we were living to load Thai goods destined for sale in Burma. Frequently, cattle were herded through on the way to Thai markets. We heard news from jade dealers; were offered stones, silver, and jewelry by gem smugglers; discussed politics with rebel army leaders, and visited their camps. We have encountered armed caravans, stumbled unwittingly across armed patrols looking for the same kinds of caravans, heard and heard of shoot-outs between contending armies, seen smugglers, merchants, and rebels purchasing rice in villages. We have seen Nationalist Chinese Army (Kuomintong, KMT) opium caravans on American built roads, observed them purchasing opium from highlanders, and even had mail delivered in remote highland villages by their supply caravans. Pictures of Chiang Kai-shek adorn many a remote village shop. The wide smooth border trails maintained by the opium traders are a relief from the steeper, muddier, and more tangled paths among the swiddens of highland villagers. Such are everyday background events in the Golden Triangle of northern Burma, Thailand, and Laos.

To understand the local details we observed, it was necessary to put them in a larger historical and regional perspective, to understand their place in a larger system. It is an area of a shadow economy and a shadow politics, a political and economic system of more than 20 years duration in its current form, which is shaped by the intersection of the national policies of Burma, Thailand, Taiwan, and the United States. The trade in opium is but one aspect of a complex political and economic system that links various peoples to each other, to the nation-states of the region, and to the world market. The current form of the Golden Triangle system is largely a consequence of Burma's economic policies, and forms a hidden dimension of Burma's way to socialism.

Other participants in the 1988 SEA conference on The Informal Economy (Wedel, Brezinski, Altman) described the dynamics of "informal" economic action in socialist states of Eastern Europe. We are more concerned with the broader international consequences of a similar internal dynamic in Burma, how similar economic policies and consequences shape the economy of a region outside Burma.

We focus on the Burma-Thailand connections and describe the trading economy of the region which brings Burman export goods—opium, antiquities, gems, and cattle—to the international market and takes Thai consumer goods into Burma. We first describe the Burman and international economic and political background which sets the stage for this trade. We then detail the outlines of the international opium trade; gem, antiquities, and cattle trade; and the export of consumer goods from Thailand. This overview provides the context for examining some of the details of trade as it passes through the Thai border in Maehongson Province.

The international context.

The international players are: Burma, Thailand, Taiwan, and the United States and in the past Britain, France, and China. We cannot detail the long history of the interrelations among these nations and the consequence this has for the present situation (see McCoy 1972 and Scott 1969). However, it is necessary to know something of what went before to understand the current situation.

Burma. Burma was a British colony, conquered in a series of three wars, the last of which ended in 1886. During the British colonial period which lasted until 1948, the lowland areas were ruled directly as a province of British India while the upland area in the north was ruled indirectly through local lords. This division presented a problem when independence was negotiated. The various minority populations were skeptical of any program that gave Burmans control over their areas. When Burma gained independence, it was constituted as a federal union with a number of states that had the right to withdraw from the union after ten years (Silverstein 1980).

The original Burman leader, Aung San, who convinced the minority groups to vote for independence as a federated state, was assassinated before independence was declared. Aung San's successor, U Nu, had less success with maintaining the union and satisfying the minorities. The Karen in lower Burma revolted almost immediately after independence as did various factions of the Burmese Communist Party. Peace was established in 1951, but no real agreement was ever reached with the minorities. In 1958 U Nu voluntarily turned the government over to General Ne Win to restore order and stability. Elections were held again in 1960; U Nu was returned with a large majority but dissension again arose. Backed by the army, General Ne Win took control of the government in 1962. He and the military continue to rule in Burma (Silverstein 1980).

Ne Win's "Burmese Way to Socialism" brought the economy under the control of the army. Land and businesses including banks were nationalized. All non-State-run newspapers were shut down and publications were censored. The frontier states were placed under direct government control (Mirante 1986).

Many ethnic groups in the border areas formed insurgent armies and rebelled against the Burmese government. These revolutionary groups have a number of goals, ranging from complete independence to the establishment of some sort of federated state. The reasons they give for fighting include: Suppression of their religion, language, and culture; imposition of a socialist economy; human rights violations; abolition of the right secede as established in the first constitution; pre-colonial territorial claims; and the perception that the Burman government wants to eliminate minorities (Mirante 1986: 13).

The Burmese Way to Socialism has provided neither goods and services nor political and economic opportunities for its minority peoples. The first creates an insatiable demand. The second contributes to the formation of revolutionary groups. The insurgent armies provision themselves by controlling or participating in the trade.

Brezinski (1988) has analyzed the internal dynamics of planned economies and suggests some of the reasons for the failure of the Burmese economic system. Burma may illustrate the process at its extreme. As MacGaffey (1988) argues for Zaire, the government is the armed forces, and the economy is operated to benefit the individuals of the armed forces. Because the economy is government controlled and organized to favor a small sector of the population at the expense of the rest, there are chronic shortages of all goods from subsistence necessities such as cooking oil to such "luxuries" as medical supplies, clothing, bicycles, and wristwatches. There is a thriving black market. Burma's "shadow economy" exists because of the insatiable demand from within Burma and the benefits to those who fulfill it.

Consumer goods from Thailand enter and gems, opium, cattle, and antiquities leave. The trade is largely controlled by the various insurgent groups that occupy most of Burma's border areas (Mirante 1986: 8).

China and Taiwan. In 1949, when China's communist revolution succeeded, remnants of Chiang Kai-shek's Chinese nationalist army in southern China fled into the Shan states of northern Burma. Initially, these remnant forces were to fight a rear guard action against the communists in Yunnan, supported by Taiwan and the United States (Taylor 1973). Never effective in this, the KMT turned to dealing in opium and fighting against the government of Burma. The presence of Burmese troops and the fighting that took place is one of the reasons given for Shan distrust and dislike of the Burmese central government (Taylor 1973).

The KMT opium connection and its reliance on direct U. S. government aid is well documented (Taylor 1973; McCoy 1972; Browning and Garrett 1971). As the United States became increasing involved in anti-communist activity in Southeast Asia, the CIA made increasing use of the KMT. In return, U.S. military transport was used to ship opium and heroin out of the area (McCoy 1972: 242-354).

United States. The United States became involved in the area through their support of Taiwan and the remnant KMT as an anti-communist force, especially during the secret war in Laos. The U.S. supported governments in both Laos and South Viet-Nam were heavily involved in the opium trade (McCoy 1972; Browning and Garrett 1971; Taylor 1973).

Thailand. Following the United States' lead, Thailand has used the KMT as a way to control local "insurgency" often labeled "communist" (Durrenberger 1975) and has allowed the KMT to operate in its northern areas. More recently, under United Nations and U.S. Drug Enforcement Agency pressure, the Thai government has attempted some control of KMT activities. Thai government policy has been to allow the insurgent armies to live on the Thai side of the border, as long as they fight on the Burma side.

Because of its concern with border definition and control, the Thai government, often with U.S. aid, has been developing the infrastructure in this area. The roads and bridges built to bring in Central Thai authority make it easy to transport consumer goods into the border areas and to ship Burmese goods out.

The Burmese demand for consumer goods brings economic prosperity to merchants in the border towns. Storekeepers accept Burmese currency, *kyat.* In 1985, when Burma demonitarized the 50 and 100 *kyat* bills, merchants rushed to an approved border market to exchange their supply during the 72 hours in which it was possible.

International trade.

Opium. Parts of the U. S. government see the opium trade simply as a "drug problem" and ignore its role in the contexts not only on the larger political (Browning and Garrett 1971) scene but also in the economic context (Mirante 1986; Durrenberger 1981a, b). Armies and bandits deal in opium because it is profitable. Rebel armies use opium to finance their wars against the Burmese government. The bandits use the money to finance their continuing involvement and buy guns, supplies, and official cooperation. On the ground both processes look similar as they involve supplying and supporting armies.

With the history of ethnic differences in Burma; the resulting problem of integration in immediate post-independence Burma (Silverstein 1980); the historical role of opium in the region (McCoy 1972); and the defeat of the nationalist Chinese, the stage is set for present day opium trade. Ne Win's "Burmese Way to Socialism" only continued the process. Because of the Burmese government's policy toward Burmanization and its ineffective economic policy, minority groups formed armies and rebelled (Lintner 1987: 47-49; Mirante 1987: 13-27). The KMT and other drug armies, like rebel groups, need money, supplies, and munitions which they get by trading opium or taxing the opium trade.

Rebel and drug armies are middlemen engaged in the taxing, transportation, and refining of opium. Their income requires both producers and consumers. Opium is grown by minority groups in Thailand, Burma, and Laos. Income from this trade affects both the internal political economic forms and the relationships of the minority groups with national governments (Jonsson 1988; Durrenberger 1975). Through their involvement in opium production, they become objects to be manipulated in changing international political relationships. Because of the illegality of opium production, the growers have no recourse when they are raided by bandits or when local Thai officials demand protection money.

With U.S. acquiescence, the KMT has encouraged opium production among minorities (McCoy 1972). Now because of the "war against drugs," the U. S. is supplying the Burman government with 2-4-D herbicides, the active ingredient in Agent Orange, to destroy opium crops. In their fight to gain control over disputed areas, the Burmans spray civilian populations and their crops causing illness and death to both livestock and people (Mirante 1987).

On the consumption side there is an increasing and insatiable demand for opium and heroin in Southeast Asia, the U. S., and the rest of the world. The contradictory U.S. government policy supported the expansion of opium production in Southeast Asia and its export to the western world (McCoy 1972; Browning and Garrett 1971). Thai government policy, supported by the U. S., encouraged infrastructure development—making it possible for Thai to secure their borders but also making it easier to transport opium and other goods.

All of these relationships are illustrated in Figure 1.

Figure 1
RELATIONSHIPS AMONG INTERNATIONAL POLICY, THE BURMESE WAY TO SOCIALISM, AND OPIUM PRODUCTION

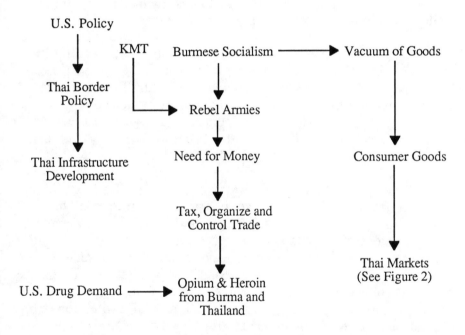

Gems, Cattle, and Antiquities. The minority areas in Burma are rich in natural resources. Ruby and sapphire mining is a Burman government monopoly and Burmans try to control the trade. Nonetheless, rubies, sapphires, and jade leave the country and enter Thailand. Indian traders smuggle gems and jewelry into Thailand. These are small and relatively easy to smuggle. Like opium, they are low volume, high value items. Jade is less easily transported. Chinese and Shan traders carry loads of jade-bearing stone. Jade comes from areas under insurgent control in Northern Burma.

As tourism has increased in Thailand, the market for antiquities has also increased. A vast array of old looking Buddha images, temple decorations, and household goods is offered in the night bazaar in Chiang Mai city. Although one cannot be sure of the "antiquity" of these, that they appear to be old and are in the market indicate the continual demand for such items. There are numerous antique shops in both Bangkok and Chiang Mai selling antiquities from Burma to tourists and Thai collectors. Buddha images, small amulets, and temple decorations come from either abandoned temples or are looted from areas under insurgent control and are a visible and obvious cargo of many horse caravans from Burma.

Cattle are walked out of Burma into Thailand, taken by truck to markets in Chiang Mai and other areas where there is insufficient local meat production to meet demand, and sold. The Thai demand for cattle is such that the Burman government broadcast at least one cautionary tale warning Shan farmers not to give into the lure of consumer goods and sell their cattle because then they would not have draft animals to plow their fields.

These products are likely to travel together. Traders bringing cattle in from Burma may also bring along antique silver, old Buddha images, or gems. Individual traders in the caravan may carry gems or whatever to sell on their own. Because of its illegality and high value and because armies control and tax the trade, opium is less likely to travel this way. Since the markets for drugs are centrally controlled, it is impossible for individuals to dispose of opium without connections to processors and protection from officials and the KMT. A highland villager who attempted free-lance transportation of opium was killed.

These products move across the border because of the lure of consumer goods available in Thailand and unavailable in Burma, one of the consequences of the Burmese Way to Socialism. The goods that move back into Burma range from the mundane (e.g., clothing and monosodium glutamate) to large-ticket items (e.g., sewing machines and motorcycles). The level of trade and its mundane nature is illustrated in a scene from Adrian Cowell's film, *Opium Warlords*. Instead of capturing an opium supply train, a rebel army captures a load of smuggled consumer goods—primarily 007 underwear (a la James Bond) and ball point pens.

Figure 2
Informal sector connections between imports and exports.

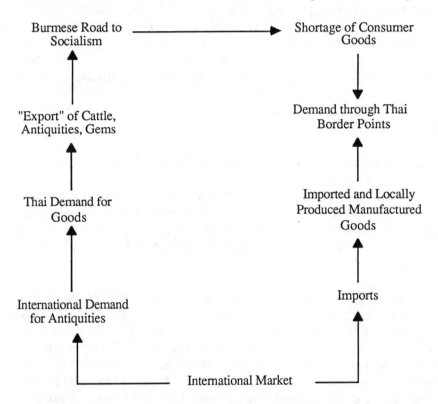

The interconnections between goods leaving Burma, the Burmese planned economy, and imports are shown in Figure 2, an elaboration of the connection between Burmese socialism and the resulting vacuum of consumption goods. This trade is not causally separate from the opium trade, illustrated in Figure 1. Both rest on the political inequalities and economic shortages that resulted from the Burmese Way to Socialism. Like the opium trade, the gem and antiquities trade respond to international market demands. The insurgent and drug armies import their supplies from Thailand along the same trade routes used to send opium out of Burma.

These systemic interconnections among the policies of the Burman, U. S., and Thai governments and the place of heroin, gems, and antiquities in the international market place structures the local organization of trade that provides the flow goods. Neither the Burman or the Thai government sanctions this trade and it is part of the "informal economy" of both States. Those people who do participate in the trade do pay taxes but to the "informal government" sector. These include local and national police both Burman and Thai and the various armies that control the border points. Income from the control of these border points is important for insurgent armies and there have been battles to gain or regain control of particular areas.

Local trade in the international context.

In the rest of this paper we examine the trade as it passes through one border area in Maehongson Province, Thailand. Our focus is on how the larger systems structure the trade relations and what effect this has on local village economies and on the provincial economy.

Maehongson Province in northwestern Thailand forms part of the border with Burma. Until recently, it has been remote and marginal to the Thai nation, economically and politically isolated from the rest of Thailand. This is changing as the Thai government has become concerned with the security of its western border with Burma and as the rustic attractions of Maehongson make it an increasingly popular destination for both Thai and foreign tourists.

There are four kinds of communities in Maehongson Province: towns with 8000-10,000 residents; lowland farming villages, mostly ethnically Shan; upland farming communities, mostly ethnically Karen, with some Hmong and Lisu; and border trading points and camps controlled by the insurgent armies. The location of these places change and there is sometimes fierce competition among the groups for control of a trading point.

Our focus is on the lowland villages. Upland villagers' involvement in this trade tends to be as producers of opium (Durrenberger 1975, 1976, 1979, 1981a, b). They may also participate in the cattle trade or like lowland villagers, work as helpers in the trading caravans.

Lowland villages serve as way stations for the traders. The opportunities this brings are not particularly stable or long term. Villagers provide food and shelter for traders or work as helpers with the livestock. During 1976-1977, traders and caravans passed frequently through Thongmakhsan, a Shan village of 35 households where we both did research. Since the road ended in Thongmakhsan, traders often camped there while a few went to town to buy goods. This brought a period of local prosperity since the villages required the traders to buy their supplies, especially rice for the horses, within the village. People who had rice to sell benefited from this. By 1979-1981, the road extended further north and the border trading point was no longer active. The caravans did not penetrate so far into Thailand, but mini-buses ladened with consumer goods regularly went to villages closer to the border.

Villagers may occasionally enter the trade by buying goods, particularly cattle, at the border points and selling them or more rarely buying consumer goods and travelling into Burma to sell them. This trade is risky since it requires more capital and connections than most villagers have. The two traders active during 1976-77 were inactive by 1979. One household split up and the trader moved to another village. The other trader succumbed to the occupational hazard of gambling and lost more than he gained. A third man became involved in the trade but he was stopped by uncompensated Thai Border Patrol Police and lost his cattle.

These villages are only stages in the route which connects traders to the larger towns where consumer goods are available in quantity. The larger towns recently connected by road to the rest of Thailand supply the consumer goods. Just as the rest of the world has an insatiable demand for opiates, Burma has an insatiable demand for mundane consumer goods. According to economists, the Burmese black market trade is three times the official trade figures and the amount coming over the Chinese border is estimated at anywhere between one and ten billion *kyat* per year (the official exchange rate for *kyat* is 6.6 to a dollar, the unofficial rate is between 30-35) (Steinberg 1988).

We do not have figures for the goods coming through the Thai border. However, the scale of the trade is indicated in the amount of goods which traders carried through Thongmakhsan during in a two-month period in 1976. Traders reported buying rubber sandals—30 dozen, 34 dozen, 150 dozen, 170 dozen, and 300 dozen. Other traders just reported that they bought sandals. They paid between 98 and 120 *baht* (US$5 to US$6) per dozen (at that time 20 *baht*=US$1.00). They expected to receive between 360-540 *kyat* (US$12-$16) per dozen, depending on where they sold them. The traders sold cattle, antiquities, gems, and tea to finance the trade. Some came into Thailand, worked as hired laborers, and used their wages to buy goods.

Control of trade is an important source of revenue for the various armies and war lords. They tax the goods leaving Burma. During 1976-1977 the tax on cattle was between 150-170 *baht* ($8.5 to $9.5) per head; on tea at 5 *baht* ($.25) per *joi* (1.6 kilograms); and 60 *baht* ($3) per horse. The income from controlling trading points is high and armies have fought one another for the power to tax and control trade. The "tax" is split between the army controlling the border point and local Thai officials.

The trade is extensive. Thongmakhsan is just one small village near the Burma border, yet large quantities of consumer goods passed through it in a short period of time. The border area is porous; there are innumerable routes into Burma. One has to multiply the trade through Thongmakhsan by all the possible routes into Burma; the extent of the demand is boggling.

The major beneficiaries of the trade are the storekeepers in the larger towns. The shopkeepers in Maehongson Town appear no more prosperous than any other shopkeepers in small provincial towns. However, the goods they display, particularly tea and jewelry from Burma, indicate that they participate in the trade. Local outlets for manufactured goods such as sewing machines and bicycles do brisk business. Salesmen in Maehongson Province win prizes in national salesmanship competitions—curious, given the general poverty and remoteness of the area. Reported sale figures indicate that every household in Maehongson should own at least one sewing machine. Obviously, these goods are not being used in Maehongson but are being exported into Burma.

Storekeepers who have sufficient capital to buy in bulk and wholesale their goods to traders are direct beneficiaries of this trade. Maehongson Town is the shipping point for cattle walked into Thailand. People who provide services (such as places to graze and take care of the cattle) also benefit as do food shop owners. Local truck drivers do a brisk business in hauling cattle farther into Thailand and consumer goods toward Burma. Local officials benefit from a steady income from gratuities from undocumented traders and others.

Other beneficiaries are those individuals and companies which manufacture and transport the goods for the Burma trade. It provides a demand for manufactured and consumer goods greater than that of Thai people alone. The Thai manufacturing sector does provide jobs for some of the urban poor although neither the wages nor the working conditions are good (Chandravithun 1982). Border villagers benefit from the trade as it passes through their area and they have access to a larger range of goods at cheaper prices than their distance from the capital would suggest.

The opium and heroin trade is completely illicit and the income opportunities much higher. Cooperation with minority armies in controlling and taxing the trade provides sources of revenue for Thai military and border personnel and brings increased income for officials along its route. U. S. sponsored drug suppression campaigns bring money and other resources which can be used to bolster the positions of government officials. These officials can win from both sides—by encouraging the trade and making it safe on the one hand, and deploring it and putting on shows of interdicting it on the other. The opium and heroin trade does not benefit lowland villagers who stay out of the way of drug caravans and their armed escorts. Small scale shopkeepers, unless they are involved in the opium network as local buyers, do not benefit from this trade.

Conclusion.

Our brief account indicates the extent of the trade in mundane consumer goods and the export of cattle, gems, and antiquities into Thailand. Burma's political and economic policies affect the surrounding countries since the vacuum of consumer goods in Burma is being filled by imports from Thailand and China. Supplying consumer goods to Burma and the border regions is a big industry. Supplying the world demand for opiates, jade, gems, and exotic antiquities is an even bigger industry. While U.S., Thai, and Taiwanese policies influence the trade, neither of these industries could have its current form without the policies known as the Burmese Way to Socialism. Only a narrow range of economic action is embraced by the official policy. The balance is "informal." Here, to ignore the "informal" because it is not recognized by government ideology and rhetoric, is to ignore most of the economic system. To make policy on the basis of such fictions dooms it to failure—as the several programs to replace, control, or eliminate opium production and trade have illustrated (Durrenberger 1981a).

References.

Altman, Yochanan
  1988   Second Economy Activity in the USSR. Paper presented at the 1988 annual meeting, Society for Economic Anthropology, Knoxville TN.

Brezinski, Horst
  1988   The Second Economy in Centrally Planned Systems. Paper presented at the 1988 annual meeting, Society for Economic Anthropology, Knoxville TN.

Browning, F. and B. Garrett
  1971   The New Opium War. Ramparts 9 (10): 32-39.

Chandravithun, N.
  1982   Thai labor: A Long Journey. Bangkok: Thai Watana Panich.

Durrenberger, E. Paul
  1975   Understanding a Misunderstanding: Thai-Lisu rela-tions in Northern Thailand. Anthropological Quarterly 48: 106-120.
  1976   The Economy of a Lisu Village. American Ethnologist 3: 633-644.
  1979   Rice Production in a Lisu Village. Journal of Southeast Asian Studies 10: 139-145.
  1981a   Opium Production and Policy in Thailand and Burma. CERES 14: 45-62.
  1981b   The Economy of a Shan Village. Ethnos 46: 64-79.

Durrenberger, E. Paul and Nicola Tannenbaum
  1983   A Diachronic Analysis of Shan Cropping Systems. Ethnos 48: 177-194
  n. d.   Analytical Perspectives on Shan Agriculture and Village Economics. Yale University Southeast Asian Studies Monograph Series, No. 37. (in press).

Fried, Morton
    1967   The Evolution of Political Society. New York: Random House.

Greenfield, S.M. and R. Prust
    1990   Popular Religion, Patronage, and Resource Distribution in Brazil: A Model of an Hypothesis for the Survival of the Economically Marginal. In M. Estellie Smith, Perspectives on the Informal Economy, 1988 SEA Proceedings. Lanham MD: University Press of America, pp. 123-145.

Jonsson, Hjorleifur
    1988   Political and Cognitive Systems in Upland Mainland Southeast Asia. M.A. thesis, University of Iowa.

Kaprow, Miriam Lee and Sharon Bohn Gmelch
    1988   The Rewards of the Underground: Spanish Gypsies and Irish Travellers. Paper presented at the 1988 annual meeting, Society for Economic Anthropology, Knoxville TN.

Lintner, Bertil
    1987   War in the North. Far Eastern Economic Review 136: 47-58.

MacGaffey, Janet
    1988   The Underground Economy in the United States and in Zaire. Paper presented at the 1988 annual meeting, Society for Economic Anthropology, Knoxville TN.

McCoy, Alfred W.
    1972   The Politics of Heroin in Southeast Asia. New York: Harper Colophon Books.

Mirante, Edith
    1986   Burma Frontier Insurgency. Cranford NJ: Project Maje Report.

1987   Adrift in Troubled Times: Recent Accounts of Human Rights Abuse in the Shan State (Burma). Cranford, NJ: Project Maje Report.

Scott, James M.
1969   The White Poppy: A History of Opium. New York: Funk and Wagnalls.

Silverstein, Josef
1980   Burmese Politics: The Dilemma of National Unity. New Brunswick NJ: Rugers University Press.

Steinberg, David I.
1988   Neither Silver nor Gold: The Fortieth Anniversary of the Burmese Economy. Paper presented at the Association for Asian Studies meetings, March 24, 1988.

Tannenbaum, Nicola
1982   Agricultural Decision Making Among the Shan of Maehongson Province, Northwestern Tahiland. Ph.D. Thesis, University of Iowa.

Taylor, Robert
1973   Foreign and Domestic Consequences of the KMT Intervention in Burma. Cornell Southeast Asia Program Data Paper 93. Ithaca NY: Cornell University.

Wedel, Janine
1988   The Hypothesis and Data on the Polish Informal Social and Economic system. Paper presented at the 1988 annual meeting, Society for Economic Anthropology, Knoxville TN.

BUNDLES OF ASSETS IN EXCHANGES: INTEGRATING THE FORMAL AND INFORMAL IN CANAL IRRIGATION[1]

Robert C. Hunt
Department of Anthropology
Brandeis University

Introduction.

In this paper I present data on exchanges in a large bureaucratically managed canal irrigation system in India, showing that some of these exchanges are in the formal economy, and some in the informal economy, and that the two are integrated with each other. The specific case presented shows that the informal economy cannot be limited to small scale exchanges, petty commerce and manufacturing, or marginal people in society. Rather, the informal part of the economy can be deeply integrated into the center of a major institution, which creates and delivers a benefit stream of prime importance to the society as a whole.

I also present an argument about exchange systems involving assets. Every actor brings to an exchange a bundle of assets.[2] Sen (1981) has written eloquently of bundles of entitlements which an economic actor can use to command access to some benefit; his emphasis is on food, but his argument is easily extended to most exchanges. I will argue for a broadening of our understanding of the structure of exchanges to include assets and, further, that a study

---

[1]This draft has had the benefit of careful readings by Arjun Appadurai, M. Estellie Smith, and Irene Winter. Robert Wade has been most generous with editorial and substantive advice and corrections. I am most grateful for the advice although I have not always accepted it.
[2]I thank Carol Bier, of the Textile Museum, Washington D.C., for suggesting the term "asset."

of the informal economy encourages the distinction among legal, non-legal and illegal.

Before presenting the specifics of the case, some discussion of entitlements, assets and exchanges is in order. In most of the writing on exchanges, the focus has been on the goods and services exchanged and on attempts to discover their relative value. Sen, in his analysis of famines and poverty (1981), has presented the view that consumers have entitlements to goods and, often, that these should not be considered individually but, rather, as bundles of entitlements. For example, in any society with both a cash economy and social security, a citizen's ability to command what food is available is a function of both cash owned and social security rights. Thus, the citizen has two entitlements to food and they form a bundle.

The notion that exchangers have bundles of things that give them the ability to command in an exchange is extremely productive. However, the connotations of entitlement make it a poor choice for the general concept. Entitlement refers to legal title, and means legal ownership (Sen 1981: 45). The terminology is tightly connected to legitimate rights. It is therefore a useful term in the context of the formal economy, but becomes very confusing when exchanges in the informal economy are involved.

I suggest that "assets" is the more general concept, with entitlements being one kind of asset. In this view, assets are what an exchanger brings to the exchange, and they are what are exchanged. Assets may, of course, be tangible, such as a spear, a vial of gold dust, or a bolt of silk. They may also be intangible, such as songs, a medical diagnostic skill, or relative social status. There are many complexities to the sociology of exchange.

Whatever else is necessary for an exchange to take place, assets must be present. Some assets are entitlements, and some are not. Some will be brought to bear on an exchange and some will not. In the case that follows, I will specify several kinds of actors, each having access to several assets. I will describe some exchanges of one dyadic pair of these roles in terms of the assets, and will then show how the formal and informal economies are intermixed.[3]

Description.

Sources. A general point about data availability, validity and reliability with respect to the informal economy needs to be made. The formal economy is the accounted one, and we normally depend upon the accounted figures for many of our data. By definition, the informal economy is not going to be a part of the accounted one. Therefore, any observation and measurement of the informal economy must be the result of special-purpose and labor-intensive observations. This raises very serious questions of sampling frames and error. There is no solution to this problem other than a careful detailed recounting of how the data were gathered. But, in turn, this may be very difficult to justify because some of the informal economy may be illegal, and the recounting may very well put informants in jeopardy. This dilemma is serious as well as perplexing for the scholar. It seems to imply that the reliability and external validity of the data on the informal economy will always be suspect.

In any empirical discussion of the informal economy it is crucial that the quality of the information be assessed. In the case from India presented below, the formal structure of the canal irrigation system is public knowledge and easily accessible to anyone who is on the spot and interested. For the structure of the informal exchanges in the operation of the system, however, a different

---

[3]A social relationship must exist for an exchange to exist and, in the vast majority of cases, such relationships endure over time. This means that recruitment, maintenance, and termination criteria play a prominent part (cf. Hunt 1971). Another factor is that some sort of propinquity must be established for the exchange to take place. Cylinder seals were one way of extending one's authority in space and time in the ancient Near East (cf. Winter 1987, Hunt 1987). Another factor is that there must be a code for discussing the exchange and, if the parties do not share the code, the technology of communication, then the exchange is hindered. Finally, there are rules of the exchange, and these must be known to both parties. Some of these pheneomena have been presented in a wide variety of contexts (cf. particularly the volume edited by Appadurai 1986). We do not yet have a general picture of the social structure of exchange.

condition obtains. Some of these informal exchanges are easily labelled "corruption," and may be called that by at least some of the people involved in them. Further, at least some of these people will also be identified as engaged in illegal activities. How, then, do we evaluate the validity and reliability of these data? In this case, at least, my major source is the publications of an economist who has done extensive field work on canal irrigation (Wade 1982, 1985). He has published two articles which provide the vast bulk of the information discussed here. However, there are other published sources (e.g., Pant 1981) that present data of the same sort.[4]

History of canal systems. Canal irrigation in India has a very long history. Irrigation is of some moment in the Rigvedas (Keith 1921:121) and was a serious matter of state administration in the Maurya Empire (Thomas 1921:428). Many systems were inaugurated or expanded in Mughal times—especially during the 16th-18th centuries (Habib 1958:26-36). The English built or expanded large canal systems to provide famine relief. They were supposed to provide enough water in times of drought so that famine would be averted (Stone 1984). For the vast majority of the colonial systems in the later 19th and early 20th centuries, there was less demand than supply of the water, and the canal water was not integrated into quotidian rural production, at least in the uplands (Wade 1982).

Since the construction of many of these pre-independence canal systems, the population of South Asia has increased fourfold, to over one billion; in India alone it has grown to over 750 million, yet the proportion of the population that lives in villages has been reduced very little (Davis 1951). Demand for agricultural land, agricultural production, and irrigation water have vastly increased. At this point in time, canal irrigation water is fully used and an integrated part of rural production. In consequence, those canal

---

[4]Knowing both of these individuals and having talked with them about these data, it is my personal judgement that the validity is high enough for us to take them seriously.

systems that formerly had a surplus of water in normal times are now said to have chronic scarcities.[5]

The empirical case described here is from a single large canal irrigation system in a state in southern India.[6] The climate is such that there is a rainy season and a dry season and the principal irrigated crops are rice and groundnuts. In some years it is possible to grow a crop of rice during the monsoon without substantial irrigation (cf. Wade 1984:180-182). Virtually any crop grown during the dry season needs some irrigation. A factor in the operation of these systems is crop zoning. The government has designated large areas (thousands of acres) as zoned for particular crops during the dry season, and these have priority for water. Rice has been the crop that farmers most want to grow. On the other hand, crop zoning frequently proscribes the growing of rice over large areas in the water-scarce dry season, especially since each hectare of rice uses much more water than the same land under many other crops.

Organization of the Canal System. Following independence in 1947, control over large canal systems was vested in the governments of the various states that make up India.[7] The authority for operating the system is now granted by the legislatures of the states, and the systems are operated through the Chief Minister, and the Minister of the appropriate department.

The state legislature is composed of Members of the Legislative Assembly (MLAs), many of whom have power bases in farming villages. They are usually members of a political party. Upon election, the majority party will form a government, with a

---

[5]Many of the exchanges involving this water are in the informal economy. It is very difficult to have any empirical knowledge of supply and demand curves in the informal exchanges. It is virtually impossible to know whether water is physically scarce or not.

[6]The material is abstracted from articles by Wade (1982, 1985).

[7]"State" is, unfortunately, an ambiguous word. If the State has sovereignty in foreign affairs, a monopoly on the use of violence, etc., the state governments in India (or Mexico, or the USA) are not States A less ambiguous term in this case would be "provinces."

Chief Minister and a number of cabinet ministers. Most of the state government budgets comes from taxes and fees paid within the state. One source is the "betterment levy" which farmers pay as a result of having lands connected to the irrigation system. A portion of the state budget is paid by the Center (National Government). Much of major construction is paid by Center funds, some of which may be borrowed abroad (e.g., from the World Bank or the Asian Development Bank).

The Irrigation Ministry itself is headed by the Minister and is staffed with a cadre of permanently employed engineers. These engineers have to have the equivalent of a BA in civil engineering (n.b., *not* agricultural or hydraulic engineering). The service accepts applications from candidates from time to time and, as part of the intake procedure, an examination is given, followed by an interview. If the candidate is accepted into the service, he is ranked among other such candidates according to how well he did in the examination and interview. Not only does this ranking stay with him for the rest of his career but later promotion is dependent upon this rank.

There are five ranks for these engineers: Junior Engineer (JE), Assistant Engineer (AE), Executive Engineer (EE), Superintending Engineer (SE), and Chief Engineer (CE). This pyramid has a very large base, and a steep slope. Only a very few of the engineers can expect to receive more than two promotions in a career. Many receive only two, the second coming close to retirement. All engineers formally retire at age 58.

If there are very few vertical ranks, there is much horizontal movement. Every engineer must be transferred out of a post before three years are up, and the usual expectation is that a post will be occupied for about two years. The transfers are managed by one's superior two ranks above. However, transfers can be, and sometimes are, ordered after only a few days in a new post. Furthermore, within the Service there are a vast number of places where one can be posted (from the state capitol to the back of beyond), and a number of different kinds of job (Operation and Maintenance, Construction, Design, etc.). The engineers are paid a salary in cash. Because this salary has been fixed for some time, it has lost purchasing power over the years.

The job of the engineer is to design and operate the canal systems. But there are also construction and maintenance to be performed. Although the latter tasks are designed and supervised by the Engineers, the actual work is performed by private contractors, who bid for the jobs. The money for the work is a part of the budget of the Irrigation System, and the engineers award the contracts, supervise the work, and authorize the payments to the contractors.

Exchanges Among Roles. There is a complex set of exchanges among several actors in the process of operating this canal system. In this section, I will briefly outline who the major actors are, what the action is about, what is being exchanged, and whether it is formal or informal. In a subsequent section, I will concentrate on one dyad, the farmer-Assistant Engineer (AE) exchange, for an analysis of assets.

The primary actors in this system are (in no particular order): the engineers, the farmers, the MLAs, the Ministers, and the contractors. The engineers have a technical education, a civil service job with tenure, receive a salary in cash, and are responsible for managing and transferring two benefit streams, (1) the water and (2) the works budget (construction and maintenance money). The farmers grow cash crops, are members of villages, pay taxes on their land which validate their water rights, and elect MLAs. The MLAs have to keep a local constituency happy, and operate in the Assembly. The Ministers are elected politicians (MLAs), appointed to the Ministry, and manage bureaucracies. The contractors are dependent upon large organizations such as the Ministry for their work, and get paid in cash for the work performed.

There are formal rules for how the benefit streams are to be distributed and exchanged. The engineers are paid a salary by the state and, in return, are to distribute water and the works budget according to technical rules. The farmers pay their taxes and, in return, are supposed to receive the water which is their right.

Contractors submit their bids and, if they submit the winning bid and do the work correctly, are supposed to be paid in cash. The MLA's and the Ministers are not supposed to be involved in these exchanges at all.

The actuality of how this works is, as one might suppose, infinitely more complex. Briefly, there is much use of money and influence in informal exchanges. Some farmers will pay money and grain to engineers to increase the probability of receiving water. Some farmers will pressure their MLA in order to try to get water. Some MLAs will pressure engineers to award a contract to a particular contractor—and some will pay money to the electorate just before an election to ensure their votes. Some Ministers will respond to pressure from MLAs to influence the transfer of engineers or the winning of a construction contract. Some Ministers will pressure engineers to award a contract and to steer the transfer of particular engineers. Some engineers take part of the construction budget directly, and then take a further percentage from the contractor. Some engineers pay their superiors (and sometimes politicians as well) for their next transfer, and accept payment from subordinates for their next transfer. In sum, there is a vast system of informal exchange going on in the operation of this canal system. These informal exchanges are integrated with the formal exchanges, which also happen at the same time.[8]

Farmer-AE exchange: An example. In what follows I have abstracted from statements made by Wade about a handful of systems. It is clear in Wade's reports that the data presented here apply to only some of the farmers and engineers in these systems. To what degree this web of informal exchanges could be said to

---

[8]Our analytic categories are less than decisive here. Throughout the 1988 SEA meeting on the informal economy, we (or, at least, I) presumed we could and were analytically separating the informal from the formal economy. This assumes some stable concept of a formal economy and, further, that there are empirical phenomena pertaining or belonging to each which can be separated with equal precision. But in the case reported here, there are exchanges which simultaneously involve formal and informal dimensions. In this case can we speak of an informal "economy"? It is clear that *the* economy can not be equated with the *formal* economy. More thought needs to be given to thse issues.

apply to other canal systems in India or elsewhere is unclear.[9] However, there is an account of similar activities in Ch'ing China (Ch'ang Hu 1955).[10] Curiously, very few cases of informal exchanges in hydraulic works seem to have entered the public record.

All of the major roles are potentially involved in every kind of transaction. For the sake of simplicity and brevity, I want to analyze just one such dyad, the farmer-assistant engineer (AE), with the primary purpose of focusing on the bundles of assets that each brings to the transactions. In this case, the primary purpose of the farmer is to get water from the system when he wants it. The primary purposes of the AE are to do his job, stay out of trouble, and make enough money to support his family.

The formal assets of the farmer include what appears to be a water right. As the owner, his land is registered and he has to pay an improvement tax which validates his water right. The farmer also grows crops, some of which he sells for cash; this cash is also an asset which he draws on to pay his taxes. So far, we have two formal assets (both entitlements), land ownership[11] and cash, that are relevant for the acquisition of water from the irrigation system.

In the struggle for water, however, there are many other assets which the farmer may have. One is the location of his lands in

[9]This is another example of the reliability and validity problems inherent in a study of the informal economy. External validity of the materials is minimal, and perhaps not significantly different from zero. I see very little that can be done about this situation, at least at the moment, and suggest that we have to learn to live with it.

[10]There are, of course, many accounts of informal exchanges in bureaucracies from all over the world (cf. Noonan 1984 for a detailed discussion of several cases from classical Rome to the English East Indian company to the U.S.). While the first draft of this article was being written, a scandal broke out in New York City over systematic bribery of the health inspectors by restaurants (*New York Times*, March 25, 1988:1). As this draft is being written in June 1988, very much in the news is the scandal of the bribery and corruption between the U.S. Department of Defense and a large number of defense contractors.

[11]Let us assume that the farmer is operating only land that he owns and on which he pays taxes. This is far from the complete picture. But the complexity that would be introduced by rented or share-cropped land does not appear to significantly change the scenario I am sketching here.

the irrigation system. If his fields are close to a main canal, and close to the head of the system, then his difficulties in getting water are much less than if he is at the end of a tiny tributary stream, way off in the tail of the system. Thus, favorable physical location is an asset. The crop zone location of his lands is also an asset; having lands located within a zone that is legally permitted to receive water is an asset for the exchange for water.

The political integration of his village is an asset. Almost no farmer can enter one of these exchanges with the AE as an individual. The AE is responsible for up to 100,000 acres, and thousands of farmers. In consequence, farmers must organize as groups to affect the distribution of water, and these groups are normally villages. So, another asset of the farmer is the willingness of his village to act as a corporate group with respect to these matters.[12] Another asset is whether a powerful person comes from a farmer's village—for example, no engineer is going to hinder water delivery to farmers in the home village of an MLA.

It is sometimes the case that farmers make informal payments to the canal system staff in exchange for water, and these payments are usually in cash or grain. Sufficient supplies of cash and grain must be available and, when they are, they are assets. Because elected politicians can be a factor in the delivery of water, influence with such politicians is an asset. Another kind of asset is the potential for creating a disturbance. If a group of angry, armed, and vociferous farmers show up at the AE's office, it is likely that some response the farmers desire will be forthcoming.

There are of course limits on the exchange value (effective demand) of any of these assets. The AEs and the politicians are not omnipotent and they must balance competing demands at all times.

The assistant engineer's assets are also complex. There is a formal asset which is compensation for his work, a salary in cash. It

---

[12]There are many other possible assets here, including known wealth level, amount of land owned, *varna*, caste, class, education, and religion. A truly fine-grained description of some of these exchanges would want to take these into account.

is paid regularly, and is an entitlement. But it is not sufficient to support some careers—and the real value has been falling as prices have risen but salaries have not. The AE legally manages two benefit streams, water and the works budget, which are extremely valuable to two other actors, the farmers and the contractors. These two benefit streams are therefore potential assets of the AE.

The benefit stream of the works budget is sometimes divided so that part is captured by the engineers, part is captured by the contractors, and part is invested in construction works. Wade states that eight and one-half percent of the works budget of the AE is taken off the top and distributed to various officers. The remainder is awarded as contracts and, of that remainder, 20%-40% will come back to the engineers as kickbacks—though, of course, always disguised as something else. Of the amount that the contractor retains, some will be invested in work and the rest will be kept (Wade 1985).

Mobility within the bureaucracy is also subject to informal exchanges. According to Wade some engineers pay for the purchase of transfers by means of the income from the works budget, but this is not sufficient in many cases to support all the cash needs of these individuals.

The second benefit stream that the engineers manage is the distribution of water. Some engineers derive cash income from the distribution of water and this involves regular exchanges with groups of farmers. Here we have several different possibilities. Because there is a general understanding that water is, or may become, relatively scarce, specific groups of farmers will, on occasion, attempt to increase their supply with extra payments to the relevant engineer. The crop zone system provides multiple opportunities for informal exchanges. For example, if an area is zoned to prohibit the planting of rice but rice is, in fact, planted, then the farmers will do their best to acquire water from the AE so as to be able to bring their rice to harvest. A series of informal payments for that water are often made. In such cases, the AE is essentially reactive. However, the AE can also be proactive: It is not difficult to create an expectation of uncertainty about water among farmers by starting rumors of scarcity. Money may then be collected from those farmers, supposedly to protect them against that uncertainty.

Other actors may get involved in these exchanges. Farmers with sufficient influence with an MLA may persuade the MLA to intervene with the AE or with the latter's superiors, so that the water allocation decisions of the AE are potentially influenced by his superiors as well as by the MLA.

There is another constraint in all of this. Some of these informal exchanges are outside the formal legal boundaries, and some of these are actually illegal. There is the omnipresent potential that someone will blow the whistle. It appears that two extremes of behavior—refusal to participate, and excessive greed—are negatively sanctioned by the participants in the informal exchanges. Engineers showing either of these extremes may be encouraged to move their behavior closer to the statistical norm.

Discussion.

From the limited cases available, several points emerge and warrant further discussion.

The first is that the informal economy, or the informal exchanges in the economy, are centrally involved in an expensive and massive infrastructure. This infrastructure is crucial to the livelihoods of a vast number of people, both rich and poor. It is therefore not a minor or marginal part of the national economy but, rather, is central to the rural economy. Furthermore, the informal and formal exchanges, or aspects of the exchanges, are intertwined with each other.

If it is granted that these large-scale and systematic exchanges are part of the informal economy, then it follows that a concept of the informal economy has to be enlarged to include such phenomena.

Secondly, I have introduced the concepts of "asset" and "bundles of assets" for describing and analyzing the capacity to engage in exchanges. As pointed out in the introduction, Sen uses the concept of entitlement and of bundles of entitlements (1981). By "entitlement" he means an asset which gives the person who has that asset the ability to command the exchange of the desired valued— which, in Sen's case, is food. By the use of the phrase "bundle of entitlement," Sen is proposing that, in many circumstances, an individual has two or more assets relevant for exchangeable goods and services.

It is productive for us to concentrate on those assets that one must have in order to command an exchange of something one wants. And it is productive to view those things not singly but as bundles. I propose then that the appropriate term for the conditions which enable exchange is "assets." In almost every case of exchange, the parties involved will have bundles of assets. Some of the assets will be brought to bear, and some will be exchanged away. Some of those assets are entitlements, backed by the full moral and judicial force of the State. But often some of those assets will not appear in any account of the formal exchanges, and some may even be illegal.

Of the assets controlled by the farmer and by the AE, in the examples sketched above, some are clearly legal entitlements—the farmer's water right, the AE's management of the water and construction funds, as well as the right to a salary. Some are apparently non-legal, such as that of the farmer coming from the village of an MLA. Some are clearly illegal; paying a bribe for water, or taking a kickback from the contractor.

A third point is the dynamic management of assets. It must be the case that parties to the exchanges are thinking strategically about the acquisition of assets, about exchanging some of one asset for some of another, and about how to invest those assets in an over-all strategy for life. Surely, the growing of rice or groundnuts this crop season is just one piece of a farmer's strategic design. And, surely, farmers vary in the time framework, complexity and scope of what they are trying to accomplish.

If location is an asset, then it seems very likely that some individuals are capable of enhancing their locational assets. It is usual for urban-based social scientists to assume that a farmer inherits a village residence, and that it is fixed for life. I suspect this is more myth than reality. There has been a vast movement of population into and out of the tube-well areas of the Punjab over the last 150 years, as irrigation has become more effective. This involves people buying and selling land, and moving (Stone 1984). It would be productive to systematically analyze the mechanisms and ease by which it may be done.

Fourthly, it is important to consider the effects of these informal exchanges on the society. Many commentators share with Wade a position that these informal transactions subtract from production and equity (for one of the opposing views, see Nye 1967). It is useful to split the discussion into, on the one hand, construction and, on the other hand, the distribution of the water. It is clear that, were the total amount budgeted for construction and maintenance actually spent on those tasks, more work would be done and, presumably, the flow of water—and thus crop production and income—would be improved. What is not clear is how such work would take place under any conditions other than a dedicated and powerful police state. If the engineers are underpaid, why is it reasonable to expect them to manage construction with perfect "honesty"?

Should not the cost of the construction include the real costs of the supervisors and those monitoring quality control? And, if these real costs are included in the works budget, then the construction budget is not as large as it appears to be for there are overhead costs hidden in it. Note that I am not arguing that the present situation is the best of all possible worlds, or even that it is functional, or functioning. I am suggesting a counter-argument to the usual (moralizing and negative) view.

On the water distribution side of the ledger, it is extremely difficult to discover exactly where and when the water is being delivered. Anyone who wants to claim that water distribution is currently less than maximally efficient has a massive data-gathering and analysis job to perform—as does anyone who wants to claim that the current picture is efficient. The data to resolve such claims simply do not exist. Collecting them would have to be done in the field, and personally.

The research design necessary for gathering the data to resolve these issues is complex, difficult to design, and very expensive to carry out. As in all cases of the informal economy, direct observation is necessary, with all of the inherent reliability and validity problems that surge along on the bow wave.

Fifthly, as we continue to probe the concepts of economic anthropology, it is clearly the case that informal versus formal will be too simple, and that we will need other, more finely focused concepts to handle all of these complexities.

In general, the informal economy is defined in contra-distinction to some *formal* economy. The latter concept has not received enough attention. It would appear to be the case that the formal economy is accounted, is legal, and is positively sanctioned by the State. If this line of thought is followed, then the formal economy in any given situation is just what a given State determines it to be. It follows from this that all studies of the informal economy will have to specify what the particular formal economy is, and that formal economy is the legitimate context for the study of some aspect of an informal economy. We might, in the future, discover that there is a substantive core to all formal economies—but we might not.

A final point: A brief survey of the literature on corruption (cf. Scott 1972, Heidenheimer's edited volume 1972, Clarke 1983; Noonan 1984) reveals two things very quickly: (1) Bribery and corruption are (at least) several thousands of years old, and may even be integral parts of the State; (2) everywhere there are rules which make certain kinds of exchanges—among certain individuals at certain times—illegal. This is a curious state of affairs. If a condition (large bundles of assets being brought to bear on exchanges, combined with a barely enforceable line between public and private benefit) is so widespread and so central to the running of the State, why is it not regarded as normal and unproblematic? Under these circumstances, the bizarre phenomenon has to be the continuous insistence that it is possible to organize things in a simple, honest and "formal" way.

One view of this situation leads to the suspicion that the laws against corruption function as a potential sanction against enemies or opponents who break some other (perhaps informal) rule. Because every participant is guilty of some sort of infraction, then everybody is potentially vulnerable to laws against infractions. Such laws may function as one of a bundle of assets which are means of social control by administrators.

Conclusion

I have argued that each participant in an exchange comes to that exchange with a bundle of assets Some of those assets are entitlements in that they are legally owned, and legally exchanged. Some of those assets are not legally owned or legally exchanged; these latter are in the informal economy.

I have presented an empirical case in which informal exchanges co-occur with formal ones, both embedded within a major part of a state organization responsible for managing a critical input to agricultural production. This suggests strongly that the informal economy may be seen as a fundamental and central part of the economy, managing and meeting important needs of many actors.

References.

Appadurai, Arjun, ed.
1986   The Social Life of Things: Commodities in Cultural
       Perspective. Cambridge: Cambridge University Press.

Ch'ang Hu
1955   The Yellow River Administration in the Ch'ing
       Dynasty. Far Eastern Quarterly 14: 505-513.

Clarke, Michael, ed.
1983   Corruption: Causes, Consequences and Control. New
       York: St. Martin's Press.

Davis, Kingsley
1951   The Population of India and Pakistan. Princeton:
       Princeton University Press.

Habib, Irfan
1963   The Agrarian System of Mughal India (1556-1707).
       New York: Asia Publishing House.

Heidenheimer, A., ed.
1970   Political Corruption: Readings in Comparative
       Analysis. New York: Holt Rinehart and Winston.

Hunt, Robert C.
1971   Components of Relationships in the Family: A Mexican
       Village. In F. Hsu, ed., Kinship and Culture.
       Chicago: Aldine, pp 106-143.
1987   The Role of Bureaucracy in the Provisioning of Cities:
       A Framework for the Analysis of the Ancient Near
       East. In M. Gibson and R. D. Biggs, eds.,The
       Organization of Power: Aspects of Bureaucracy in the
       Ancient Near East: Studies in Ancient Oriental
       Civilization No 46. Chicago: The Oriental Institute of
       the University of Chicago, pp. 161-192.

Keith, A.B.
1921   The Period of the Later Samhitas, the Brahmanas, the
        Aranyakas, and the Upanishads. The Cambridge
        History of India I: 102-133.

Noonan, J. T.
1984   Bribes. New York: Macmillan.

Nye, J.
1967   Corruption and Political Development: A Cost-Benefit
        Analysis. American Political Science Review 61: 417-
        427.

Pant, Niranjan
1981   Some Aspects of Irrigation Administration. Calcutta:
        Debesh Dutta.

Scott, James
1972   Comparative Political Corruption. Englewood Cliffs
        NJ: Prentice- Hall.

Sen, Amartya
1981   Poverty and Famines. An Essay on Entitlement and
        Deprivation. Oxford: Oxford University Press.

Stone, Ian
1984   Canal Irrigation in India. Cambridge: Cambridge
        University Press.

Thomas, F. W.
1921   Political and Social Organization of the Maurya
        Empire.The Cambridge History of India I: 427-445.

Wade, Robert
1982   The System of Administrative and Political
        Corruption: Canal Irrigation in South India. Journal
        of Development Studies 18: 287-328.

1984   Managing a Drought With Canal Irrigation: A South
        Indian Case. Agricultural Administration 17: 177-
        202.
1985   The Market for Public Office: Why the Indian State is
        Not Better at Development. World Development 13:
        467-497.

Winter, Irene J.
1987   Legitimation of Authority Through Image and
        Legend: Seals Belonging to Officials in the
        Administrative Bureaucracy of the Ur III State. In M.
        Gibson and R. D. Biggs, eds., The Organization of
        Power: Aspects of Bureaucracy in the Ancient Near
        East. Studies in Ancient Oriental Civilization, No. 46.
        Chicago: The Oriental Insititute of the University of
        Chicago, pp. 69-116.

A CROSS-CULTURAL TREATMENT
OF THE INFORMAL ECONOMY[1]

Rhoda H. Halperin
Department of Anthropology
University of Cincinnati

Sara Sturdevant
Department of Anthropology
University of Pittsburgh

Introduction.

This paper proposes a model of the informal economy that can be used as a heuristic device for dealing with variability, plurality and change in economic systems across cultures and over time. It is meant to explore the potentials of the concept by drawing upon a range of cultural systems—from hunter-gatherers to third world and post-industrial States.

Most discussions of the informal economy have been restricted to the marginal, hidden or illegal segments of urban, State-level societies (Arizpe 1977; Babb 1985; Bromley 1978a, 1978b, 1985; Davies 1979; Dow 1977; Gaertner and Wenig 1985; Hoyman 1987; Mattera 1985; Obregon 1980; Peattie 1980, 1982). Whether under capitalism, or in centrally planned economies (Grossman 1988; Sampson 1985/6, 1987; Wedel 1986; Bloch 1985/86), the primary foci have been industrialized societies or the urban sectors of developing countries (Gerry 1987; Hart 1973; Miller 1987; Trager 1985, 1987).

The rural parts of State systems have not received attention from analysts of the informal economy. For the most part,

[1]Thanks to Sandi Cannell and Beth Remer for typing and editing this manuscript. Barry Isaac,M. Estelle Smith, and Sidney Holtzman were extremely helpful in, especially, the initial and final stages.

discussions have used ethnographic materials from rural and non-State societies as quaint examples of small scale systems, or as indications that principles such as kin-based reciprocity (Mauss 1954; Lévi-Strauss 1969; Polanyi 1957; Sahlins 1972) are universal, with variations in different cultural contexts (Gaughan and Ferman 1987). With a few exceptions, exchange processes have been emphasized to the exclusion of processes of production or consumption (Simon and Witte 1982; Lomnitz 1988; Gaughan and Ferman 1987).

Most importantly for our purposes, these focused treatments have not used their discussions of the informal economy to inform the subfield of economic anthropology as the scientific study of economies across cultures (Halperin 1988). As a result, some confusions are in evidence. For example, the domain to which the concept of the informal economy applies is not at all clear. The concept has been used in both the developed and the underdeveloped world, but to which parts? Are the rural parts automatically excluded—or are they assumed to constitute the informal sectors? If, on the other hand, the rural as well as urban parts of industrial and pre-industrial or industrializing States have both formal and informal sectors, how should these be considered? Any treatment requires a concept of the informal economy that is cross-culturally and historically based.

In this paper, we take a broad-based, cross-cultural perspective and attempt to develop a model to explore the utility of a concept of the informal economy as a cross-cultural concept. The wording, "explore the utility" is important because our aim here is to examine the potentials of a concept of the informal economy for understanding pattern, variability, and change in processes of production, distribution, and consumption in a range of sociocultural types. That is, we develop the concept of the informal economy as a heuristic device or model—a conceptual tool that can be used to understand aspects of economic processes that would remain hidden without such an analytic instrument. We use the concept of the informal economy to deal with processes of production as well as with processes of distribution, in particular, problems of the organization of the productive resources, land, labor, and credit (Long 1978; Illich 1981; Henry 1987). To summarize thus far: (1) We need a concept of the informal economy that can be used across cultures and over time; (2) this paper is intended to indicate how such a cross-cultural concept of the informal economy can be formulated. Below, we outline a model of the informal economy and present some examples of how the model can be used in different cultural contexts.

Definitions and assumptions.

Formal economy as mainstream economy. First, some definitions and assumptions. If we assume that all economies have both formal and informal components, then, logically speaking, the informal economy can be understood analytically as the opposite of the formal economy. Any treatment of a concept of the informal economy, then, requires a prior definition of what constitutes the formal economy. For definitional purposes, we can say that the formal economy is the mainstream economy. By "mainstream economy" we mean what Polanyi called the dominant mode of economic integration, or, more simply, the major, recognized and accounted for (by either qualitative or quantitative mechanisms) principles organizing a given economic process or set of processes. Since the issue of accountability has been discussed at some length elsewhere (Smith 1989), we will not dwell on it here. The formal economy is, in this sense, both a folk and an analytic concept. In its folk meaning, the formal economy is recognized in a given cultural system as the officially sanctioned and expected way of doing things, in either the normative or the statistical sense—or both. Analytically, the formal economy may be a model that is set up for scientific purposes only, say, as a set of ideals, or as a set of expectations under known or controlled conditions. As will become clear below, the analytical meaning of informal economy can be understood in similar terms. From both folk and analytic perspectives, the formal economy may generally be understood as follows: In State level economies, the formal economy may be organized by the polity itself in its many pre-industrial or industrial forms, by the capitalist market mechanism, or by some combination of the two. In pre-State societies, kinship principles or principles involving age sets, for example, may dominate the organization of economic processes. Notice that the definition of the formal economy here does not refer only to bureaucratic mechanisms, but includes a range of structures and institutions, both bureaucratic and non-bureaucratic (Hart 1973).

Informal economy as anti-economy. Given the above framework for the formal economy, the informal economy is the opposite of the formal economy, what we will call the "anti-economy." The anti-economy can be defined as follows: locational and appropriational movements outside of the mainstream economy (Polanyi 1957; Halperin 1989). Locational movements involve physical changes, such as the movement of goods from one place to another; appropriational movements involve changes in organizational principles, primarily the nature of the rights and obligations associated with a given economic process.

The term "anti-economy" is meant to indicate tension between the formal and the informal elements of economic processes, whether the tension takes the form of deviance from the mainstream economy (as in breaking the rules of the mainstream economy by secret or illegal activity), or whether the tension takes the form of alternative economic institutions that operate in parallel to the mainstream economy. Whatever its form, we can assume that there is always tension between the formal and the informal components of economic processes. In some instances, for example, only some of the folk will have access to knowledge of the workings of the informal economy. Still others may have access to the goods of the informal economy. There is a tug-of-war between the formal and the informal economies that operates on several levels. This framework allows for the fact that what at one time may have been an informal sector may become formal and dominant; or there may be changes in both formal and informal components of economies such that both change qualitatively and quantitatively.

To summarize thus far: Defined operationally in this way, the concept of the informal economy is not necessarily restricted to State systems, but can be used across cultures and over time. If we assume that variability in principles of economic organization exists in all economies—that no economy is without variability—then the advantage of a cross-cultural concept of the informal economy is that it provides an analytical tool for gaining some insight into the nature of the variability. We might note here that, especially for kin-based economies, the assumption that principles of economic organization (e.g., reciprocity) operate consistently and homogeneously is a holdover from British structural-functionalism and has prevented the examination of variability. Malinowski (1922) used terms such as "reciprocity" to describe many different kinds of economic exchanges. Raymond Firth (1929, 1939) followed in his footsteps. Helen Codere (1968) wrote of social economies as organized by reciprocity, and political economies as organized by redistribution. Even Morton Fried (1967), whose framework was evolutionary rather than functionalist, wrote of egalitarian societies having reciprocal economies—without any attention to the variability inherent in these economies and polities. This concept of the informal economy as anti-economy is designed to get at some of the variability.

We can use the concept of the informal economy then, to question conventional canons about economic organization, especially about the homogeneity of small scale economic systems. In short, a concept of the informal economy, if used heuristically in a cross-cultural framework, allows us to ask certain kinds of questions that are difficult to ask otherwise. For example, the division of labor by age and sex has commonly been thought to operate in all small scale egalitarian societies in an exclusive and consistent fashion. But what happens if we use a concept of the anti-economy to ask such questions as: What are the conditions under which men and women, young and old, reverse economic roles? What are the economic rituals of rebellion? Who is exempt, either permanently or temporarily, from the conventional economic rules and roles? We find that some very interesting answers emerge. One is that we not only find deviation and flexibility in small scale systems, but complexity and variability that, when recognized, lead to a series of other questions: How much informality is allowed? How much deviation from the mainstream economic principles can exist before the system changes radically or falls apart? How many alternative forms of economic organization are possible?

325

In all cultures mechanisms outside of the mainstream provide both flexibility and variability. A concept of the informal economy as anti-economy allows us to examine relationships between different kinds of economic activities, i.e. those organized by different principles. These relationships have been handled in a rather cumbersome manner, e.g. as "articulating modes of production" (Foster-Carter 1978; Taussig 1980).

Pre-State societies: The informal economy as a barometer of variability, conflict and change.

Our basic hypothesis is that, in pre-State systems, the model of the informal economy can be used as a barometer of variability that may lead to conflict and, ultimately, change.

The !Kung and the Jivaro. At the band level, it is difficult to conceptualize or imagine how an informal, anti-economy might work except as a barometer of conflict and change. The inimitable, non-shareable coke bottle that falls out of the sky in the film, "The Gods Must be Crazy" is one very clever, but highly symbolic example of what happens when egalitarian cultures become suddenly integrated into nation-State capitalist systems. The bottle represents exclusivity, indeed, private property, and cannot, without extremely rapid and radical change in the economic system, coexist in an economy of sharing and generalized reciprocity. Similarly, once the !Kung have been placed on a reservation, their sedentary existence renders them reliant upon government rations (the distasteful mealie-mealie). Since there is a scarcity of this food, it cannot be shared (Marshall 1980). The fact that the !Kung woman, N!ai, becomes a street beggar who sells her songs for cash is an example of the development of an informal economy. Her exclusive access to songs, and thus, cash, creates as much, if not more conflict as the Coke bottle.

An example of an informal economic arrangement operating in parallel to the mainstream economy of reciprocity is that of the accumulative economy of the Jivaro shamans. The shamans exemplify the anti-economy. They are the only people who are exempt from the dominant economy of reciprocity in goods and

326

labor. They are the only people allowed to engage in accumulation. For example, Harner reports that, for an ordinary Jivaro, a request for a gift cannot be denied without the one refusing "losing face." This makes it difficult for the majority of persons to hoard quantities of possessions (1973: 117). Non-shamans badger one another continually for gifts, but these ordinary people almost never ask a shaman for gifts. The shaman's ability to accumulate appears to be important for political relations with neighboring groups since shamans, "frequently use their wealth and social influence to secure specific services from their non-shaman neighbors, including hosting neighbors to help in land clearing" (1973: 118). It is interesting to note that according to the ideological system, this acquisition of services with the expectation of a return effort is understood as reciprocal cooperative labor, but, says Harner, "the shaman's neighbors are reluctant to ask him to work for them in turn" (1973: 118). In addition, Harner reports several cases in which shamans received daughters in marriage, but were exempt from both bride service and bride price (Harner 1973: 118).

Among the many interesting elements in the Jivaro case, is that the anti-economy is so public and political. It allows the shaman to play both political (alliance-forming) and economic (goods and services obtaining) roles. It is also of note that one out of every four adult men is a shaman, a significant portion of the male population. They cannot be discounted as rarities or deviants. In short, non-mainstream economic activities are not insignificant. Rather, what we have here is a case in which the concept of the informal economy can be used to indicate heretofore unrecognized variability in an Amazon Basin economy. These economies have conventionally been treated as homogeneous reciprocal economies.

The Tiv. For the African Tiv, the Bohannans are much more specific about some of the informal elements of the economy, particularly the informal elements of women's work, stands in contrast to the more formally organized men's work. The formal rules of work organization consist of the following: (1) brothers tend to work together; (2) co-wives work separately, unless they are attached to senior wives.

Ordinarily, work groups of women tend to be smaller, and more circumscribed than those of men. Women's work groups are composed of a senior woman, those junior wives who are "put into her hut," and her daughters-in-law (1968: 70). According to the Bohannans, the important facts about such female groups are as follows: (1) The optimal, day-to-day size of a working group of women is three or four women (1968: 71); (2) if there are more, they tend to form two groups; (3) women who find themselves in an uncongenial group leave their husbands.

There is one condition under which women deviate from this pattern. This is for weeding. The Bohannans describe what is involved in extremely tentative terms so as to indicate irregularity:

All of the women of one compound, or of several nearby compounds, may band together two or three times a year for a hoeing party to weed the fields of each of them. Such a hoeing party is "called" by a senior woman, who supplies food and beer....These groups are usually composed of between fifteen and twenty women, but there may be as many as thirty-five. The important point is that this is the major form of agricultural cooperation among women; other forms are rare (1968: 73).

In contrast to the irregular and sporadic nature of large cooperative work groups for women, men cooperate regularly, systematically, and in a formal manner:

Cooperation in agricultural tasks is more formally developed among men and has no equivalents among women....When hoeing mounds (of yams) in large groups each man makes a diagonal row of mounds, but all work together in a single vertical row. This enables them to mound the field with regularity. As soon as a man's diagonal row reaches the side of the field, he goes to the other end of the line. Between forty and fifty men mounded about five acres of yams in two days (1968: 73-74).

It is difficult to know how many groups of this type have similar combinations of formal and informal arrangements of large-scale cooperative labor. One suspects that such informal ways of organizing work are quite common. Ethnographers tend to deal only with the dominant forms of work organization, however, and do not look for the variability. In addition, in the Tiv case, it is possible to contemplate a whole range of deviations from the clearly articulated forms of production and particularly exchange. The systems of conveyances and convergences, described in great detail by the Bohannans, can be and probably are, subject to a variety of irregular forms.

We can begin to see one important point from the Tiv example, a point that will be further elaborated below. That is, the institutional context determines whether a given form of organization is informal or not. In one institutional context, large groups of workers, organized along kinship lines, may be dominant and, therefore, represent the mainstream (formal) economy. In others, household based groups are dominant. Deviations from the dominant form constitute the informal elements of the economy.

State systems: The informal economy as a barometer of pluralism and change.

In State systems, the informal economy is not only a barometer of variability and change, but of pluralism. By "pluralism" we mean numerous economic sectors and economic activities operating simultaneously. Complicating the systems at the State level is the fact that the informal sector itself is heterogeneous with many different types of economic activities, e.g., street vendors, small market traders, small shops as well as many different categories of workers (Trager 1987). The importance of the overall institutional context in determining the informal economy becomes even more clear. We will use three examples to illustrate the utility of a cross-cultural concept of the informal economy as the anti-economy outside of the dominant capitalist contexts and in rural and non-bureaucratic settings: The first involves centrally planned economies; the second treats stores and storekeepers in a rural

Appalachian community; the third considers marketplace systems in rural Kentucky as they articulate with other modes of distribution.

Centrally planned economies. The utility of, first, defining the informal economy as the anti-economy and, then, using the concept as a heuristic device is nowhere made more clear than in the case of centrally planned economies in the Soviet Union and Eastern Europe. In this context, there are several anti-economies operating simultaneously both in conjunction with and in opposition to the mainstream centrally planned economy. We draw here on the work of Steven Sampson because he deals with varying forms of the informal economy, from

> ...capitalist entrepreneurship: the peasant who cultivates her private plot and sells the produce on the free market, speculative trading, middleman fees, renting property, money, lending, and operating a private firm...[to] producing or selling illegal goods such as narcotics or providing illegal services such as prostitution; pilfering from the workplace...conducting unregistered or untaxed trade; and paying off police or inspectors to ignore such activities...[to] second economy activities that are neither typically capitalist nor universally illegal...underground factories; paying bribes or tips in order to buy something in a store or to induce planners and controllers to revise plans; buying and reselling goods obtained from shops for foreigners; and selling scarce or rationed goods taken from the State (1987: 121).

Sampson argues that these second economies must be understood within the context of the total economic system: "The second economy is an integral part of the official, planned economy, sometimes complementing it, sometimes hindering it directly, sometimes competing with it" (1987: 122). A cross-cultural definition of the informal economy is essential for dealing with this variability. All of these are forms of the informal economy, but to define the informal economy only in terms of exchange and not production, for example, rules out underground factories. To define the informal economy as only those activities that are illegal rules out all of the alternative forms that are legal, but non-mainstream.

330

A rural Appalachian economy. The operation of informal mechanisms in rural, non-bureaucratic settings is often quite secretive and always full of subtlety and nuance. In this essentially kin organized subsistence economy, storekeepers engage in certain kinds of informal economic arrangements which produce tension in the system. The rural Appalachian community under consideration here is that of Little Laurel, described by George Hicks in the book *Appalachian Valley* (1973). Little Laurel is a community typical of many in the Appalachian region: It is small (population 1300 at the time of fieldwork) and its economy is oriented to subsistence farming combined with daily and weekly, as well as seasonal, migration to towns and cities for factory-based wage labor. Loyalty to kin is a primary principle of social and economic organization and store patronage is patterned along kinship lines. Trade in both livestock and other goods has existed for at least a century.

Storekeepers in Little Laurel are the intermediaries between the subsistence and the cash economy. They control the flow of goods and cash both into and out of the rural community. Storekeepers also compete with one another for clientele. For example, galax, a fern gathered in Little Laurel by men, women, and children alike, and used as background greenery in flower arrangements, is sold to florists outside of the community for cash. Storekeepers distribute galax to the outside by obtaining galax from clients and converting it into credit against a person's account. As Hicks describes it, when a galacker who is known to be a regular customer of store A, in which his galax would be converted into credit only, wants cash for his galax in store B, storekeeper B must not reveal this cash transaction to store owner A to whom the galacker owes money. This secret economic transaction is part of the informal economy in this small community.

Storekeepers also have other sorts of knowledge about economic matters. While Hicks notes that the secrets are often short-lived, there is a short-run economic advantage for the people involved. For example, Hicks reports:

> Locations of good patches of galax, prices paid for land and livestock, the whereabout of individuals at various times, and

the income of families are all matters about which storekeepers have a great deal of knowledge. They find it to their own advantage not to spread their knowledge too freely.

Indeed, the successful operation of a store in the Little Laurel depends very much upon the storekeeper's adeptness in controlling the flow of information among himself and his customers. Privy to many secrets, he can choose what part of them to put into circulation.... By protecting his customers—keeping wives from knowing what husbands are doing or government officials from knowledge of certain illegal activities in the valley—he earns their gratitude and attaches them more firmly to his store. Information about the plans and activities of his competitor businesses is, thus, in appreciation for past favors, taken in and used to financial advantage (1973: 87).

Here, mechanisms of kinship and friendship are part of the informal economy, but the consequences of violating kinship obligations, a distinct possibility where multiple stores are used by clients, are unclear. This example raises questions about the relationships between informality, secrecy, and even corruption, and the position of a person or group in the local and the regional stratification system.

A periodic marketplace system in eastern Kentucky. Periodic marketplace systems can be the primary and dominant mode of extra-community (non-local) distribution; this has been true in much of the preindustrial third world. Examples from China (Skinner 1964) and Mexico (Cook and Diskin 1976; Malinowski and de la Fuente 1982) are common. On the other hand, periodic marketplace systems can be the key components of the informal economy. Our work in Eastern Kentucky illustrates this point. At the rural urban interface the periodic marketplace system is a major source of cash as well as an outlet for locally produced goods. The marketplace system is, however, only one component, albeit an important component, of a system of multiple livelihood strategies that consists of three sectors: (1) the informal (periodic marketplace) sector; (2) the formal (market economy) sector; (3) the subsistence sector, which is neutral from the point of view of formal and informal principles of economic organization (Halperin, n.d.).

The example of the informal economy in eastern Kentucky raises some important points associated with our hypothesis that informal economies are barometers not only of variability, but also of pluralism and change in the organization of economic systems. First, the system of marketplaces has grown enormously during our two years of fieldwork. The numbers of vendors in each major marketplace, and the number of actual market places has increased markedly. In one of the major marketplaces, for example, the number of stalls, both interior and exterior, grows on a weekly basis. When we first began the fieldwork, there were several empty aisles inside the converted tobacco warehouse; now all booths are occupied and the marketplace has expanded. Ironically, perhaps, it is located in an area adjacent to a large shopping mall in which many identical items are sold for as much as ten times the price. Many of the vendors in the market are themselves owners of stores and shops in both urban and rural areas. It could be argued that the existence of such an alternative system of distribution is what makes it possible for the large numbers of working class people to live at the rural/urban interface. These workers provide the temporary labor for the growing numbers of (light industry) factories. Alternative sources of distribution for goods are essential in this context, otherwise people would either have to retreat back to the deep rural areas or move to the cities and become totally dependent upon cash from low level jobs or welfare. The fact that the interface provides so many livelihood alternatives, and that people utilize multiple strategies, is an indicator of pluralism that appears on the increase and, for the near future, likely to remain.

Conclusion.

We have argued here that if we define the informal economy as the anti-economy, then all economies have informal components (institutional arrangements). In this framework, the concept of the informal economy is a heuristic device designed to handle variability, pluralism and change in economic systems.

Informality is not necessarily "a residue of traditionalism" (Lomnitz 1988: 42). Informal components may represent the newest economic form, or at least a sophisticated set of adaptations at various levels of local, regional and national economies. What is informal, or even corrupt, at the local level may simply be normal and regular in the upper echelons of the State bureaucracy. The abilities of local elites in Mexico to monopolize resources by using their ties to the State come immediately to mind.

It is clear that, as an analytic tool for cross-cultural analysis, the concept of the informal economy tells us different things in different types of economies, capitalist and non-capitalist, State and non-State. The informal components of economies are organized; they are instituted in complex and changing ways. In this framework, informal economies are not marginal, but represent variability and alternitivity across cultures and over time.

References.

Arizpe, Lourdes
    1977   Women in the Informal Sector: The Case of Mexico City. Signs: Journal of Women in Culture and Society Fall: 45-59.

Babb, Florence E.
    1985   Middlemen and "Marginal" Women: Marketers and Dependency in Peru's Informal Sector. In S. Plattner, ed., Markets and Marketing, Monographs in Economic Anthropology 4. Lanham, MD: University Press of America, pp. 287-308.

Bloch, Andrzej
    1985/6 The Private Sector in Poland. Telos 66: 129, 131.

Bohannan, Paul and Laura Bohannan
    1968   Tiv Economy. London: Longmans.

Bromley, Ray
    1978a Introduction. The Urban Informal Sector: Why is it Worth Discussing? World Development 6: 1033-1039.
    1978b Organization, Regulation and Exploitation in the So-Called "Urban Informal Sector": The Street Traders of Cali, Columbia. World Development 6: 1161-1171.

Bromley, Ray, ed.
    1985   Planning for Small Enterprises in Third World Cities. Oxford: Pergamon Press.

Codere, Helen
    1968   Exchange and Display. In D. Sills, ed., International Encyclopedia of the Social Sciences. New York: Free Press, pp. 239-245.

Cook, Scott and Martin Diskin, eds.
    1976   Markets in Oaxaca. Austin: University of Texas Press.

Davies, R.
1979   Informal Sector or Subordinate Mode of Production?
A Model. In R. Bromley and C. Gerry, eds., Casual
Work and Poverty in Third World Cities. New York:
John Wiley and Sons, pp. 87-104.

Dow, Leslie M., Jr.
1977   High Weeds in Detroit: The Irregular Economy
Among a Network of Appalachian Migrants. Urban
Anthropology 6: 111-128.

Ferman, Louis A., S. Henry, M. Hoyman, eds.
1987a The Informal Economy. The Annals of the American
Academy of Political and Social Science. Newbury
Park CA: Sage Publications.
1987b Preface. The Informal Economy. The Annals of the
American Academy of Political and Social Science.
Newbury Park CA: Sage Publications, pp. 10-14.

Firth, Raymond
1929   Primitive Economics of the New Zealand Maori. New
York: Dalton.
1939   Primitive Polynesian Economy. London: Routledge.

Foster-Carter, A.
1978   The Mode of Production Controversy. New Left
Review 107: 47-78.

Fried, Morton
1967   The Evolution of Political Society. New York:
Random House.

Gaertner, Wulf and Alois Wenig, eds.
1985   Economics of the Shadow Economy. New York:
Springer-Verlag.

Gaughan, Joseph P. and Louis A. Ferman
1987   Toward an Understanding of the Informal Economy.
        In L. A. Ferman, S. Henry, M. Hoyman, eds., The
        Informal Economy. The Annals of the American
        Academy of Political and Social Science. Newbury
        Park CA: Sage Publications, pp. 15-25.

Gerry, Chris
1987   Developing Economies and the Informal Sector in
        Historical Perspective. In L. A. Ferman, S. Henry, M.
        Hoyman, eds., The Informal Economy. The Annals of
        the American Academy of Political and Social
        Science. Newbury Park CA: Sage Publications, pp.
        100-119.

Grossman, Gregory, ed.
1988   Studies in the Second Economy of Communist
        Countries. Berkeley: University of California Press.

Halperin, Rhoda
1988   Economies Across Cultures. London: McMillan Press.
1989   Ecological and Economic Anthropology Reconsidered:
        Changing Place vs. Changing Hands. In Barry L.
        Isaac, ed., Research in Economic Anthropology 11.
        Greenwich CN: JAI Press (in press).
n. d.   The Livelihood of Kin: Making Ends Meet "The
        Kentucky Way." Austin: The University of Texas
        Press (in press).

Harner, Michael
1973   The Jivaro. New York: Anchor Books.

Hart, Keith
1973   Informal Income Opportunities and Urban
        Employment in Ghana. Journal of Modern African
        Studies 11: 61-89.

Henry, Stuart
  1987   The Political Economy of Informal Economies. In
          L.A. Ferman, S. Henry and M. Hoyman, eds., The
          Informal Economy. The Annals of the American
          Academy of Political and Social Science. Newbury
          Park CA: ```11Sage Publications, pp.137-153.

Hicks, George L.
  1973   Appalachian Valley. New York: Holt, Rinehart and
          Winston.

Hoyman, Michele
  1987   Female Participation in the Informal Economy: A
          Neglected Issue. In L. A. Ferman, S. Henry, M.
          Hoyman, eds., The Informal Economy. The Annals of
          the American Academy of Political and Social Science.
          Newbury Park CA: Sage Publications, pp. 100-119.

Illich, Ivan
  1981   Shadow Work. London: Marion Boyars.

Lévi-Strauss, Claude
  1969   The Elementary Structures of Kinship.   Boston:
          Beacon Press.

Lomnitz, Larissa A.
  1988   Informal Exchange Networks in Formal Systems.
          American Anthropologist 90: 42-55.

Long, Norman and Paul Richardson
  1978   Informal Sector, Petty Commodity Production, and the
          Social Relations of Small-Scale Enterprise. In John
          Clammer, ed., The New Economic Anthropology.
          New York: St. Martin's Press, pp. 176-209.

Malinowski, Bronislaw
  1922   Argonauts of the Western Pacific. London: Routledge
          and Kegan Paul.

Malinowski, B. and J. de la Fuente
    1982   The Economics of a Mexican Market System. London:
            Routledge and Kegan Paul [original 1957].

Marshall, John
    1980   N!ai: The Story of a !Kung Woman [ethnographic
            film]. Odyssey Television Series.

Mattera, Philip
    1985   Off the Books: The Rise of the Underground
            Economy. New York: St. Martin's Press.

Mauss, Marcel
    1925   Essai Sur le Don: Frome et Raison de l'Exchange dans
            les Societes Archaiques. L'Annee Sociologique 1: 30-
            186 (for 1923-24). [Republished in 1954 as The Gift:
            Form and Functions of Exchange in Archaic Society,
            transl. Ian Cunnison. London: Cohen and West.]

Miller, S. M.
    1987   The Pursuit of Informal Economies. In L. A. Ferman,
            S. Henry and M. Hoyman, eds., The Informal
            Economy. The Annals of the American Academy of
            Political and Social Science. Newbury Park CA: Sage
            Publications, pp. 26-35.

Obregon, Anibal Quijano
    1980   The Marginal Pole of the Economy and the Margin-
            alized Labor Force. In H. Wolpe, ed., The
            Articulation of Modes of Production: Essays from
            Economy and Society. Boston: Routledge and Kegan
            Paul, pp. 254-288.

Peattie, Lisa R.
    1980   Anthropological Perspectives on the Concepts of
            Dualism: The Informal Sector, and Marginality in
            Developing Urban Economies. International Regional
            Science Review 5: 1-31.

1982   What is to be Done with the "Informal Sector"? A Case Study of Shoe Manufacturers in Columbia. In Helen I. Safa, ed. Towards Political Economy of Urbanization in Third World Countries, Delhi, India: Oxford University Press, pp. 201-217.

Polanyi, Karl
1957   The Economy as Instituted Process. In K. Polanyi, C. M. Arensberg and H. W. Pearson, eds., Trade and Market in the Early Empires. New York: The Free Press, pp. 234-269.

Sahlins, Marshall
1972   Stone Age Economics. Chicago: Aldine.

Sampson, Steven
1985/6 The Informal Sector in Eastern Europe. Telos 66: 44-66.
1987   The Second Economy of the Soviet Union and Eastern Europe. In L. A. Ferman, S. Henry and M. Hoyman, eds., The Informal Economy. The Annals of the American Academy of Political and Social Science. Newbury Park CA: Sage Publications, pp. 120-136.

Simon, Carl P. and Ann D. Witte
1982   Beating the System: The Underground Economy. Boston: Auburn House.

Skinner, William G.
1964   Marketing and Social Structure in Rural China. Journal of Asian Studies 24: 3-43.

Smith, M. Estellie
1989   The Informal Economy. In S. Plattner, ed., Economic Anthropology. Stanford, CA: Stanford University Press (in press).

Taussig, Michael
1980   The Devil and Commodity Fetishism in Latin America. Chapel Hill: The University of North Carolina Press.

Trager, Lillian
1985   From Yams to Beer in a Nigerian City: Expansion and Change in Informal Sector Trade Activity. In Stuart Plattner, ed., Markets and Marketing. Monographs in Economic Anthropology 4. New York: University Press of America, pp. 259-286.
1987   The Urban Informal Sector in West Africa. Canadian Journal of African Studies 21: 238-255.

Wedel, Janine
1986   The Private Poland. New York: Facts on File.

INDEX

A

Aage, H., 235, 247, 249
Accra, 33-34, 49, 99
Accumulation, 327
Activist groups, *See* Collective
   action
Adaptation, 141-42, 149, 186,
   197, 199, 211-13, 224-25
   265, 291-92, 293, 326,
   333, 334
Adas, M., 51, 70
Affluence, 40, 187, 197
Africa, 3, 5, 11, 33-34, 49-71,
   99, 128, 162, 251, 252,
   265, 268, 286, 326, 327-
   29
Age marking, 3, 5, 7, 36, 37, 40,
   41, 51, 110, 154, 156, 246,
   256, 266, 325
Agriculture, 53, 54, 293-95,
   301-19, 327-29, 331-32
Alderson-Smith, G, 37, 43
Aldrete-Haas, J. A., 75, 95
Allum, P. A., 131, 143
Altman, Y., 284, 297
Amin, S., 184, 201
Anderson, M., 35, 43
de Andrade, S. M. B. V., 106, 119
Appadurai, A., 303, 317
Appalachia, 331-32
Arensberg, C. M., 340
Argentina, 26, 30, 31
Arias, P., 28, 43
Arizpe, L., 321, 335
Arnould, E. J., 21
Aron, R., 1
Ascher, R., 123, 144
Asia, 3, 13, 251-79, 281-99,
   301-19

Asian Development Bank, 306
Assets, 301-03
Associations, *See* Collective
   action

B

Babb, F. E., 321, 335
Bach, R., 186, 187, 200, 203
Bairoch, P., 184, 201, 251, 272
Bands, foraging, 326-27
Banjerjee, N., 251, 272
Banfield, E. C., 3, 16
Banfield, L. F., 3, 16
Barcelona, 212
Barter, 3, 4, 8, 216, 241, 310,
   331-32
Bastide, R., 128, 143
Batley, R., 77, 93
Beavon, K. S. O., 251, 252, 268,
   277
Bell, D., 1
Belo Horizonte, 107
Beltrán Antolín, J., 207, 232
Benaria, L., 29, 43
Benedict, P., 6, 16
Bennett, J. T., 9, 16
Bennett, J. W., 119
Benton, L., 43, 47, 201
Berliner, J., 2, 16
Bernard, R. M., 203
Bertaux, D., 272
Bertaux-Wiame, I., 272
Bienefeld, M., 208, 232
Biggs, R. D., 317, 319
Bilbao, 212
Birbeck, C., 184, 201, 252, 272
Blanes, J., 40, 43
Blitzer, S., 46
Bloch, A., 321, 335

Boeke, J. H., 32, 43, 98, 119
Boesen, J., 54, 55, 70
Bohannan, L., 327, 328, 329, 335
Bohannan, P., 327, 328, 329, 335
Boileau, J., 202
Bolivia, 40
Bonke, J., 235, 247
Bonny, Y., 202
Bowen, J. R., 119
Brant, V. C., 96
Brazil, 11, 26, 28, 31, 36, 40, 73-96, 97-122, 123-45
Breman, J., 23, 44
Brezinski, H., 284, 286, 297
Brokers, 131, 139-40, 225-26, 288, 330, 331-32
Bromley, R., 34, 44, 149, 158, 162, 178, 184, 201, 210, 232, 251, 252, 272, 273, 278, 321, 335, 336
Brown, D. DeG., 127, 128, 130, 140, 143
Brown, E. H. P., 254, 255, 273
Browning, F., 286, 287, 289, 297
Brush, S., 6, 16
Budgets/budgeting, 2, 3, 246, 306, 311, 314
Bureaucracy/bureaucrats, 7, 60, 63, 66, 74, 77, 78, 81, 85, 86, 87, 90, 91, 126-27, 128-30, 134-38, 165, 211,219-220, 228, 237, 245,263, 301-19, 324, 334
Burma, 13, 281-99

C
Cali, 184, 252
de Camargo, C. P. F., 127, 143
Campos Romero, M. L., 208, 232
Camus, A., 1
Canada, 194
Canton, 265
Capital, 24, 77, 87, 89, 107, 113-14, 124, 164, 169-70, 174, 200, 213, 225, 252, 254, 256-57, 264, 265, 266, 270, 293, 295
Capitalism and the capitalization process, 98, 103-09, 118,124, 250, 161, 162-64,165, 175, 252, 254, 261,262, 267, 321, 323, 326,329
Cartaya F., V., 162, 178
Carter, W. E., 143, 144
Castells, M., 43, 47, 201
Centrally planned economies, See Socialism
Chandravithun, N., 295, 297
Ch'ang, H., 309, 317
Change and innovation, 28, 42, 52, 54, 56, 62-63, 75, 123, 141-42, 163, 211, 326, 333, 334
Chen, E. K. Y., 254, 273
Chevalier, J., 252, 273
Child labor, See Age marking
Chile, 26, 38
China/Chinese, 191, 251-79, 283, 290, 294, 296, 332
Chiu Chau, 265
Church, role of, 81, 85, 88, 128
Cities, 4, 6, 11, 12, 15, 23 ff., 49 ff., 74 ff., 97 ff.,

123 ff., 147 ff., 161 ff.,
183 ff., 207 ff., 242,
251 ff.
Civil servants and civil service,
See Bureaucracies and
bureaucrats
Clammer, J., 18, 274, 276, 338
Clark, G., 6, 16, 278
Clark, J., 186, 203
Clarke, M., 315, 317
Class, 51, 87, 89, 114, 118,
124, 150, 185, 187, 220,
265, 269, 271
Codere, H., 325, 335
Collective action, 38, 52, 53,
79, 80-83, 85, 88, 90,
130, 227, 310, 327-29
Collectivization, 53
Collier, D., 74, 77, 93
Colombia, 27, 76, 184
Commoditization, 118, 326
Competition, 28, 29, 35
Conflict, *See* Confrontations/
open conflict
Confrontations/open conflict,
79-82, 90, 310
Consumption/consumerism,
90, 246, 285, 286, 287,
288, 289, 294
Cook, S., 332, 335
Cooley, M., 190, 201
Cooper, E., 254, 273
Cooperatives, 24
Cornelius, W., 44, 46, 47, 94
Corral Raya, J., 208, 232
Corruption, 49, 9, 15, 40, 55,
60,63, 64, 67, 86, 89,
262, 293, 294, 295, 308,
309, 311, 313, 315, 330,

332, 334
Cottrell, R., 255, 273
Cramer, J. S., 8, 16
Credit, 5, 59, 137, 140, 169,
170, 173, 176, 187, 212,
264
Crises, 26, 55, 57, 107, 147-59,
207-33, 253, 255, 258
Cuba/Cubans, 12, 183 ff.
Currency, money, cash, 8, 212,
239, 269, 287, 309, 333
Curtis, J., 46

D
Dar es Salaam, 50-69
Davies, R., 149, 158, 251, 273,
321, 336
Davis, K., 304, 317
Decision making, 1, 2, 27, 33,
34, 99, 114, 115-16, 215,
263, 266, 267, 271, 313
Demographic variables, *See*
Age marking; Gender
marking; Education; Family
and kinship; Health and
medical care; Households;
Income; Population change
Denmark, 13, 235-49
Dependency theory, 162-63, 177
De Soto, H., 23, 44, 165, 178
Despres, L. A., 11, 12, 97-122
Development/development
theory, 3, 5, 6, 28, 73, 97,
98-99, 100 ff., 123, 147-
48, 165, 211-13, 251-52
Dietz, H. A., 77, 93
DiLorenzo, T. J., 9, 16
Diniz, E., 94
Dirksen, E., 1

Diskin, M., 332, 335
Distribution systems, 107, 123-45, 167-68, 174, 215, 261, 282, 283, 287-94., 301-19, 322, 324, 333
Dominican Republic, 12, 161-81
Dow, L.M., Jr., 321, 336
Drakakis-Smith, D., 251, 273
Drucker, P. F., 1, 17
Drug Trade, 13, 40, 183, 186, 283-84, 286-89, 295-96, 330
Dual economy, model and theory, 5-7, 32, 75-76, 98, 99, 109-110, 162-63, 175, 199
Duarte, I., 168, 179
Durand, G., 190, 210
Durrenberger, E. P., 13, 281-99

E

Eckstein, S., 34, 44, 74, 77, 93, 149, 158
Ecology, *See* Environment
Economic efficiency, 32, 33, 114, 170, 241, 257, 263, 266, 270, 271, 314
Economic 'facts', 1, 6, 282
Economic restructuring, 100-14, 123-24, 147-48, 156-57, 163, 166, 176, 189, 190, 191, 192, 207 ff., 211-13, 224, 253-55, 258
Ecuador, 36
Education, 26, 61, 103, 111, 153, 168, 169, 187, 242, 265, 267, 269, 270-71, 306
Egmose, L., 247

Egmose, S., 245, 247
Eisenstadt, S. N., 145
Elderly, *See* Age marking
Elites, 76, 103-04, 106, 107, 334
Employment, 8, 9, 12, 13, 23, 27, 31, 58, 59, 73, 97-122, 149, 152, 213, 221, 224, 228, 243-46, 251-79, 282
England, J., 256, 274
Entitlements, 5, 7, 8, 9, 15, 27, 29, 30, 31, 34, 35, 42, 59, 124, 126-27, 132-34, 149-51, 153, 169, 170, 171-72, 192, 194, 195, 211, 224, 235-49, 256, 257, 268, 301-19, 333
Entrepreneurs/entrepreneurialism, 5, 13, 33, 35, 74, 78, 87, 89, 104, 109. 173, 184, 186-87, 192, 195, 196, 198, 200, 266, 330
Environment, 9, 15, 75, 106, 288, 331-32
Escobar, A., 27, 44
Ethical issues, 10, 303
Ethnicity, 4, 12, 103, 174, 183-205, 265, 284, 285, 288
Europe, 12, 30, 35, 42, 207-33, 235-49, 284, 330
Evers, T., 74, 76, 77, 83, 84, 85, 93
Exchange, social structure of, 303
Exploitation, 23, 63, 76, 151, 164, 176, 184, 185, 188, 191,193, 194, 200, 252, 256, 268-69

Exports, *See* Imports/Exports

F

Family and kinship, 35, 36, 37, 38, 39, 49, 51, 58, 60, 63, 105, 107, 117, 125-26, 135-36, 138, 147-59, 163-64, 169-70, 174-5, 188, 190, 221, 229-30, 238, 267, 268, 270, 322, 323, 327-28, 331-32
Fapohunda, L., 251, 274
Faria, V., 74, 93, 114, 119
Favelas, *See* Squatter settle-ments
Feige, E. L., 7, 8, 17
Fendt, R., Jr., 123, 145
Ferdandez-Kelly, P., 186, 201
Ferman, L. A., 4, 7, 8, 17, 19, 69, 70, 322, 336, 337, 338, 339, 340
Ferman, P. R., 4, 7, 17
Firth, R., 325, 336
Foreign trade, *See* Imports/Exports
Forman, S., 131, 143
Foster-Carter, A., 252, 274, 326, 336
Frank, A. G., 98, 120
French, K., 147-59
Fried, M., 281, 298, 325, 336
Frobel, F., 261, 274
Fry, P., 39, 44
de la Fuente, J., 332, 339
Futurology, 1, 6

G

Gabriel, C. E., 128, 143
Gaertner, W., 321, 336
Garcia, A., 186, 201

García, B., 167, 169, 179
Garreau, J., 185, 202
Garrett, B., 286, 287, 289, 297
Gaughan, J. R., 322, 337
Geertz, C., 3, 17, 32, 44, 98, 120, 149, 158
Gender marking, 3, 26, 38, 51, 60, 68, 110, 148-49, 151-52, 168, 189, 190, 196, 197, 198, 220, 242, 255, 265, 266, 281, 325, 327-28
Gerry, C., 34, 44, 120, 158, 201, 251, 272, 273, 278, 321, 336, 337
Ghai, D., 49, 70
Ghana, 5, 33-34, 99
Gibson, M., 317, 319
Gifts and reciprocity, 4, 131-40, 237-38, 239, 295, 322, 325, 327, 332
Gilbert, A., 178, 272
Gmelch, S. B., 282, 298
GNP/GDP, 6, 7, 125, 149, 212-13, 236, 237, 240, 242-43, 255, 261
Goodman, F., 145
Gottdiener, M., 74, 91, 93
Graham, D. H., 123, 144
Grazia, R. D., 247
Greenfield, S. M., 11, 123-45, 282, 298
Grossman, G., 3, 17, 321, 337
Growth, 6, 198, 100-01, 102-08, 123-24, 163, 173, 176, 187, 211
Guadalajara, 28, 37
Guatemala, 37-38, 76
Guatemala City, 37-38, 76

Gutmann, P. M., 7, 8, 17, 244, 247
Gypsies, 229, 282

H

Habib, I., 304, 317
Haiti/Haitians, 183 ff.,
Halperin, R., 14, 321-41
Hansson, I., 235, 242, 247
Hardoy, J. E., 178
Harner, M., 327, 337
Harrison, J., 211, 212, 213, 232
Hart, K., 4, 5, 6, 7, 17, 33, 34, 44, 73, 93, 97, 98, 99, 120, 158, 162, 179, 184, 202, 251, 274, 321, 324, 337
Haug, M., 186, 202
Havnevik, K., 55, 70
Health and medical care, 64, 66-68, 126-27, 133-40, 171-72, 193, 258
Heidenheimer, A., 315, 317
Heinrichs, J., 274
Helleiner, G. K., 49, 70
Henney, J., 145
Henry, S., 17, 19, 69, 70, 322, 336, 337, 338, 339, 340
de las Herâs, J., 209, 232
Herskovits, M. J., 128, 144
Hicks, G. L., 6, 331, 338
Ho, S. F., 261, 274
Ho, Y-p., 276
Hockett, C. F., 123, 144
Hong Kong, 13, 251-79
Hopkins, K., 254, 273, 275
Households, 5, 34, 39, 41, 49, 58-59, 76, 103, 107, 108, 147-59, 163-64, 169-70,
171, 236, 237-38, 327-28, 329
Housing, 73-96, 102, 154-55, 156-57, 199, 259
Hoyman, M., 6, 17, 19, 69, 70, 321, 336, 337, 338, 339, 340
Hsu, F., 317
Hunt, R. C., 13, 301-19
Hunter-gatherers, 321
Hutchinson, B., 131, 144
Hyden, G., 53, 71

I

Ideology, 1, 1, 23, 39-41, 60-61, 63-66, 68, 80-81, 116-18, 128-31, 162-65, 170, 171, 190, 229-30, 262, 268, 281-82, 296, 313, 314, 327
Illich, I., 322-338
Imports/Exports, 54, 56, 103, 185, 212, 213, 253-55, 258, 283-96
Income, 24, 26, 27, 31, 38, 39, 41, 42, 49, 51, 58, 59, 62, 63, 64-5, 66, 68, 73, 74, 86, 99, 110-13, 116, 118, 151, 152-53, 156, 166, 168-73, 186, 192, 194, 196, 197-98, 199, 239, 241, 242, 245, 256-57, 267, 306-08, 310-12, 314, 332
India, 13, 252, 255, 268, 289, 301-19
Indians, South American, 326-27
Indonesia, 32

ndustrial production and
industrialization, 28, 31,
35, 54, 100 ff., 123, 141,
163, 212, 253-56, 262
nflation, 49, 147, 148, 166,
167, 172-73, 212, 224
nformal economy, definitions,
10, 14, 23 ff., 73, 98, 99,
124, 149-50, 161-62,
164-65, 184, 188, 210,
237, 260, 281-82, 308,
315, 323-25
nformal economy, linkages with
formal, 6-7, 10, 13-14,
15, 25, 30-31, 32, 33-36,
41, 42, 51, 60, 62 ff., 76-
79, 87-89, 91-92, 98,
107 ff., 125, 141, 150-54,
156-57, 162-66, 167,
171-77, 184-87, 193,
196, 210-11, 222-27,
229, 230-31, 235-49,
251-79, 301-19, 330,
332-34
nformal economy, methodology/
modeling/analysis, 9-10,
12, 14, 23-48, 75, 91-92,
97-99, 100-110, 124,
148, 161-67, 174-77,
184, 199, 210, 235-459,
251, 252, 269-71, 281-
84, 301-03, 308, 309,
312-16, 321-34
nformal economy, studying, 10,
42, 50, 78-79, 91-92,
99-100, 162-67, 235-49,
252-53, 281-84, 303-04,
309, 321-34
nformal economy, terms for

3, 235
Informal economy, validity of
data, 237-39, 242, 243,
244, 246, 303-04
Institutions, 6, 13, 88, 128-30,
301, 329, 333
International Labor Office, 23
24, 45, 97, 149, 158, 161,
162, 179, 255, 275
International Monetary Fund,
50
International trade, 8, 13; See
also Imports/Exports
Ireland, 282
Isaac, B. L., 337
Isachsen, A. J., 235, 242, 244,
247
Italy, 36

J
Jacobi, P., 94
Jivaro, 326-27
Joinville, 97, 102-06, 109, 112,
115, 117
Jones, Y. V., 6, 18
Jonsson, H., 288, 298
Jorge, A., 186, 202
Joshi, H., 251, 275
Juiz de Fora, 97, 106-09, 111,
112-15, 117

K
Kaprow, M. L., 282, 298
Keely, C. B., 203
Keith, A. B., 304, 318
Kenya, 162
Kim, M-H., 152, 153, 154, 158
Kinship, See Family and kinship
Kirschgässner, G., 243, 248

Klovland, J. T., 247
Kohn, M., 47
Koponen, J., 70
Kowarick, L., 74, 76, 77, 94
Kreye, O., 274
Krischke, P., 93
Kritz, M. M., 203
!Kung, 326

L

Labor conditions, 9, 27, 17, 187,
    193, 256, 257, 268-69,
    295
Labor force, 78, 100-18, 187,
    253-56
Lachapelle, J., 202
Lacombe, M., 202
Lamoureaux, C., 202
Laos, 281 ff.
Latin America, 3, 11, 12, 23-48,
    73-96, 97-122, 123-45,
    185, 187, 251
Lau, S., 260, 275
Lavallee, R., 202
Laverdiere, M., 190, 202
Law and laws, *See* Regulations,
    laws, and rules
Leacock, E., 45
Leaders, 56, 125, 131-40, 326-
    27
Lee, R. P., 276
Leeds, A., 34, 45, 74, 76, 77, 94
Leeds, E., 74, 76, 77, 94
Leeming, F., 275
Legitimacy, 64, 67, 89
Leisure, 6
Lemarchand, R., 145
Lerch, P., 131, 144
Lessinger, J., 251, 252, 268, 275

Lethbridge, D., 273
Levine, B., 185, 202
Lévi-Strauss, C., 322, 338
Lewis, O., 34
Licences/licensing, 59-60, 61,
    62, 66, 162, 209, 219-20,
    221, 224, 226-29, 230,
    231, 260-64, 306
Lieberman, S., 211, 212, 213,
    233
Lim, K. C., 267, 275
Lima, 37
Lin, T-b., 255, 256, 276
Lintner, B., 288, 298
Loescher, G., 194, 202
Lomnitz, L. A., 6, 18, 38, 45, 73,
    74, 76, 77, 94. 118, 120,
    251, 276, 322, 334, 338
Long, N., 6, 7, 18, 43, 252, 276,
    322, 338
Lorenzo Quintela, M. A., 232
Loyola, M. A. R., 106, 120
Lozano, B., 229, 233
Lubell, H., 274, 275
Lui, T. L., 255, 276
Luytjes, J., 185, 202

M

Macao, 265
MacGaffey, J., 286, 298
Macumba, 128
Madras, 268
Madrid, 207-33
Malinowski, B., 325, 332, 338,
    339
Malloy, J., 31, 45
Manaus, 97, 100-02, 105, 108,
    109, 110, 111, 112-13,
    115, 117

Manning, R., 186, 203
Manufacturing, 101 ff., 123, 176, 254, 333
Marginality thesis, 109-14
Margolis, M. L., 143, 144
Market places, 32, 167, 197, 207-33, 331-33
Market system, 4, 53, 213, 237, 255, 257, 266, 283, 289, 291, 296, 323, 332
Marshall, A., 27, 29, 30, 45
Marshall, J., 326, 339
Martínez Saez, M. V., 232
Marxist theories/marxism, 75, 90, 97, 98, 141-42, 150, 162-64, 165, 174-75, 251-79
Masotti, L., 94
Mattera, P., 14, 18, 321, 339
Mauss, M., 322, 339
Mayer, P., 6, 18
McCoy, A. W., 284, 286, 287, 288, 289, 298
McGee,T. G., 6, 18, 98, 120, 251, 258, 259, 261, 262, 265, 266, 268, 276
McGuire, T. R., 21
Mehenna, S., 6, 20
Meillassoux, C., 6, 19
Mejía, M., 167, 169, 179
Men, See Gender marking
Merrick, T. W., 123, 144
Mertens, W., 46
Mexico, 12, 26, 28, 31, 36, 37, 76, 147-59, 332, 334
Mexico City, 28, 38, 76
Miami, 12, 183-205
Middle class, 25, 50, 58, 65-68, 74, 76, 78, 87, 88, 110,

197
Migration and migrants, 6, 13, 27, 33-4, 35, 36, 37, 38, 102, 105, 106, 107, 108, 110-13, 124, 155-57, 163, 169, 184, 185-87, 188, 194-95, 212, 221-22, 251, 252, 254, 258-59, 265, 268, 269-71, 314
Miller, J. C., 194, 203
Miller, S. M., 321, 339
Mingione, E., 19, 35, 36, 45, 98, 120, 228, 233
Mintz, S., 6, 19
Mirante, E., 285, 286, 287, 288, 298, 299
Mode of production model, 252, 326-29
Modernization, See Change and innovation; Development/ development theory; Economic restructuring; Growth.
Mohl, R., 185, 203
Moley, J., 275
Moncarz, R., 186, 202
Monopolies/monopsonies, 53, 54, 62, 334
Monterrey, Mexico, 28
Montevideo, 27
Montreal, 194
Morris, E. W., 147-59
Moser, C. O. N., 23, 45, 97, 98, 114, 121, 164, 179, 251, 252, 276
Multinationals, 104
Murphy, A. D., 12, 147-59
Murphy, M. F., 12, 161-81
Myanmar, 281-99

N

Nacken, J., 264, 277
National accounts, 6, 149, 237, 282, 288, 294, 312
Nattrass, N. J., 98, 121
Networks, 35, 37, 38, 39, 63, 66, 85, 89, 125 ff., 134-40, 173, 209, 238, 264, 266, 267, 270, 282, 290, 293, 308, 310, 331-33
New York City, 186, 189, 191, 194
Ng, S-h., 256, 277
Noonan, J. T., 309, 315, 318
Norris, W. P., 11, 73-96
Norway, 13, 242, 244
Nun, J., 98, 121, 164, 180
Nye, J., 314, 318

O

Oaxaca, 12, 147-59
Obregon, A. Q., 321, 339
Odgaard, R., 70
Olanrewaju, J., 274
de Oliveira, F., 74, 76, 95
de Oliveira, P., 106, 121
Oliver-Smith, A., 207-33
Olwig, K. F., 248
Opportunity structure, 265
Ordinances, See Regulations, laws and rules
Ortiz, R., 128, 145

P

Pahl, R. E., 6, 13, 19, 225, 233, 244, 248
Pant, N., 304, 318
Paraguay, 28
Patronage and patrons, 11, 17, 123-45
Pearson, H. W., 340
Peasants, 4, 53, 271, 290, 301-19, 330
Peattie, L. R., 34, 46, 73, 74, 75, 76, 95, 98, 121, 251, 277, 321, 339-40
Pedruelo Pedruelo, M. T., 232
Perez, L., 186, 203
Periodic markets, 207-33, 331-33
Perlman, J., 74, 76, 95
Peru, 27, 31, 36, 37, 77, 252
Petersen, H-G., 244, 248
Petty commodity production, 3, 5, 7, 51, 55, 64, 67, 98, 99, 107, 108, 111, 113, 114, 118, 163, 189, 191, 195, 196-97, 200, 252, 261
Planned economies, See Socialism
Plattner, S., 20, 21, 275, 335, 340, 341
Poland, 282
Polanyi, K., 60, 71, 322, 323, 324, 340
Political economy, 2, 24, 29, 31, 54 ff., 74, 77, 91-92, 98, 109, 149, 150, 164, 211, 212-13, 222-25, 261-63, 281-99, 312
Politics, politicians and political parties, 31, 50-51, 56, 60, 61, 63, 74, 76, 77, 79, 86, 88, 90, 127, 136-37, 224, 305-06, 307-08, 310, 327
Population, changes in, 24, 100-01, 102, 105, 107, 123-24,

186, 191, 192, 251, 254, 258, 259, 264, 265, 267, 304

Portes, A., 26, 27, 29, 30, 43, 46, 47, 73, 86, 95, 98, 121, 161, 164, 176, 180, 184, 185, 186, 187, 188, 195, 196, 200, 201, 202, 203, 204, 205, 261, 262, 277

Poverty, 24, 34, 40, 97, 102, 124-25, 164, 171, 196, 212, 220, 230, 251, 252

Power, 89, 114

Pressel, E. J., 128, 145

Pre-state societies, 326-29

Prestige, 302, 310

Prices and pricing, 53, 54, 66, 164, 174, 175, 224, 228, 236-37, 244, 261, 294, 295, 333

Privatization, 15, 39, 56, 61, 67

Production/productivity, 53, 255-56, 330

Profit, 164, 174, 175, 226

Proletarianization, 252, 256, 271

Prust, R., 123-45, 282, 298

Przeworski, A., 33, 46

Public Policy, 29, 42, 50, 51, 52 ff., 77, 87, 91, 97, 109, 148, 164-65, 171-72, 194, 212, 219-20, 227, 230, 246, 256, 260-63, 281-82, 304, 305, 315

Public Services, 9, 13, 15, 30, 36, 38, 53, 54, 56, 59, 67, 74, 77, 89, 90, 102, 109, 124, 197, 211, 259

Q

Quijano, A., 98, 121, 164, 180

R

Rabushka, A., 255, 277

Racism/ethnic antagonism, 184, 190, 193, 194, 200

Ramíerez, R., 178

Ray, V., 19

Rear, J., 256, 274

Recessions, 27, 147-48, 154, 192

Recife, 124 ff.

Reciprocity, See Gifts and reciprocity

Records and record keeping, See Statistics and record keeping

Redclift, N., 19

Redistribution, 325, 331. See also Taxes

Rees, M., 12, 147-59

Regulations, laws, and rules, 24, 29, 53, 57, 60-61, 63, 77, 83, 86, 91, 101, 137-38, 151, 164-66, 171-72, 188, 190, 193, 211, 212, 219-220, 227, 230, 231, 257, 260-63, 305

Religion, 11, 39, 123-45, 282

Remy, D., 251, 277

Resettlement, forced, 54, 57, 59

Rice, B. R., 203

Richardson, H. W. ,98, 122

Richardson, P., 6, 7, 18, 252, 276, 338

Riedel, J., 255, 277

Riegelhaupt, J. F., 131, 143

Rio de Janeiro, 40, 77, 107, 128,

134, 140
Risen, J., 191, 204
Risk, 5, 32, 114-17, 187
Roberts, B., 11, 23-48, 74, 75,
  76, 96, 98, 122, 149, 150,
  159,177
Rogerson, C. M., 251, 252, 268,
  277
Roldan, M., 29, 43
Romer's Rule, 124, 141
Roniger, L., 131, 145
Rosell Vaquero, M. D., 232
Rural peoples, 4, 49, 54-55,
  301-19, 329-30, 331-33
Rural-urban linkages, 49, 53,
  57, 67, 103-09, 110, 123,
  169, 198, 208, 209, 221,
  242, 290, 292-96, 312,
  321-22, 331-32, 333, 334

S
Safa, H., 272, 277, 340
Sahlins, M., 322, 340
Salanzar-Camillo, J., 123, 145
Salmon, K., 213, 233
Sampson, S., 19, 248, 321, 330,
  340
San Sebastian, 212
Santiago, 38
Santo Domingo, 12, 161-81
de Santos, C. N. F. , 84, 85, 96
Santos, M., 6, 19, 76, 96
Sanz Garcia, J. M., 208, 232
São Paulo, 83-85, 101, 107
Sassen-Koob, S., 46, 73, 95, 161,
  176, 180, 184, 185, 186,
  196, 203. 204
Saunders, L., 6, 20
Saving and savings, 76

Scandinavia, 13, 235-49
Scanlan, J., 194, 202
Scotta, A. McE., 252, 278
Scott, J., 50, 51, 52, 71, 284,
  299, 315, 318
Sebba, H., 143
Selby, H., 147-59
Sen, A., 301, 302, 312, 313, 318
Sethuraman, S. V., 6, 20
Shaidi, L. P., 57, 71
Shanghai, 254
Shankland, G., 6, 20
Sills, D., 335
Silverstein, J., 284, 285, 288,
  299
Simon, C. P., 243, 244, 248, 322,
  340
Simonis, U-E., 276
Sinclair, S., 251, 278
Singer, P., 85, 96
Sit, V. F. S., 254, 259, 275, 276,
  278
Skinner, W. G., 332, 340
Slums, See Squatter settlements
Smart, J., 13, 251-79
Smith, M. E., 1-22, 159, 298,
  323, 340
Smuggling, 284-96
Social costs, 9
Socialism, 49-71, 118, 161,
  281-99, 321, 323, 329,
  330
Social movements, 78
South Africa, 252, 268
South Korea, 254-55
Souza, P. R., 98, 122, 163, 180
Soweta, 252
Spain, 12, 31, 207-33, 282
Spiritism, 128, 134

Squatter settlements, 37, 73-96, 102, 106, 109. 124, 126, 256

Stack, C. B., 4, 20

State, control by and policy of, 53 ff., 62, 74 ff., 88, 163-65, 166, 194, 211-12, 259, 260, 261-64, 285, 288, 289, 290, 291, 292, 296, 315, 334

State, defined 281, 305

State, legitimacy of 55, 63-65, 89

State polities, 9, 11, 14, 15, 23,. 42, 49-71, 77, 89, 150, 162, 184, 185, 210, 211, 224, 227, 281-2, 284, 301-19, 321-22, 324, 329-30

State, relations with internal components, 78, 284-91

State, resistance to, 13, 50-53, 61-62, 69, 79-80, 88, 227, 262, 264, 285, 287, 288, 310

Statistics and record keeping, 5, 6, 8, 101, 107, 108, 149, 150, 162, 163, 191, 193, 194, 195, 209, 220, 224, 226, 228, 237, 241, 242, 246, 259, 281-82, 303-04, 309, 323

Steinberg, D. I., 294, 299

Stepick, A., 12, 183-205

Stetkär, K., 235, 243, 248

Stone, I., 304, 314, 318

Strategies and strategizing, 12, 27, 34, 49, 51-52, 56, 60, 74, 76, 84, 86, 88, 91, 98, 117-18, 151-52, 155-56, 170, 185, 188, 191, 199, 215, 225, 241, 244, 251, 257, 259, 263, 264, 266, 268-71, 313, 332

Street hawking and vendors, 3, 12, 13, 40, 57 ff., 105, 114, 162-75, 188, 197, 207-33, 251-79, 329

Strickon, A., 144

Strøm, S., 235, 242, 244, 247

Structural-functionalism, 325

Sturdevant, S., 14, 321-41

Surplus labor dynamics/theory of, 97, 99, 101, 102, 108, 109, 112, 113, 124, 162-64, 174, 184, 253, 333

Surplus value, 3, 261

Sweatshops, 188, 189, 191, 256

Sweden, 12, 242

Swetnam, J. J., 6, 20

Swift, M. G., 3, 21

Sze Yap, 265

T

Taiwan, 283, 287, 296

Tamames, R., 228, 233

Tannenbaum, N., 13, 281-99

Tanzania, 11, 49-71

Tanzi, V., 8, 9, 21, 247, 248

Tardanico, R., 179

Taussig, M., 326, 341

Taxes, 7, 8, 13, 29, 60, 61, 66, 84, 149, 166, 188, 211, 227, 231, 239, 241, 245, 289, 290, 294, 295, 306, 307, 330

Taylor, R., 286, 287, 299

Technology, 13, 24, 28, 29, 301-19
Ternes, A., 106, 122
Thailand, 281-99
Thomas, F. W., 304, 318
Tironi, E., 38, 47
Tiv, 327-29
Tokman, V., 25, 26, 27, 47, 98, 114, 122, 163, 180, 181
Tomasi, S., 203
Tourism, 101, 148, 152, 156, 193, 213, 290, 292
Trager, L., 6, 7, 21, 321, 329, 341
Transportation, 61-62, 107, 167, 174, 185, 198, 207-08, 215, 225, 287, 293, 295
Tremblay, J., 202
Tripp, A. M., 11, 49-71
Trueblood, F., 44, 46, 47, 94
Tse, F. Y., 251, 278

U

Udy, S. H., Jr., 21
Umbanda, 127-40
Union of Soviet Socialist Republics, 118, 330
Unions, 189, 190, 191, 192, 193, 194
United Kingdom, 13, 31, 244, 256, 284
United States, 7, 12, 26, 183-205, 241, 243, 244, 283, 286-89, 295, 296, 309, 329-30, 331-33
Urban infrastructure, 80-84, 90, 100, 102, 109, 124, 259
Urbanization, 31, 36, 73, 83, 91, 102, 105-07, 118, 123-4, 141, 163, 262, 267
Uruguay, 27
Uzzell, J. D., 6, 21, 269, 279

V

Valladares, L., 74, 75, 77, 85, 86, 96
Van Dikj, P., 6, 21
Vélez-Ibañez, C., 6, 21, 77, 96
Viby Mogensen, G., 13, 235-49
Vietnam, 287
Vinay, P., 6, 22
Vitoria, 212

W

Wade, R., 304, 305, 308, 311, 314, 318-19
Wage work, 5, 39, 40, 73, 83, 99, 100 ff., 108, 109, 110-13, 115-17, 150, 168, 171, 184, 187, 188, 189, 190, 191, 192, 196, 199, 210, 213, 215, 251-79, 294, 295, 301-19, 329, 331, 333
Wallace, C., 6, 19
Walton, J., 29, 30, 43, 46, 94, 98, 121, 164, 176, 180, 261, 262, 277
Wealth, See Affluence
Wedel, J., 6, 22, 282, 284, 299, 321, 341
Wenig, A., 321, 336
West Germany, 241, 243, 244
Willems, E., 127, 145
Wilson, K., 186, 205
Winter, I., 303, 319
Winter, M., 147-59

Wirth, J., 44
Witte, A. D., 243, 244, 248, 322, 340
Wolpe, H. 339
Women, *See* Gender marking
World Bank, 306
World economy, 56, 177, 213, 253, 254, 257, 263, 266, 281-96
Woronoff, J., 254, 255, 256, 279

Y
Yeung, Y. M., 251, 265, 276

Z
Zaire, 286
Zaluar, A., 40, 41, 48
Zucker, N. F., 194. 205

A a
Aage, H., 235, 247, 249